ISBN: 978129024795

Published by:
HardPress Publishing
8345 NW 66TH ST #2561
MIAMI FL 33166-2626

Email: info@hardpress.net
Web: http://www.hardpress.net

THE MOON

PRINTED BY
SPOTTISWOODE AND CO., NEW-STREET SQUARE
LONDON

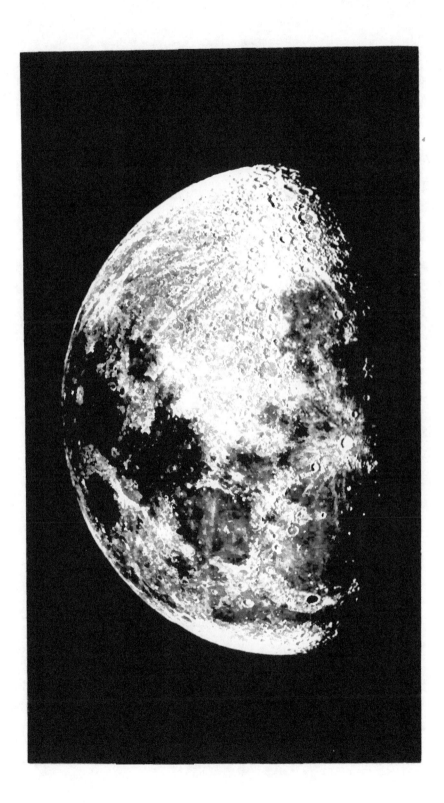

THE MOON

HER MOTIONS, ASPECT, SCENERY, AND PHYSICAL CONDITION

BY

RICHARD A. PROCTOR

AUTHOR OF 'THE SUN' 'SATURN AND ITS SYSTEM' 'THE ORBS AROUND US'
'ESSAYS ON ASTRONOMY' 'OTHER WORLDS THAN OURS' ETC.

*Wandering companionless
Among the stars that have a different birth—
And ever changing, like a joyless eye
That finds no object worth its constancy'—*SHELLEY

*WITH TWO LUNAR PHOTOGRAPHS BY RUTHERFURD
AND MANY ILLUSTRATIONS*

THIRD EDITION

LONDON

LONGMANS, GREEN, AND CO.

1886

21966

13/2/92

PREFACE

TO

THE SECOND EDITION.

—————•◇•—————

ALTHOUGH I have had no occasion to be dissatisfied with the reception given to the first edition of this work, yet I have found reason to believe that portions of the original work were too difficult for the general reader. I have therefore removed from the present edition the matter relating to details of the lunar theory (leaving the general account of the moon's motions) and also the more difficult parts of Chapter III. The illustrations, which in the former edition were arranged in plates of diagrams, lithographed, appear here as woodcuts.

The last chapter, on the moon's physical condition, has been considerably enlarged.

RICHARD A. PROCTOR.

LONDON : *July* 1878.

CONTENTS.

CHAPTER I.

THE MOON'S DISTANCE, SIZE, AND MASS.

CHAPTER II.

THE MOON'S MOTIONS.

CHAPTER III.

THE MOON'S CHANGES OF ASPECT, ROTATION, LIBRATION, ETC.

CHAPTER IV.

STUDY OF THE MOON'S SURFACE.

CHAPTER VI.

CONDITION OF THE MOON'S SURFACE.

TABLES.

INDEX TO THE MAP OF THE MOON.

LIST OF ILLUSTRATIONS.

———•◦•———

———————

DIRECTIONS TO BINDER.

Plates IV. and V. to lie the same way, the top of each towards
the left, to admit of being studied simultaneously.

Plate VI. to be placed so that when opened it shall face the
same way as pages 1, 3, 5, &c.

THE MOON.

CHAPTER I.

THE MOON : DISTANCE, SIZE, AND MASS.

ALTHOUGH the sun must undoubtedly have been the first celestial object whose movements or aspect attracted the attention of men, yet it can scarcely be questioned that the science of astronomy had its real origin in the study of the Moon. Her comparatively rapid motion in her circuit around the earth afforded in very early ages a convenient measure of time. The *month* was, of course, in the first place, a lunar time-measure. The *week*, the earliest division of time (except the day alone) of which we have any record, had also its origin in the lunar motions. Then the changes in the moon's appearance as she circles round the earth must have led men in very early times to recognize a distinction between the moon and all other celestial objects. While inquiring into the nature of these changes, and perhaps speculating on their cause, the first students of the moon must have soon begun to recognize the fact that she traverses the stellar vault

B

so as to be seen night after night among different star-groups. To the recognition of this circumstance must be ascribed the origin of astronomy properly so called. Until the varying position of the moon among the stars had been noticed, men must certainly have failed to notice the changes in the aspect of the stellar heavens night after night throughout the year. In examining the moon's motions among the stars, they must have been led to study the annual motion of the stellar sphere. Thence presently they must have learned to distinguish between the fixed stars and the planets. And gradually, as the study of the stars, the moon, and the planets continued, the fundamental problems of astronomy must have presented themselves with increasing distinctness, to be for centuries the object of ingenious speculation, more or less based on the actual results of observation.

It would be difficult to form just ideas respecting the order in which the various facts respecting the moon and her motions were ascertained by ancient astronomers. Indeed, it seems probable that among the different nations to whom the origin of astronomy has been attributed, the moon's changes of appearance and position were studied independently, the order of discovery not being necessarily alike in any two cases. We are free, therefore, in considering the knowledge of the ancients respecting the moon, to choose that arrangement of the various facts which seems best suited to the requirements of the student.

The first, as the most obvious peculiarity of the

moon, is that continually varying aspect which has led men in all ages to select the lunar orb as the emblem of change. 'The inconstant moon, that nightly changes in her circled orb,' must, in the first place, have appeared as a body capable of assuming really different shapes; and it is far from unlikely that this apparent evidence of power, associated with the moon's rapid change of place among the stars, may have led to the earliest forms of Sabæanism. Yet in very early times the true explanation of the peculiarity must have been obtained. The Chaldæan astronomers undoubtedly recognized the moon as an opaque orb, shining only because reflecting the sun's light; for otherwise we should be unable to explain the care with which they studied the moon's motions in connection with the recurrence of lunar and solar eclipses. Their famous cycle, the Saros (of which I have spoken more particularly in my treatise on Saturn), shows that they must have paid very close attention to the moon's movements for a long period before the Saros was determined, and for a much longer period before the cycle was made known to other astronomers of ancient times. Moreover, as they recognized in the moon the occasion of solar eclipses, though they could see her waning as she approached the sun's place, and waxing from the finest crescent of light after passing him, it is clear that they must have understood that the lunar phases indicate no actual change of shape. Nor can we imagine that reasoners so acute as the Chaldæan astronomers failed to recognize how all the phases could be explained by the varying amount of the moon's illuminated hemisphere turned at different times towards the earth.[1]

Quite early, then, the moon must have been recognized as an opaque globe illuminated by the sun. It would be understood that only one half of her surface can be in light. And apart from the fact that the moon was early recognized as causing solar eclipses by coming between the earth and the sun, it would be understood by the fineness of her sickle when near the sun's place on the celestial vault that she travels in a path lying within the sun's. That fine sickle of light shows that at such times the illuminated half is turned almost directly away from the earth ; and therefore the illuminating sun must at such times lie not far from the prolongation of a line carried from the earth's centre to the moon's.

It is not improbable, indeed, that the acute Chaldæans deduced similar inferences respecting the moon's nature from a careful study of her face ; for the features of the moon when horned or gibbous obviously correspond with those presented by the full moon, in such sort that no one who considers the phenomenon attentively can doubt for a moment that the moon

---

[1] It is remarkable, however, that Aratus, writing about 230 B.C., long after the time when the Chaldæans established their system of astronomy, refers to the lunar phases in a way which implies either ignorance or forgetfulness of their real cause ; for he speaks of the significance of the position in which the horns of the new moon are seen, regarding this position, though obviously a necessary consequence of the position of the sun and moon, as in itself a weather portent.

undergoes no real change when passing through her phases. It may also be imagined that the same astronomers who recognized the fact that Mercury is a planet, though he is never visible except in strong twilight, must have repeatedly observed that the whole orb of the moon can be seen when the bright part is a mere sickle of light. Nay, it is even possible that in the clear skies of ancient Chaldæa[1] the chief lunar features might be discerned when the dark half of the moon is thus seen.

The comparative nearness of the moon was probably inferred very early from her rapid motion of revolution around the earth. Almost as soon as observers noticed that the celestial bodies have different apparent motions, they must have learned that the moon's daily change of place among the stars is much greater than that of any other orb in the heavens. It would seem almost, from the distinction drawn in Job between the sun and the moon, that for some time the moon was regarded as the only body which actually moves over the celestial vault ; for he says, ' If I beheld the sun when it shined, or the moon walking in brightness' (Job xxxi. 26); and the recognition of the sun's annual circuit of the heavens most probably preceded the

[1] It is not very easy to determine what was the true site of the region spoken of in Judith (v. 6), as the land of the Chaldæans. The verse here referred to shows clearly that the region was not in Mesopotamia. From astronomical considerations I have been led to suppose that the first Chaldæan observers occupied a region extending from Mount Ararat northward as far as the Caucasian range. See Appendix A to *Saturn and its System*, and the Introduction to my *Gnomonic Star-atlas*.

discovery of the motions of the planets. Be this, however, as it may, astronomers must quite early have ascertained that among the more conspicuous orbs not one travels so quickly over the celestial vault as the moon. Accordingly, we find that even in the very earliest ages of astronomy the moon was regarded as the orb which travels nearest to the earth; and in the system of Pythagoras, in which musical tones were supposed to be produced by the revolution of the spheres bearing the planets, we find the *neate,* or highest tone of the celestial harmony, assigned to the moon.

Whether the Chaldæan astronomers ever ascertained the moon's distance observationally, is a question we have no means of answering satisfactorily. If they did, it is probable that the determination arose from the careful study of the moon's peculiarities of motion, such study being pursued with the object of rendering the prediction of eclipses more trustworthy. So far as is known, however, the first actual determination of the moon's distance, as compared with the dimensions of the earth's globe, must be ascribed to the astronomers of the Alexandrian school. Aristarchus of Samos (B.C. 280) had attempted to compare the distances of the sun and moon by a method of observation altogether inadequate to the requirements of that very difficult problem.[1] But he does not appear to have investigated the subject of the moon's distance. Somewhat more than a century and a quarter later, Hipparchus attacked both problems; the first with no better success than

---

[1] His method is described in my treatise on *The Sun* (p. 7).

had rewarded Aristarchus, but the second by a method which was probably very successful in his hands, though it is from his successor Ptolemy that we learn the actual results of observations applied according to the ideas of Hipparchus.

It would appear that the scrutiny of the moon's motions,—with the object of determining her path among the stars, and the exact laws according to which she traverses that path,—led Hipparchus to attack the problem of determining the moon's distance. We know that his observations were so carefully pursued that he determined the eccentricity of the moon's path, and its inclination to the sun's annual path on the star-vault. It is also highly probable that he detected a certain peculiarity of the moon's motion, called the *evection*, which will be described further on. Whether this is so, or whether the discovery should be ascribed to Ptolemy, it is certain that the labours of Hipparchus could not have led to the results actually obtained, without his having noticed certain effects due to the relative nearness of the moon as compared with the other celestial bodies. The study of these effects probably enabled him to form a fair estimate of the moon's distance.

We have, however, no record of the results actually obtained by Hipparchus, and we must turn to the pages of the great work, the 'Almagest,' written by Ptolemy about two centuries and a half later, for the first exact statement respecting the moon's distance, and the means used for determining it by the astronomers of old times.

The fundamental principle on which the measurement of the distance of any inaccessible object depends, is a very simple one. If a base-line (A B, fig. 1) be measured, and the bearing of the inaccessible object C from A and B (that is, the direction of the lines A C, B C, as compared with the line A B) be carefully estimated, then the distances A C and B C can, under ordinary circumstances, be determined. For, in the triangle A B C, we know the base-line A B, and the two base angles at A and B ; so that the triangle itself is completely determined. Therefore,

Fig. 1.

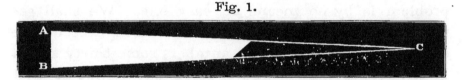

the ordinary formulæ of trigonometrical calculation,— or even a careful construction,—will give us the sides A C and B C.

If in all such cases we could determine A B and the base angles at A and B *exactly*, we should know the exact lengths of A C and B C. But even in ordinary cases, each observation must be to some extent, greater or less, inexact. Accordingly, the estimated distance of the object must be regarded as only an approximation to the truth. Setting aside mistakes in the measurement of the base-line, mistakes in determining the angles at A and B will obviously affect more or less seriously the estimate of either A C or B C. And a very brief consideration of the matter will show that the greater the distance of C as compared with the base-line A B,—in other words, the smaller the angle C,—the more serious will be the effect of any error in the observation of the angles A and B.

The difficulty experienced by the astronomer in the application of this direct method to the determination of the distances of celestial objects, consists chiefly in this: that his base-line must always be exceedingly small compared with the distance which he wishes to determine. It is, indeed, only in the case of the moon that the astronomer can apply this method with the least chance of success; and even in her case the problem is by no means an easy one. We shall see presently that the distance of the moon exceeds the earth's diameter in round numbers some thirty times. If the reader draw a figure, as in fig. 1, but so that each of the lines A C and B C is about thirty times as long as A B, he will see that the angle at C is very small, insomuch that a very slight error in the determination of either of the base angles at A and B would lead to a serious error in the estimate of the distance of C, even supposing a full diameter of the earth could be taken as the base-line.

When we remember that the ancient astronomers were unable to undertake long voyages for the purpose of determining the moon's distance, and that, even though they could have set observers at widely distant stations, they had not the requisite acquaintance with the geographical position of different places to know what base-line they were making use of, it may appear

same considerations which he would apply to the moon regarded as at rest.   He would still be able to compare together the periods during which the moon is above and below the horizon, since her own motion would cause *both* these periods to be correspondingly affected.

The actual problem is rendered somewhat less simple by the fact that the moon's motion takes place in a path inclined to the plane of the circle *e* E *e'*.   But it is obviously in the power of mathematics to take into consideration all the effects due to the moon's real motion, and thus, as in the simpler case imagined, to deduce the relation between E P and P M.

But we may now look at the problem in a somewhat different light.   Hitherto we have only considered the effect of the earth's size in causing an apparent want of uniformity in the moon's rate of motion.   We can see, however, from fig. 2, that what in reality happens is that the moon is not seen in the same direction from points on the earth's surface as from the centre of the earth ; and that the apparent displacement is greater or less according as the moon is nearer to or farther from the horizon.   She is seen in the same direction from E as from P.   But when she is seen from *e* or *e'* she is seen as though ninety degrees from the point overhead, whereas, as seen from P, she would be less than ninety degrees from that point : that is, she is seen from E lower down than she is in reality.

But it is clear that this is equally true, wherever the station of the observer may be.   The moon is always seen below the place she would occupy if she could be observed from the earth's centre, except when she is actually overhead; and she is more depressed the nearer she is to the horizon.

Thus let M, fig. 3, represent the moon's place when she is 50 degrees above the horizon; then, as 'seen

Fig. 3.

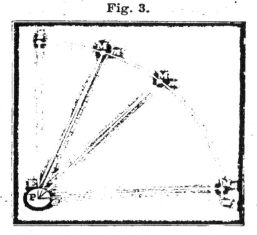

ILLUSTRATING LUNAR PARALLAX.

from P, she would lie in the direction P M; but from E she is seen in the direction E M, which is the same as P m (drawing P m parallel to E M). Thus the actual displacement, measured as an arc in the heavens, is represented by the arc M m. The displacement when the moon is on the horizon is represented by the arc M_H m_h, which is clearly greater than M m. If M' represents the moon's place when she is 70 degrees above the horizon, then M' m', her displacement, is less again than M m.

This displacement is called the lunar parallax, and the displacement when the moon's centre is on the horizon is called the lunar horizontal parallax.

Now the moon's apparent diurnal path at any station on the earth would precisely resemble the apparent diurnal path of a star at the same distance from the pole, if it were not, *first*, for the moon's actual motion amongst the stars, and *secondly*, for this effect, by which she is depressed below her true place, more or less according as she is nearer to or farther from the horizon. The first circumstance could be taken into account so soon as the general course of the moon's motion came to be known. Her true path among the stars at any particular time could be ascertained. And *then* it would only remain to determine how much she seemed to depart from that path when on the horizon, and again when high above it. This could be done by means of any contrivance which would enable the observer to follow the moon in the same way that the sun or a star can be followed, by means of a suitable pointer, carried round the axis on which the celestial vault seems to rotate in what is called the diurnal motion ; that is, around an axis directed to the true pole of the heavens. Such a pointer directed once upon a star would follow the star from rising to setting (neglecting the effects of atmospheric refraction); but directed on the moon, and corrected from time to time, so that the moon's actua motions among the stars should be taken into account, the pointer would not follow the moon by a mere rotation around its polar axis. If pointed on the moon when she first rose above the horizon, it would be found to point *below* the moon when carried (round its axis) towards the place occupied by the moon when high above the horizon; for it would have to be depressed by the full amount of the horizontal parallax when the moon was on the horizon, and this depression would be too great when the moon was high above the horizon. In like manner, if the pointer were directed upon the moon when she was high above the horizon, it would be carried to a place above that occupied by the moon when setting beyond the western horizon.

It was in this way that the moon's distance was first ascertained. The reader will recognize in the description just given the principle of the equatorial telescope, which, turning around a polar axis, follows a star by a single motion. But the astronomical principle of this instrument was understood and applied long before the telescope itself was invented. Ptolemy, who is usually credited with the invention of the equatorially mounted pointer, was the first to apply the instrument to the determination of the moon's displacement or parallax.[1] The result contrasts strikingly with the ill success which he and other ancient astronomers experienced when they attempted to apply this and other methods to the determination of the sun's distance. He assigned 57' as the moon's parallax when she is on the horizon; in other words, his observations led him to the conclusion that the angle

---

[1] A trace of this early application of the principle remains in the name *parallactic instrument*, still sometimes given to the equatorial. The principle of the instrument is explained in the *Almagest*, and the instrument, as made before the telescope was invented, was sometimes called *Ptolemy's Rule*.

E M_H P, fig. 3, is one of 57', a value which would
set the moon's distance at almost exactly sixty times
the earth's radius. We shall see presently that this is
very close to the true value.[1] Other observations were
made by this method ; and it is probable that the
value given for the lunar parallax in the Alphonsine
Tables, viz. 58', was deduced from a comparison of
many such observations. This would give a distance
somewhat exceeding 59 times the earth's radius, or
more exactly, with the present estimate of the earth's
dimensions, 235,000 miles.

Tycho Brahé, from his own observations, based on
the same principle, found for the moon's horizontal
parallax 61', corresponding to a distance somewhat less
than 223,000 miles.

But a more satisfactory method of determining the
moon's distance is that which is based simply on the
considerations discussed at pp. 8, 9—in other words,
the method of observing the moon from two distant
stations whose exact position on the earth's globe has
been ascertained.

[1] Before this Aristarchus of Samos had set the moon's distance
at two million *stadia*, which, according to Buchotte's estimate of
the length of the Greek stadium, would be equal to about 230,000
miles. The method by which he deduced this result is not well
known ; but it is believed to have been based on the consideration
of the length of time occupied by the moon in passing from horizon
to horizon ; in fact, it would seem to have been a modification of
the method hypothetically considered in pp. 10–12. If so, it
corresponded to a certain degree with the method he applied to
determine the sun's distance. (See my treatise, *The Sun*, p. 25.)
Hipparchus considered that the moon's distance lay between 62
and 72½ times the radius of the earth. The above evaluation of
ptolemy is inferred from the numbers given at p. 211 of Prof.
Grant's *History of Physical Astronomy*.

Let us suppose, for convenience of illustration, that one station is ·the Greenwich Observatory, and the other the Observatory at the Cape of Good Hope. These two stations are not on the same meridian. At present, however, we shall not take into account the difference of longitude.

Let fig. 4 represent a side view of the earth at night, when Greenwich is at the place marked G. Let H h be a north and south horizontal line at Greenwich, G Z the vertical, G p (parallel to the earth's polar axis) the polar axis of the heavens; and let us suppose that the moon, when crossing the meridian, is seen in the direction G M; then the angle p G M is the moon's north polar distance.

Again, let us suppose C to be the Cape Town Observatory. In reality it has passed from the edge of the disc shown in fig. 4, by nearly 1¼ hour's rotation: but let us for the moment neglect this, and suppose the station C to be at the edge of the disc. Let H' C h' be the north and south horizontal line at C, C Z' the vertical, C p' (parallel to the earth's polar axis) the polar axis of the heavens (directed necessarily towards the south pole); and let us suppose that the moon, when crossing the meridian, is seen in the direction C M'. Then, since the lines G M and C M' are both pointed towards the moon's centre, they are not parallel lines, but meet, when produced, at that point.

Let fig. 5 represent this state of things on a smaller scale, M being the moon, G Greenwich, and C the Cape of Good Hope; then G C M is just such a

triangle as we considered at p. 8. The base-line
G C is of course known; and it is very easily seen that
the angles at G and C are known from the observations

Figs. 4 and 5.

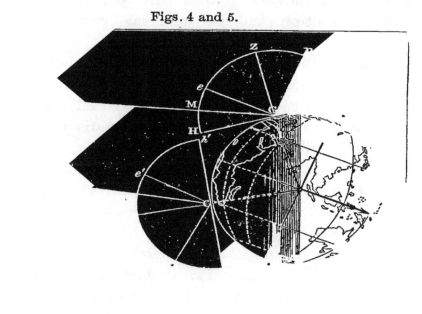

MEASUREMENT OF THE MOON'S DISTANCE.

pictured in fig. 4.[1] Thus M C and M G can be calculated.

[1] The distance from Greenwich to Cape Town is not in question,
but the distance between Greenwich and the point C on the meridian of Greenwich; for any effects due to the difference of longitude of Cape Town and Greenwich are readily taken into account
astronomically. Now the distance C G is the chord of a known arc
of a great circle of the earth. Thus C G is known, and the angles
O G C, O C G, are equally known. Again, the angle M G C is the
sum of the angles M G H and H G C; and of these M G H is the

Such is the general nature of the method for determining the moon's distance by observations made at different stations, and either simultaneously or so nearly simultaneously that the correction for the moon's motion in the interval can be readily made.[1]

One of the earliest series of observations directed to the determination of the moon's distance was that undertaken by Lacaille when he visited the Cape of Good Hope in 1750. From a comparison of his results with observations made in Europe, he deduced the value 57' 13·1" for the moon's mean equatorial horizontal parallax. This corresponds to a mean distance of 238,096 miles. But it is to be noticed that Lacaille was not acquainted with the true shape of the earth. He supposed the earth's compression to be greater than it really is; in fact, he supposed the equatorial to exceed the polar diameter in the propor-

moon's observed meridian altitude at Greenwich, while H G C is the complement of the known angle O G C. Hence M G C is known. In like manner M C G is known. So that we have the base-line and the two base angles of the triangle M C G known, and therefore M C and M G can be calculated. In reality the angle C M G is about 1½ degree.

[1] If such an instrument as the equatorial were as trustworthy as a meridional instrument, it would be easy to make the observations simultaneously, determining the polar distances of the moon at Greenwich and Cape Town respectively. But as a matter of fact it is absolutely necessary to observe the moon when she is on the meridian. What then is done is to deduce from the observed north polar distance of the moon when on the meridian at Cape Town (or from the moon's place at that time, with respect to some known star) her position at the moment when she is on the meridian of Greenwich.

tion of 200 to 199, whereas in reality the proportion is approximately 300 to 299 ; in other words, the compression is $\frac{1}{300}$. If this correction is taken into account, Lacaille's results give for the lunar parallax 57′ 4″·6, corresponding to a distance of 238,679 miles. Lalande, by comparing Lacaille's observations with his own, made simultaneously at Berlin,[1] found for the lunar parallax the value 57′ 3″·7, corresponding to a distance of 238,749 miles. It will be noticed that as Berlin is more than 13 degrees east of Greenwich, observations made on the moon when in the meridian, at Cape Town and at Berlin, are more nearly simultaneous than corresponding observations at Cape Town and Greenwich.

Bürg, by comparing Lacaille's observations with those made at Greenwich, deduced for the moon's parallax the value 57′ 1″, corresponding to a distance of 238,937 miles.

Henderson, the first who determined the distance of the celebrated star Alpha Centauri, made a series of lunar observations at the Cape of Good Hope in 1832 and 1833, with very imperfect instrumental means. From a comparison of these observations with others made at Greenwich and Cambridge, he deduced 57′ 1″·8 for the value of the moon's parallax.

---

[1] Lacaille was born on March 15, 1713, and Lalande on July 11, 1732, so that Lalande was nineteen years younger than Lacaille, who was himself but a young man when he made his observations. In fact, Lalande was but nineteen years old when he was sent to Berlin for the purpose of observing the moon simultaneously with Lacaille at the Cape of Good Hope.

The corresponding distance amounts to 238,881 miles.

Airy, from a discussion of the whole series of Greenwich observations, deduced the value 57′ 4″·94, corresponding to a distance of 238,656 miles.

But probably the most accurate value is that which has been deduced by Professor Adams from a comparison of Mr. Breen's observations at the Cape of Good Hope, with others made at Greenwich and Cambridge. Professor Adams deduced for the lunar parallax the value 57′ 2″·7, corresponding to a distance of 238,818 miles.

One other method of determining the moon's distance remains to be mentioned: it cannot, however, be called a strictly independent method, since it is based on the theory of gravity, which could not have been established without an accurate determination of the moon's distance.

In showing that the earth's attraction keeps the moon in her observed orbit, Newton had to take into account the moon's distance. He reasoned that the earth's attraction reduced as the square of the distance would be competent at the moon's distance to cause the observed deflection of the moon from the tangent to her path. He assumed the lunar parallax to be 57′ 30″, corresponding to a distance of 237,000 miles; and he found that the terrestrial attraction calculated for that distance corresponded so closely with the observed lunar motions as to leave no doubt of the truth of the theory he was dealing with. But now, when once the theory of gravity is admitted, we have in the observed

lunar motions the means of forming an exact estimate
of the earth's attraction at the moon's distance, and as
we know her attraction at the earth's surface, we are
enabled to infer the moon's distance. In passing, it
may be observed that this process is not, as it might
seem at a first view, mere arguing in a circle. Observation had already given a sufficiently accurate estimate
of the moon's distance to supply an initial test of the
theory that it is the earth's attraction reduced as the
square of the distance which retains the moon in her
orbit. This theory being accepted, and other tests
applied, we may fairly reason back from it in such sort
as to deduce the exact distance of the moon.

In this process, however, the mass of the moon would
have to be taken into account. In fact, as will be seen
in the next chapter, we must add the moon's mass to
the earth's in considering the actual tendency of the
moon towards the earth ; so that, if we know the moon's
mass, the earth's size, and the moon's period, we can
deduce the moon's distance.

Burckhardt, applying this method, on the assumption
that the moon's mass is $\frac{1}{75}$ of the earth's, deduced the
parallax 57' 0'', corresponding to a distance of 239,007
miles. Damoiseau, taking the moon's mass at $\frac{1}{74}$ of the
earth's, deduced a parallax of 57' 1'', corresponding to
a distance of 238,937 miles. Plana, assuming the
moon's mass to be $\frac{1}{87}$, found for the mean lunar parallax
the value 57' 3''·1 corresponding to a distance of
238,792 miles.

We shall throughout the rest of this work assume

that the moon's mean equatorial horizontal parallax is
57' 2''·7, and her distance, therefore, 238,818 miles,
the earth's equatorial diameter being assumed equal to
7,925·8 miles.

Now it follows from this that, as seen from the
moon at her mean distance, the earth's equatorial
radius subtends an angle of 57' 2''·7 ; that is, the
equatorial diameter of the earth covers on the heavens
an arc of 1° 54' 5''·4, as seen from the moon at her
mean distance. If the moon's orbit were circular,
the earth's equatorial diameter would always cover such
an arc. But the moon traverses a path of considerable
eccentricity. Its mean shape (for it varies in shape) is
exhibited in fig. 6, where C is the centre of the orbit,
E the earth, M the place of the moon when nearest
to the earth, or in perigee, M' her place when farthest
from the earth, or in apogee, m and m' her positions
when she is at her mean distance (in other words, m m'
is the minor axis of the moon's orbit). Thus E C is
the linear eccentricity of the orbit.[1] E C is about the
eighteenth part of C M, and is thus not at all an
evanescent quantity even on the small scale of fig. 6.
The distance E C is equal to about 13,113 miles. It
will be observed, however, that though the *eccentricity*
of the orbit is shown in fig. 6, the *ellipticity*—that is,
the departure from the circular shape—is not indicated.

[1] The true eccentricity is represented by the ratio of E C to
E M ; that is, in the case of the lunar orbit, it is about $\frac{1}{18}$ when the
orbit is in its mean condition. When the orbit has its maximum
eccentricity, the ratio rises to about $\frac{1}{15}$, and when the eccentricity
is at its minimum, the value is about $\frac{1}{22}$.

In reality, it would not be discernible on the scale of fig. 6.[1] ✓

But the eccentricity of the moon's orbit is not con-

Fig. 6.

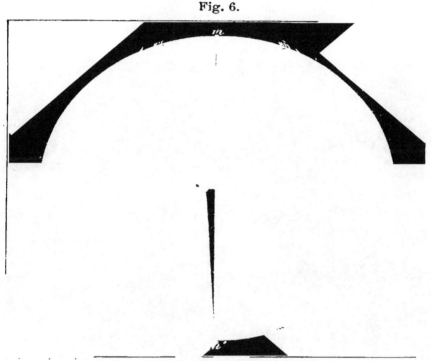

THE MOON'S ORBIT (MEAN ECCENTRICITY).

stant. Owing to the perturbations which the moon undergoes (as explained in the next chapter), her path

[1] By a well-known property of the ellipse, the distances E m and E m' are equal to C M and C M'. Hence C m is easily found. If, for convenience, we represent C M or E m by the number 18, E C will be represented by unity. Hence C m will be represented by $\sqrt{(18)^2-1}$, or by $\sqrt{323}$, or by .17·9722. The semi-axes C M and C m may be approximately represented by the numbers 1,800 and 1,797 ; that is, by the numbers 600 and 599 ; or C m is less than C M by less than 1-600th part of either.

changes in shape, the mean distance remaining throughout nearly constant. The shape of her path when it is
most eccentric, as well as when it is least eccentric, would
not differ appreciably from m M M', fig. 6, and therefore, so far as this relation is concerned, no new figure

Fig. 7.

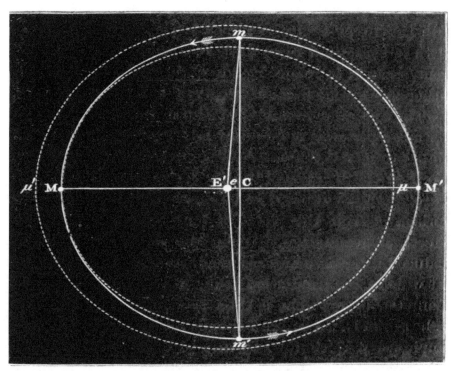

THE MOON'S ORBIT (MAXIMUM ECCENTRICITY).

is required. But for another purpose, presently to be
explained, it is convenient to have a picture exhibiting
the moon's path around the earth when the eccentricity
is a maximum. It is therefore shown in fig. 7, the
centre being at C and the earth at E', and M M' the

moon's path.   The point *e* shows the position occupied
by the earth's centre when the eccentricity is a minimum.   The distance E′ C is 15,760 miles, while *e* C is
10,510 miles.   Thus the difference, E′ *e*, is 5,250 miles,
or about two-thirds of the earth's diameter.   Owing to
the peculiarities of the lunar perturbations, however,
these numbers are not to be strictly applied in dealing
with the lunar orbit.   In fact, her distance from the
earth is somewhat more increased, owing to perturbations, than it is reduced—when the maximum effects
either way are compared.

The apparent diameter of the moon when she is at
her mean distance is found by telescopic observation (at
night) to be 31′ 9″, or 1,869″ (when reduced to correspond to the distance of the earth's centre ; or, approximately, when supposed to be made on the moon in the
horizon).   But this value is partly increased by the
effects of irradiation.   When the moon's diameter is
deduced from observations made during solar eclipses
(at which time irradiation tends to reduce her apparent
diameter, because she is then seen as a dark body on a
light ground), the value depends partly on the telescope
employed.   With instruments of average power it is
about 30′ 55″, or 1,855″.   From a careful discussion of
the occultations of stars by the moon, as observed
at Greenwich and at Cambridge, Sir George Airy
inferred that the length of the moon's mean apparent diameter is 31′ 5″·1, or 1,865″·1.   This is the
value assumed throughout the present work.   (It is a
useful aid to the memory to notice that the number of

seconds of arc in this value gives the number of
the year in which Sir George Airy announced his
results.)

There is no apparent flattening of the lunar orb as
seen from the earth; the most careful measurement
presents it as circular. Since the earth's semi-diameter
subtends from the moon an angle of 57′ 2″·7, or
3,422‴·7, while the moon's diameter subtends from the
earth an angle of 1,865‴·1, it follows that the moon's
diameter is less than the earth's radius (or 3,962·9
miles) in the proportion of 18,651 to 34,227. Thus it
is readily calculated (by rule of three) that the moon's
real diameter (or at least any diameter square to the
line of sight from the earth) is 2,159·6 miles. It
chances that this is the exact value adopted by Mädler,
though obtained by employing a different value (1) of
the lunar parallax, (2) of the lunar apparent diameter,
and (3) of the earth's real diameter.

It follows that the earth's equatorial diameter exceeds the moon's in the proportion of about 3,670 to
1,000; or, if we represent the earth's equatorial diameter by 10,000, then the moon's would be represented
by 2,725. Assuming the moon's shape to be globular,
and the earth's compression $\frac{1}{300}$, it follows that the
earth's surface exceeds the moon's in the proportion of
about 13,435 to 1,000; or if we represent the earth's
surface by 10,000, the moon's will be represented by
744. Lastly, on the same assumption as to the moon's
shape, the earth's volume exceeds the moon's in the
proportion of about 49,441 to 1,000; or, if the earth's

volume be represented by 10,000, the moon's will be represented by 209.

Roughly, we may take the moon's diameter as two-sevenths of the earth's, her surface as two twenty-sevenths, her volume as two ninety-ninths. Of these proportions, the most interesting is that between the moon's surface and the earth's; for neither the diameter nor the volume of the moon is specially related to her condition as a globe comparable with our earth in regard to those features which affect our own requirements. But the surface of the moon's globe obviously affects her fitness, in one important respect, to be the abode of living creatures. Now the actual surface of the moon is rather more than two twenty-sevenths of the earth's, and the surface of the earth is about 196,870,000 square miles: hence the moon's surface is about 14,600,000 square miles. This is about the same as the areas of Europe and Africa together (exclusive of the islands usually included with these continents). It is almost exactly equal to the areas of North and South America, exclusive of their islands. The portion of either hemisphere of the earth lying on the polar side of latitude 58° 23′, is equal to the whole surface of the moon. The arctic and antarctic regions together exceed the moon in area in about the proportion of 10 to 9. Lastly, it may be noticed that, reckoning the Russian empire (in Europe and Asia) at 7,900,000 square miles, and the British dominions at 9,100,000, these two empires together exceed the whole surface of the moon by no less than 2,400,000 square miles. The part of the moon actually visible to us (taking her librations into account) is somewhat more extensive than the Russian empire, while the part totally concealed from us is equal in area to about seven-tenths of the British empire.

It should be noticed that, under all circumstances, whether the moon is at her mean distance, or nearer to or farther from the earth (in fact, whatever the size of her disc may be), the earth's disc, as supposed to be seen at the moment from the moon, is nearly 13½ times larger.

But the variation of the moon's apparent size, according to her varying distance, must also be carefully taken into account. It is much greater than is commonly supposed. The observed telescopic mean diameter of the moon is, as already stated, 31′ 9″, while 31′ 5″·1 is taken as the true mean diameter,—that is, the telescopic diameter reduced for the effects of irradiation. Now, the telescopic semi-diameter when the moon is at her nearest to the earth,—that is to say, not merely in perigee, but in perigee at a time when her orbit has its greatest eccentricity,—is found to be 33′ 32″·1 ; while, when the moon is farthest from the earth, the observed diameter is 29′ 22″·9. These values, reduced for the effects of irradiation, give for the diameter,—

(1) When the moon is nearest to the earth, 33′ 30·1″, or 2,010·1″
(2)   ,,   ,, at her mean distance, 31 5·1, or 1,865·1
(3)   ,,   ,, farthest from the earth, 29 20·9, or 1,760·9

It has been already mentioned (p. 26) that the mean

distance is not the arithmetic mean between the greatest and least distances ; it necessarily follows that the mean apparent diameter is not the arithmetic mean between the greatest and least apparent diameters.

The apparent surface of the lunar disc varies, not as these diameters, but as the squares of these diameters. It is easily calculated that if the size of the lunar disc, when the moon is at her mean distance, is represented by the number 10,000, then, when she is nearest to the earth, her disc presents a surface of 11,615 ; while, when she is farthest, the apparent surface is but 8,914. Or, if we call the surface of the moon's disc when nearest to us 10,000, then, when she is farthest from us, the surface of her disc would be represented by the number 7,674. We may very nearly represent the apparent size of the moon's disc when she is nearest to us, and when she is farthest from us, by the numbers 4 and 3 ; in other words, when the moon is full and farthest from the earth, she gives only three-fourths of the amount of light which she gives when full and nearest to the earth. But there is a very convenient way of representing the relative dimensions of the moon's disc when she is at her nearest and farthest. It is very easily shown that if we describe circles M μ and M' μ' about E' as centre, fig. 7, p. 25, and passing through the points M and M', then the circles M μ and M' μ' represent the dimensions of the lunar disc when the moon is at M' or M respectively. In like manner we could compare the dimensions of the lunar disc when the moon is in perigee and apogee, and the eccentricity has its least value (*i.e.* the earth as at *e*, fig. 7); or when the eccentricity has its mean value (the earth as at E, fig. 6).[1]

It remains only that we should consider the subject of the moon's mass,—that is, of the quantity of matter contained in her globe, whose volume or size is already known to us.

There are four different ways in which the moon's mass may be determined.

First, since, as we have already mentioned (and shall explain further in the next chapter), the moon's motion under the earth's attraction is calculable when the size of the earth, the value of terrestrial gravity, and the moon's distance and mass are known, it follows that as the size of the earth, the earth's gravity, and the moon's period are very accurately known, and as the moon's distance has been determined by independent observations, her mass may be inferred by the consideration of her observed motions ; in fact, precisely as, in the method for determining the moon's distance, described at p. 21, we infer the distance when the mass is known, so, if the distance be independently deter-

---

[1] This is a very convenient method of comparing the apparent dimensions of the same orb seen at different distances. We take these distances, and with them describe circles ; then these circles represent the relative apparent dimensions,—the largest, of course, corresponding to the appearance of the globe as seen at the least distance, and *vice versâ*. Thus suppose that we wish to compare the size of the sun as seen from two planets, which we may call, for convenience, P and P', and that we have a chart of orbits including the orbits of these planets ; then if the orbit of P represent the size of the sun as seen from P', the orbit P' represents the size of the sun as seen from P.

mined, we can infer the mass.   And it is to be observed
that although, if these two methods alone. existed for
determining the mass and distance, they would leave
both problems indeterminate ; yet, as other methods
exist, these two afford very useful tests of the accuracy
of the results deduced by the other methods.

Laplace, adopting the value 57′ 12″·03 for the lunar
parallax, deduced for the moon's mass, by this method,
the value $\frac{1}{74\cdot9}$, the earth's mass being unity.

Another method for determining the moon's mass is
based on the theory of the tides.   If the height of the
tides at any place be observed carefully for a long period
of time, and then the mean height of the spring tides
be compared with the mean height of the neap tides,
we can infer the relative efficiency of the sun and moon
when acting together to raise the tidal wave, and when
their actions are opposed.   The problem is, indeed,
rendered difficult by theoretical and practical considerations of much complexity.   But presenting the
problem roughly, we may say that, after careful attention to the observations, we obtain $L + S$ and $L - S$,
where L is the lunar action and S the sun's ; the first
at spring tides, the second at neap tides.   Now, the
sum of these compound actions is 2L, and the difference 2S ; so that we can infer L the lunar action, and
S the solar action.   These enable us to infer the relation between the moon's mass and the sun's.   Newton
was led, by comparing the results of his theory with
the observed height of the tides, to the conclusion that
the moon's mass is $\frac{1}{39\cdot788}$, the earth's being represented
by unity.   Laplace was led by the observation of the

tides at Brest to the theory that the moon's mass is $\frac{1}{56\cdot6}$ of the earth's. He considered, however, that this result, although less than Newton's, might still be considerably too large, since he judged that the height of the tides at Brest might be influenced by several local circumstances. It seems obvious that this method cannot be susceptible of very great accuracy, since the shape of the ocean masses, as well with respect to their horizontal as to their vertical proportions, renders the direct application of the theory of the tides impracticable.

Another method depends on the circumstance that the earth circuits once in each lunation round the centre of gravity of her own mass and the moon's. Owing to this circumstance, the earth is sometimes slightly in advance of, and sometimes slightly behind, her mean place in longitude. In fact, we know that the moon, circling around the same centre of gravity, but in a much wider orbit, is sometimes in advance of the earth and sometimes behind the earth—regarding these orbs as two planets severally pursuing their courses round the sun ; and if we look upon the earth's motion as representing very nearly the motion of a planet at her distance and undisturbed by a satellite (which is not far from being the case), then we see that the moon, owing to her motion in an orbit 477,600 miles in diameter round the earth, is alternately 238,800 miles in advance of, and as many behind, her mean place in longitude. So that, since the earth circuits round the common centre of gravity

D

of the two bodies, in a smaller orbit, she will be alternately in advance of and behind her mean place [1] by the radius of that orbit. Obviously the effect of this will be that the sun, round which the earth is thus moving, will seem to be alternately in advance of and behind the mean place due to his apparent annual motion round the heavens. His apparent place will obviously not be affected at all when the moon is on a line with the sun and earth, or *in syzygy,* as it is called (that is, when it is either *new* moon or *full*), for then the earth's displacement is on the same line, and the only effect is that the sun appears either very slightly larger (when the moon is ' full ' and the earth most displaced *towards* the sun), or very slightly smaller (when the moon is ' new ' and the earth most displaced *from* the sun). Both effects would be quite inappreciable. But when the moon is at her first quarter, the earth is displaced towards the side occupied by the moon at her third quarter ; that is, she is at her maximum displacement *in advance* of her mean place, and the sun also appears accordingly at his maximum displacement *in advance* of his mean place in his apparent annual motion round the heavens. In like manner, when the moon is at her third quarter, the sun appears at his maximum displacement *behind* his mean place. It is easy to ascertain what the sun's displacement should be, on any given assumption

[1] The mean place here referred to is that place which the earth would have if she were travelling alone round the sun, and not, as is actually the case, under the perturbing influence of a satellite.

as to the moon's mass. Suppose the moon's mass, for example, to be $\frac{1}{80}$th of the earth's, then the centre of gravity of the. earth and moon lies eighty times farther from the moon's centre than from the earth's. Hence the distance of this centre of gravity from the earth is $\frac{1}{81}$st part of 238,818 miles, or 2,949 miles. Thus the sun may be displaced from his mean place by the angle which a line 2,949 miles long subtends at the earth's distance from the sun. Since the equatorial semidiameter of the earth is 3,963 miles, this displacement of the sun is equal to about $\frac{3}{4}$ths of the small arc called the solar parallax, or is rather more than 6″·6, if we assume 8″·9 to be the mean value of the solar parallax. This quantity is about $\frac{1}{290}$th part of the sun's apparent diameter.

But obviously if the exact amount of the maximum displacement can be ascertained, we can infer precisely what proportion the distance of the earth's centre from the centre of gravity of the earth and moon ·bears to the earth's mean diameter. We shall have to make an assumption as to the value of the solar parallax (that is, in effect, as to the sun's distance); but that is an element which has been determined with a satisfactory degree of accuracy in many different ways. Hence the moon's mass can be determined with a corresponding degree of accuracy, if only the observations of the sun's displacement are accurately made.

From a great number of observations of the moon, Delambre deduced for the sun's maximum displacement

(called the *sun's parallactic inequality*) the value
$7''\cdot5$. Hence Laplace deduced the value $\frac{1}{69\cdot2}$ for the
moon's mass. With the values at present adopted for
the distances of the sun and moon, he would have
deduced $\frac{1}{72}$ as the value of the moon's mass.

In recent times the meridional observations of the
sun have been so numerous and exact, that the means
of determining the moon's mass by this method are
much more satisfactory. Thus we can place very
great reliance on Leverrier's estimate of the parallactic
inequality, viz. $6''\cdot50$. Professor Newcomb, of Washing-
ton, deduces from a yet wider range of observations the
value $6''\cdot52$. These values lie so close together as to
show that the observations on which they have been
based suffice for the very accurate determination of this
quantity.

Now the value of the moon's mass which we should
infer from the mean ($6''\cdot51$) of these two estimates,
will depend on the value we assign to the solar
parallax. If we estimate the mean equatorial horizontal solar parallax at $8''\cdot91$, it would follow that the
distance of the centre of gravity of the earth and moon
from the earth's centre is $\frac{651}{891}$sts of the earth's equatorial semidiameter, or $\frac{651}{891}$sts of 3,963 miles; that is,
about 2,895 miles. Thence it follows that the moon's
mass is to the sum of the masses of the earth and moon
as 2,895 to 238,818, or—

Moon's mass : Earth's mass :: 2895 : 235923
::   1 :   81·5

that is, the earth's mass exceeds the moon's $81\frac{1}{2}$ times.

In calculating the sun's distance from the solar parallactic inequality, the Greenwich observers have adopted $\frac{1}{81\cdot45}$ for the moon's mass. Leverrier adopted the value $\frac{1}{81\cdot48}$ (originally, owing to an error of calculation, Leverrier adopted the value $\frac{1}{81\cdot84}$). Professor Newcomb has adopted the value $\frac{1}{81\cdot08}$.

These values were deduced by an independent method, the last remaining to be described, and on the whole perhaps the most satisfactory. Owing to the attraction of the sun and moon on the bulging equatorial parts of the earth, the axis of the earth undergoes the disturbance called precession. Now this disturbance, whose period is about 25,868 years, depends on the inclination of the earth's equator-plane to lines drawn from the sun and moon. The portion due to the moon's action depends on the inclination of the equator-plane to a line from the moon. Of course this inclination varies during the moon's circuit of the earth, because she twice crosses the celestial equator in such a circuit, and at these times the moon's action vanishes. But *these* changes are comparatively unimportant so far as the progress of the displacement of the earth's axis is concerned, simply because the displacement during a month is exceedingly small. There is, however, a change which, having a much longer period, is clearly recognisable. The moon's orbit is inclined to the ecliptic by rather more than five degrees. If the orbit thus inclined had a constant position, its inclination to the earth's equator (assumed also to have a constant position, which is approximately the case) would also be constant. But we shall see in the next chapter that the direction of the line in which the moon's plane intersects the ecliptic makes a complete revolution once in about 18½ years. Hence the inclination of the moon's orbit to the equator is affected by an oscillation of rather more than five degrees on either side of the mean inclination, which is the same as that of the ecliptic to the equator, or about 23½ degrees. Thus the inclination passes in the course of rather more than 18½ years from about 18½ degrees to about 28½ degrees, and thence to about 18½ degrees again. Obviously the lunar action varies accordingly; and, moreover, it is to be remembered that if the lunar action were alone in question, the pole of the equator would circle, not about the pole of the ecliptic, but about the pole of the moon's orbit-plane; and as this pole is itself circling about the pole of the ecliptic in a period of rather more than 18½ years, it is readily seen that there arises a fluctuation in the motion of the pole of the heavens, having the same period. This fluctuation is necessarily small, because in 18½ years the whole motion due to precession is small,[1] and this fluctuation is only a minute portion of the whole motion. It is found to amount, in fact, to about 9″·2, by which amount the pole of the heavens, and with it the apparent position of every star in the heavens, is, at a maximum, displaced from the mean

---

[1] The 1360th part of the complete circuit made by the pole of the heavens round the pole of the ecliptic (less than 16′ of a small circle of the heavens having an arc-radius of 23½ degrees), or about 6¼′ of arc.

position estimated for a perfectly uniform precessional motion. Now, since this displacement (called *nutation*) is solely dependent on the moon's mass, it follows that when its observed value is compared with the formula deduced by theory, a means of determining the moon's mass is obtained.

Laplace, adopting Maskelyne's value of the maximum nutation—namely, $9''\cdot6$,—inferred for the moon's mass $\frac{1}{72}$ (the earth's being regarded as unity). Professor Newcomb, adopting $9''\cdot223$ for the lunar nutation, and $50''\cdot378$ for the annual luni-solar precession, deduces the value $\frac{1}{81\cdot06}$. Leverrier, with the same values, deduces $\frac{1}{81\cdot45}$. Mr. Stone, in his latest calculation, with the same values, deduces for the moon's mass $\frac{1}{81\cdot36}$.[1]

In the present work we adopt $\frac{1}{81\cdot40}$ (or $0\cdot01228$) as the moon's mass, the earth's being regarded as unity. Taking the moon's volume as $\frac{1}{49\cdot26}$ (the earth's as unity), it follows that the moon's mass bears a smaller proportion to the earth's than her volume bears to the earth's volume, in the ratio of 4,925 to 8,140. Hence the moon's mean density must be less than the earth's in this ratio. So that if we express the earth's density by unity, the moon's will be expressed by $0\cdot6052$. If the earth's mean density be held to be $5\cdot7$ times that of water, the moon's mean density is rather less than $3\frac{1}{2}$ times the density of water.

Such are the main circumstances of the long process of research by which astronomers have been enabled

---

[1] To these values may be added Lindenau's estimate, $\frac{1}{87\cdot7}$, and the estimate obtained by MM. Peters and Schidlowski, $\frac{1}{81}$.

to pass from the first simple notions suggested by the moon's aspect and movements, to their present accurate knowledge of the distance, diameter, surface, volume, and weight of this beautiful orb, the companion of our earth in her motion round the sun.

CHAPTER II.

THE MOON'S MOTIONS.

ALTOGETHER the most important circumstance in what may be called the history of the moon is the part which she has played in assisting the progress of modern exact astronomy. It is not saying too much to assert that if the earth had had no satellite the law of gravitation would never have been discovered. *Now* indeed that the law has been established, we can see amid the movements of the planets the clearest evidence respecting it; insomuch that if we could conceive all that has been learned respecting the moon blotted out of memory, and the moon herself annihilated, astronomers would yet be able to demonstrate the law of gravity in the most complete manner. But this circumstance is solely due to the wonderful perfection to which observational astronomy on the one hand, and mathematical research on the other, have been brought, since the law of gravitation was established, and *through* the establishment of that law. It needs but little acquaintance with the history of Newton's great discovery to see that only the overwhelming evidence he was able to adduce from the moon's movements could have enabled him to compel

the scientific world to hearken to his reasoning, and
to accept his conclusions.   We can scarcely doubt that
he himself would never have attacked the subject as
he actually did, with the whole force of his stupendous
intellect, had he not recognised in the moon's movements the means of at once testing and demonstrating
the law of the universe.   Had the evidence been one
whit less striking, the attention of his contemporaries
would soon have been diverted from his theories,
which indeed could barely have risen above the level
of speculations but for the lunar motions.   Astronomy
would never have attained its present position had
this happened.   It would have seemed vain to track
the moon and the planets with continually increasing
care, if there had been no prospect of explaining the
peculiarities of motion exhibited by these bodies.
Kepler had already done all that could be done to
represent the planetary *motions* by empirical laws,—
the planetary *perturbations* could be explained in no
such manner.   The application of mathematical calculations to the subject would have been simply useless;
and there would have been nothing to suggest the
invention of new modes of mathematical research, and
therefore nothing to lead to those masterpieces of
analysis by which Laplace and Lagrange, Euler and
Clairaut, Adams, Airy, and Leverrier, have elucidated
the motions of the heavenly bodies.

The history of the progress of investigation by
which Newton established the law of gravitation is full
of interest.   And although a high degree of mathe-

matical training is requisite fully to apprehend its significance, yet a good general idea of the subject may
readily be obtained even by those who are not pro-
foundly versed in mathematics.

It had been recognised long before Newton's time
that this globe on which we live possesses a power
of drawing to itself objects left unsupported at any
distance above the earth's surface. It is, indeed, very
common to find the recognition of this fact ascribed
to Newton, who is popularly supposed to have asked
himself *why* a certain apple fell in his orchard. But
the fact was thoroughly recognised long before his
time. Galileo, Newton's great predecessor, had instituted a series of researches into the law of this terrestrial attraction. He had found that all bodies are
equally affected by it, so far as his experimental inquiries
extended ; and he established the important law that
the velocity communicated to falling bodies by the
earth's attraction increases uniformly with the time of
falling ; so that whatever velocity is acquired at the end
of one second, a twofold velocity is acquired at the end
of the next, a triple velocity at the end of the third,
and so on.

In order to estimate the actual velocity which
gravity communicates to falling bodies, Galileo caused
bodies to descend slightly inclined planes. He showed
that the action of gravity was diminished in the proportion which the height of the plane's summit bears
to the sloped face ; and by making the slope very
slight, he caused the velocity acquired in any given

short time to be correspondingly reduced. To reduce friction as much as possible, he mounted the descending bodies on wheels, and made the inclined planes of hard substances perfectly polished. But other and better methods were devised : and when Newton's labours began, men of science were already familiar with the fact that a falling body, if unretarded by atmospheric resistance or other cause, passes in the first second over $16\frac{1}{10}$ feet, and has acquired at the end of the second a velocity of $32\frac{1}{5}$ feet per second ; by the end of the second second it has passed over $64\frac{2}{5}$ feet in all, and has acquired a velocity of $64\frac{2}{5}$ feet per second ; at the end of the third it has passed over $144\frac{9}{10}$, and has acquired a velocity of $96\frac{3}{5}$ feet per second ; and so on,—the law being that the space fallen varies as the square of the number of elapsed seconds,[1] while the velocity varies as this number directly.

So much, as I have said, was known before Newton began to inquire into the laws influencing the celestial bodies; so that, if there is any truth in the story of the apple, Newton certainly did not inquire *why* the apple fell to the earth. It is not impossible that on some occasion, when he was pondering over the motions of the celestial bodies—and perhaps thinking of those inviting speculations by which Borelli, Kepler, and others had been led to regard the celestial motions as due to attraction—the fall of an apple may have suggested to Newton that terrestrial gravity afforded a

---

[1] The spaces traversed in successive seconds are proportional to the numbers 1, 3, 5, 7, &c.

clue which, rightly followed up, might lead to an explanation of the mystery. If the attraction of the sun rules the planets, the attraction of the earth must rule the moon. *What if the very force which drew the apple to the ground be that which keeps the distant moon from passing away into space on a tangent to her actual orbit !*

Whether the idea was suggested in this particular way or otherwise, it is certain that in 1665, at the age of only 23 years, Newton was engaged in the inquiry whether the earth may not retain the moon in its orbit by the very same inherent virtue or attractive energy whereby she draws bodies to her surface when they are left unsupported.

In order to deal with this question, he required to know the law according to which the attractive force diminishes with distance. Assuming it to be identical in quality with the force by which the sun retains the several planets in their orbits, he had, in the observed motions of the planets, the means of determining the law very readily. The reasoning he actually employed is not quite suited to these pages. I substitute the following, which the reader may, if he please, omit (passing to the next paragraph), but it is not difficult to grasp. Let us call the distance of a planet (the earth, suppose) unity or 1, its period 1, its velocity 1. Let the distance of a planet farther from the sun be called D; then the third law of Kepler tells us that its period will be the square root of D × D × D, or will be D$\sqrt{D}$. But regarding the orbits as circles around the sun as centre, the circumference of the larger orbit will exceed that of the smaller in the proportion of D to 1 ; hence, if the velocity of the outer planet were equal to that of the inner, the period of the outer planet would be D. But it is greater, being $D\sqrt{D}$ (that is, it is greater in the proportion of $\sqrt{D}$ to 1); hence the velocity of the outer planet must be less, in the proportion of 1 to $\sqrt{D}$. Now the sun's energy causes the direction of the earth's motion to be changed through four right angles in the time 1 ; that of the outer planet being similarly deflected in the time $D\sqrt{D}$; and we know that a moving body is more easily deflected (*in direction*) in exact proportion as its velocity is less ; so that the outer planet, moving $\sqrt{D}$ times more slowly, ought to be deflected $\sqrt{D}$ times more quickly if the sun influenced it as much as he does the nearer one. Since the outer planet, instead of being deflected $\sqrt{D}$ times more quickly, is deflected $D\sqrt{D}$ times less quickly, the influence of the sun on the outer planet must be less than on the earth $\sqrt{D} \times D\sqrt{D}$ times,— that is, $D \times D$ (or D^2) times less. In other words, the attraction of the sun diminishes inversely as the square of the distance.

Newton had therefore only to determine whether the force continually deflecting the moon from the tangent to her path is equal in amount to the force of terrestrial gravity reduced in accordance with this law of inverse squares, in order to obtain at least a first test of the correctness of the theory which had suggested itself to his mind. Let us consider how this was to be done; and in order that the account may agree as closely as possible with the actual history of the discovery, let us employ the elements actually adopted by Newton at this stage of his labours.

Newton adopted for the moon's distance in terms of the earth's radius a value very closely corresponding to that now in use. We may, for our present purpose, regard this estimate as placing the moon at a distance equal to sixty terrestrial radii. ' Thus the attraction of the earth is reduced at the moon's distance in the proportion of the square of sixty, or 3,600, to unity. Now, let us suppose the moon's orbit circular, and let $m \, m'$, fig. 8, be the arc traversed by the moon in a

Fig. 8.

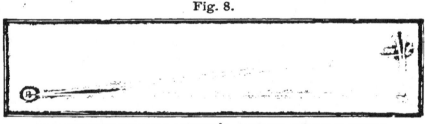

ILLUSTRATING THE EARTH'S ACTION ON THE MOON.

second around the earth at E ($m \, m'$ is of course much larger in proportion than the arc really traversed by the moon in a second), then when at m the moon's course was such, that if the earth had not attracted her, she would have been carried along the tangent line $m \, t$; and if t be the place she would have reached in a second, then $m \, t$ is equal to $m \, m'$, and E t will pass almost exactly through the point m'. Thus $t \, m'$, which represents the amount of fall towards the earth in one

second, may be regarded as lying on the line t E.[1]
Now m' E is equal to m E, and therefore t m' represents
the difference between the two sides m E and t E of
the right-angled triangle m E t. Newton adopted the
measure of the earth in vogue at the time, according
to which a degree of arc on the equator was supposed
equal in length to 60 miles, or the earth's equatorial
circumference equal to 21,600 miles. This gave for
the circumference of the moon's orbit 1,296,000 miles,
and for the moon's motion in one second rather less
than half a mile. Thus t m and m E are known, for
m E is equal to thirty terrestrial diameters ; and thus
it is easy to determine t E.[2] Now Newton found, that
with the estimate he had adopted for the earth's dimensions, t E exceeded m E by an amount which, increased
3,600-fold, only gave about 14 feet, instead of $16\frac{1}{10}$ feet,
the actual fall in a second at the earth's surface.

This discordance appeared to Newton to be too
great to admit of being reconciled in any way with the
theory he had conceived. If the deflection of the
moon's path had given a result *greater* than the actual
value of gravity, he could have explained the discrepancy as due to the circumstance that the moon's own

---

[1] In the account ordinarily given, t m' is taken as lying parallel
to m E. This is *also* approximately true. As a matter of fact the
point m' lies a little outside t E (that is, on the side away from m)
and a little within the parallel to m E, through t. But the angle
t E m is exceedingly minute. This angle as drawn represents the
moon's motion for about half a day instead of a single second of
time.

[2] By Euc. I. 47 the square on t E is equal to the squares on t m
and m E.

mass adds to the attraction between the earth and herself. But a *less* value was quite inexplicable. He therefore laid aside the investigation.

Fourteen years later Newton's attention was again attracted to the subject by a remark in a letter addressed to him by Dr. Hooke, to the effect that a body attracted by a force varying inversely as the square of the distance would travel in an elliptic orbit, having the centre of force in one of the *foci*. I do not at present pause to explain this remark, which is indeed only introduced here to indicate the sequence of Newton's researches. It is to be noted that Hooke gave no proof of the truth of his remark; nor was there anything in his letter to show that he had established the relation. He was not, indeed, endowed with such mathematical abilities as would have been needed (in his day) to master the problem in question. Newton, however, grappled with it at once, and before long the idea suggested by Hooke had been mathematically demonstrated by Newton. Yet, even in ascribing the idea to Hooke's suggestion at this epoch, we must not forget that Newton, in the very circumstance that he had discussed the moon's motion as possibly ruled by the earth's attraction, had implicitly entertained the idea now first explicitly enunciated by Hooke: for the moon does not move in a circle around the earth, but in an ellipse.

In studying this particular problem, Newton's attention was naturally drawn again to the long-abandoned theory that the earth's attraction governs the moon's motions. But he was still unable to remove the discrepancy which had foiled him in 1665.

At length, however, in 1684, news reached him that Picard [1] had measured a meridional arc with great care, and with instrumental appliances superior to any which had been hitherto employed. The new estimate of the earth's dimensions differed considerably from the estimate employed by Newton before. Instead of a degree of arc at the equator being but 60 miles in length, it now appeared that there are rather more than 69 miles in each degree. The effect of this change will be at once apparent. The earth's attractive energy at the moon's distance remains unaffected, simply because the proportion of the moon's distance to the earth's diameter had alone been in question. Newton, therefore, still estimated the earth's attraction at the moon's distance as less than her attraction at her own surface, in the proportion of 1 to 3,600. But now all the real dimensions, as well of the earth as of the moon's orbit, were enlarged linearly in the proportion of $69\frac{1}{2}$ to 60. Therefore the fall of the moon per second towards the earth, increased in the proportion of 3,600 to 1, was enlarged from rather less than 14 feet to rather more than 16 feet—agreeing, therefore, quite as closely as could be expected with the observed fall of $16\frac{1}{10}$ feet per second in a body acted upon by gravity and starting from rest.

It is said that as Newton found his figures tending

---

[1] Picard died at Paris in 1682, two years before the news of his labours had reached the ears of Newton.

to the desired end, he was so agitated that he was compelled to ask a friend to complete the calculations. The story is probably apocryphal, because the calculations actually required were of extreme simplicity Yet if any circumstance could have rendered Newton unable to proceed with a few simple processes of multiplication and division, undoubtedly the great discovery which was now being revealed to him might have led to such a result. For he clearly recognised the fact that the interpretation of the moon's motion was not what was in reality in question, nor even the explanation of the movements of all the bodies of the solar system; but that the law he was inquiring into must be, if once established, the law of the universe itself.

If we consider the position in which matters now stood, we shall see that in reality the law of gravitation had already been placed on a somewhat firm and stable basis. Newton had shown that the motions of the planets are conformable to the theory that the sun attracts each planet with a force inversely proportional to the square of the planet's distance. The motions of Jupiter's satellites (the only scheme known to Newton) agreed similarly with this law of attraction. And now he had shown that, in the case of our own moon, the attraction exerted by the central body round which the moon moves is related to the attraction exerted by this body, the earth, on objects at her surface, according to precisely the same law. Furthermore, it was known that all bodies are attracted in the same way by the earth, let their condition or elementary constitution

be what it may.   The inference seemed abundantly
clear that the law of attraction—with effects directly
proportional to the attracting masses, and inversely
proportional to the square of the distances separating
them—is the general law of matter, and prevails as
far as matter prevails—that is, throughout the universe.

But Newton was sensible that a law of this nature
could not be established unless some special evidence,
suited to attract the attention of scientific men to the
subject, were adduced and insisted upon.   The discovery
must throw light on some facts hitherto unexplained—
must, in effect, achieve some striking success—before
men could be expected to look favourably upon it.

What Newton determined to do, then, was this.
The law had been shown to accord with the general
features of the moon's motions.   But these motions
are characterised by many peculiarities.   At one time
she takes a longer, at another a shorter time, in circling
around the earth, than that average period called the
sidereal lunar month.   At one time she is in advance
of her mean place, calculated on the supposition of a
simple elliptic orbit ; at another time she is behind her
mean place.   The inclination of her path is variable,
as is the position of its plane ; so also the eccentricity
of her path and the position of her perigee are variable.
Newton saw that if the law of gravitation is true, the
moon's motion around the earth must necessarily be
disturbed by the sun's attraction.   If he could show
that the peculiarities of the moon's motions vary in

accordance with the varying effects of the sun's perturbing influence, and still more if he could show that the
extent of the lunar perturbations corresponds with the
actual amount of the sun's perturbing action, the law
of gravitation would be established in a manner there
could be no disputing.

Let us consider the general nature of the moon's
perturbations caused by the sun's attraction.

In the first place, I may mention a fact which
will perhaps seem surprising to many. Though the
sun's disturbing influence on the moon is such that the
moon's course around the earth is not very different in
any single revolution from that which she would have
if the sun's attraction had no existence ; yet the sun
actually exerts a far more powerful influence on the
moon than the earth does. As we shall have to consider the relation between the two forces, we may as
well proceed at once to prove this excess of power on
the sun's part.

The law of gravitation enables us at once to compare the sun's mass with the earth's. For precisely as
we have been able to show that under the influence of
terrestrial gravity the moon, at her distance, should
follow such a path as she actually traverses, so we can
determine how much a body should be deflected per
second at the earth's distance from the sun if his mass
were equal to the earth's ; and by comparing this amount
with the actual deflection, we can compare the sun's
mass with the earth's.

Or we may proceed in this way :—

The earth, at a distance of 238,800 miles from the moon, has power to deflect the direction of the moon's motion through four right angles in 27·322 days, the moon moving with a velocity which we may represent by $\frac{238,800}{27\cdot322}$.[1] The sun, at a distance from the earth equal to about 92,500,000 miles, has power to deflect the direction of her motion through four right angles in 365·256 days, the earth moving with a velocity which we may represent by $\frac{92,500,000}{365\cdot256}$. Now *first*, since gravity varies inversely as the square of the distance, the sun would require (if other things were equal) to have an attractive power exceeding the earth's in the ratio $\left(\frac{92,500,000}{238,800}\right)^2$ to produce the same effect on her that she produces on the moon; and *secondly*, since the deflection of a body's line of motion is a work which will be done at a rate proportional to the force which operates, the sun's power (if other things were equal) should be less than the earth's in the ratio $\frac{27\cdot322}{365\cdot256}$, to accomplish in one year what the earth accomplishes in a month; and *lastly*, since the faster a body moves the greater is the force necessary to deflect its course through a given angle in a given time, it is obvious that the sun's attractive power should exceed the earth's in the proportion of $\frac{92,500,000}{365\cdot256}$ to $\frac{238,800}{27\cdot322}$,—that is, in the ratio $\frac{92,500,000 \times 27\cdot322}{238,800 \times 365\cdot256}$, to produce a given change of direction in the case of the quickly-moving earth, in the same

[1] We need not consider the velocity in miles per hour, or the like ; because, throughout the paragraph, relative and not absolute velocities are in question. Hence we can represent the moon's velocity by the radius of her orbit divided by her period, provided we represent the earth's velocity round the sun in like manner.

time that the earth produces such a change in the case of the less swiftly-moving moon. We have only to combine these three proportions,[1] which take into account every circumstance in which the sun's action on the earth differs from the earth's action on the moon, in order to deduce the relation between the sun's attractive energy and the earth's,—at equal distances from the centre of either. This gives the proportion $\left(\frac{92,500,000}{238,800}\right)^3 \times \left(\frac{27 \cdot 322}{365 \cdot 256}\right)^2$ to unity—which reduces to 325,082 : 1,—in which proportion the sun's attractive energy exceeds the earth's. We may take 325,000 as representing this proportion in round numbers, with an accuracy at least equal to that with which the sun's distance has been determined.

Now in order to see whether the sun or the earth has the greater influence on the moon, we have only to compare the masses of the first-named two orbs and the influence of their respective distances from the moon. We thus have, *first,* the proportion 325,000 to 1, in which the sun's attraction exceeds the earth's at equal distances ; and *secondly,* the proportion $(238,800)^2$ to $(92,500,000)^2$, in which the attraction due to the sun's distance falls short of that due to the earth's. Thus we have this relation,—the sun's actual influence on the moon bears to the earth's the proportion which $325,000 \times (238,800)^2$ bears to $(92,500,000)^2$, or approximately a proportion of 15

[1] The whole process corresponds exactly to an ordinary problem in double (or rather multiple) rule of three.

to 7.[1] Thus the sun's influence on the moon is more
than twice as great as the earth's.

It may be asked, then, how it is that the moon
does not leave the earth's company to obey the sun's
superior influence? In particular it might seem that
when the moon is between the earth and the sun (or as
placed at the time of a total solar eclipse), our satellite,
being then drawn more than twice as forcibly from
the earth towards the sun as she is drawn towards the
earth from the sun, ought incontinently to pass away
sunwards and leave the earth moonless.

The answer to this enigma is, simply, that the sun
attracts the earth as well as the moon, and with almost
the same degree of force, his pull on the earth sometimes slightly exceeding, at others slightly falling
short of, his pull on the moon, according as the distance of the moon or earth from him is greater at the
moment. Thus the earth, in order to prevent the
escape of her satellite, has not to overcome the sun's
pull upon the moon, but only the excess of that pull
over the pull he exerts upon the earth herself. This
excess, as will presently appear, is always far less than
the earth's own influence on the moon.

But it may be noticed, that in considering the
moon's course round the sun we recognise the inferiority
of the earth's influence in a very evident manner. The
moon seems well under the earth's control when we

---

[1] The actual proportion is 2·1421 : 1, correct to the fourth decimal
place. The proportion 15 to 7 is equal to 2·1429, which for ordinary
purposes is sufficiently near.

consider only the nature of the lunar orbit round the
earth ; but if for a moment we forget that the moon
is circling round the earth, and consider only the
fact that the moon travels as a planet round the sun,
with perturbations produced by the attractions of

Fig. 9.

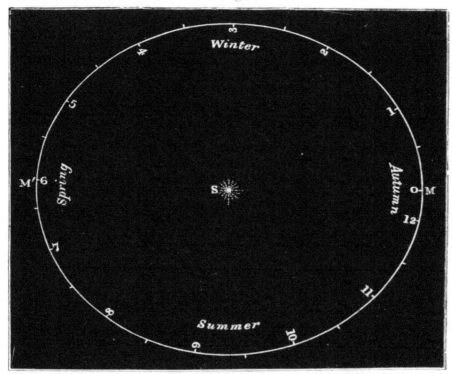

another planet—our own earth,—we can readily test
the extent of these perturbations. Thus, let the circle
M M′ (fig. 9) represent the moon's path round the sun
S, and let us suppose that at 0 the moon is between the
earth and sun, and again similarly placed at 1, 2, 3 . . . .
11, and 12,—being therefore on the side away from the

sun at the intermediate stations marked with a small
line outside the circle M M' ; then the moon's orbital
course is a serpentine or waved curve, having its
minima of distance from the sun at 0, 1, 2, 3 . . . . 11, 12,
and its maxima of distance at the intermediate points.
But on the scale of fig. 9 the whole of this serpentine
curve would lie within the breadth of the fine circular
line M M'. Thus it will readily be understood that
the curvature of the moon's path remains throughout
concave towards S, even when, as at the points, 0, 1, 2, 3,
&c., the convexity of the orbital path round the earth
is turned directly towards the sun. In other words,
as the moon travels in her orbit round the sun her
course is continually being deflected inwards from the
tangent line, or always towards the sun. It is to be
noticed, however, that the earth's perturbing influence
is an important element in determining the moon's real
orbit. For when the earth and sun are on the same
side of the moon, or at the time of full moon, the pull
on the moon is the sum of the pulls of the earth and
sun, or exceeds the sun's pull alone in the ratio 22
to 15 ; and on the other hand, when the earth and sun
are on opposite sides of the moon, or at the time of
new moon, the pull on the moon is the difference of
the pulls of the sun and earth, or is less than the sun's
pull alone in the proportion of 8 to 15. Thus at the
time of full moon the moon is acted on by a force
which exceeds that acting on her at the time of new
moon in the ratio of 22 to 8 or 11 to 4. And though
at the time of full moon the moon's actual velocity

(that is, her velocity in her orbit round the sun) is at a maximum, being then the sum of her mean orbital velocity round the sun and of her velocity round the earth ; yet this by no means counterbalances the effects of the greatly increased pull on the moon ;[1] so that the curvature of her path when she is 'full' greatly exceeds the curvature at the time of new moon.

It was necessary to say so much about the moon's path round the sun, and the sun's real influence upon our satellite, because a great deal of confusion very commonly prevails in the student's mind on this subject. He is exceedingly apt, when his attention is chiefly (and in the first instance) directed to the sun's perturbing influence, to suppose that our earth plays the chief part in ruling the motions of the moon, whereas the sun's influence is in reality paramount at all times.

In considering the moon's motion around the earth, however, we may leave out of consideration the common influence of the sun upon both these orbs, and need consider only the difference of his influence upon the earth and moon, since this difference can alone affect the moon's motion around the earth.

Now we are enabled to deal somewhat more readily with this case than with the general problem of three

---

[1] The earth's velocity in her orbit being about 65,000 miles per hour, and the moon's about 2,000 miles per hour, the extreme variation of the moon's motion in her orbit round the sun lies between the values 67,000 and 63,000 miles, or (roughly.) between values in about the ratio of 110 to 103. But the attractive force on the moon varies in the ratio of 110 to 40, as above shown.

bodies, because the moon is always very close to the earth as compared with the distance of either from the sun.   On this account lines drawn to the sun from the earth and moon enclose so small an angle that they may be regarded as appreciably parallel.   Again, these lines are at all times so nearly equal, that in determining the relative pull on the earth and moon we may employ a simple method available with quantities that are nearly equal.   Thus, suppose two bodies placed at distances represented by 100 and 101 respectively from a certain centre of force, then the attractions on the two bodies are inversely proportional to the squares of 100 and 101, or are in the ratio 10,201 to 10,000 ; but this ratio is appreciably the same as the ratio of 102 to 100.   Therefore in this case, and in all such cases where the distance from one body exceeds the distance from the other by a relatively minute quantity, we can obtain the relative *forces* by representing them as lines having a relative distance *twice* as great.[1]

Now let us apply this principle to the moon and earth.   Suppose E (fig. 10) to be the earth, M the moon, and that the lines E *s*, M *s'* (appreciably parallel) are directed towards the distant sun.   We may suppose the globe S to represent the sun, and we may regard S *s'* and S *s* as the prolongations of M *s'*

[1] The student should test this assertion by a few calculations. Thus he can take the numbers 45,681 and 45,682, and show that the ratio of the squares of these numbers is approximately represented by the ratio 45,681 to 45,683 ; and therefore the inverse ratio of the squares by the ratio 45,683 to 45,681.   We may equally well take 45,680 to 45,682 for the ratio of the squares, and 45,682 to 45,680 for that of the inverse squares.

and E s, if we recognise the fact that the gap at $s\,s$ would, on the scale of our figure, be some ten yards across. Now suppose that the sun's attraction on a unit of the moon's mass [1] is represented by the line joining S

Fig. 10.

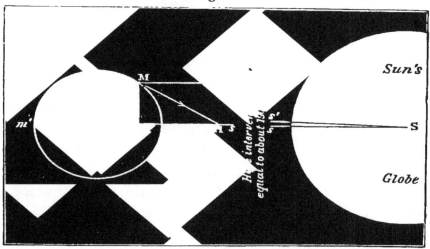

and M, then the line joining S and E will be too large to represent the sun's attraction on a unit of the earth's

---

[1] Throughout the explanation it must be carefully borne in mind that when the attraction on the moon or earth is spoken of, what is really to be considered is the attraction on each unit of the mass of either body. The attraction of the sun on the whole mass of the earth is always far greater than his attraction on the whole mass of the moon; but this circumstance in no way concerns us in studying the lunar perturbations. For that excess of attraction which depends on the earth's greater mass is strictly compensated by the circumstance that the mass affected by it is correspondingly great. The case may be compared to that of two unequal masses let fall at the same moment from the same height above the earth. Here the earth's attraction on the greater mass is greater than her attraction on the less. Yet the greater mass falls at no greater rate; because that greater attraction is employed to move a correspondingly greater mass.

mass, for E is farther away from S than M is (in the
state of things represented by the figure), so that the
attraction on E is less than the attraction on M.   If we
draw M K square to E *s*, we have the distance of K
from S appreciably equal to the distance of M from S.
K E is then the excess of the distance of E from S over
the distance of M from S.   If the sun's attraction
diminished as the distance increased—that is, if it
were simply as the inverse distance,—we need only
take off K L equal to this excess E K, in order to get
the line from S to L representing the attraction of the
sun on the earth at E.   But as the force is inversely as
the square of the distance, we must (from what was
shown in the preceding paragraph) take K H equal
to twice the excess E K, in order to have the distance
from S to H representing the sun's attraction on the
earth at E.

Now, let us make a separate figure to indicate the
actual state of things in such a case as we have considered.   There is the sun at S (fig. 11) pulling at the

Fig. 11.

moon with a force which we have represented by M S;
and he is pulling at the earth with a force which we
represent on the same scale by S H.   This last force,
so far as the moon's place with respect to the earth is
concerned, is clearly a force tending to keep the moon
and earth together.   It may be represented then, *in*

this sense, by the line S H, or as a force tending to thrust the moon from the sun (almost as strongly and directly as the direct action on M tends to draw the moon *towards* the sun).[1] Thus the moon is virtually acted on by the two forces represented by M S and S H; and therefore, by the well-known proposition called the triangle of forces, we have, as the resultant perturbing action on the moon, a force represented by the line M H.[2]

Thus we have an exceedingly simple construction for determining the sun's perturbing action on the moon (as compared with his direct action) when she is in any given position. We have merely to draw M K (see fig. 10) square to the line joining E and S, to take K H equal to twice E K, and to join M H; then M H is the perturbing force, where the line joining M and S represents the sun's direct action on the moon.[3]

[1] Of course the sun's action on the earth does not really amount to a force thrusting or repelling the moon from the sun. But in determining the sun's perturbing action on the moon, we have in effect to take the excess or defect of the sun's full action on the moon as compared with his full action on the earth, so that the latter action necessarily comes to be viewed in a sense contrary to its real nature, precisely as in ordinary arithmetic a sum which is positive in itself is considered to be negative when it has to be subtracted.

[2] If the student is more familiar with the parallelogram of forces than with the same property under the form called the triangle of forces, he should draw a line from M parallel and equal to S H; he will find that M H is the diagonal of a parallelogram having this line and M S as adjacent sides.

[3] Practically M H may be taken to represent the sun's perturbing action on the moon when the line joining E and S represents the sun's direct action on the earth; for the proportion of M S to either E S or H S is very nearly unity under all circumstances.

Let us now figure the various degrees of perturbing
force exerted on the moon when she is in different
parts of her orbit, neglecting for the present the inclination of her path to the ecliptic; in other words,
regarding all such lines as M H (fig. 11) as lying in
one plane. The ellipticity of the moon's orbit is also
for the moment neglected. In fig. 12 this has been
done. To avoid confusion, the different points where
the action of the perturbing force is indicated have
not been all lettered. Nor has the construction for
obtaining the lines indicating the perturbing force

Fig. 12.

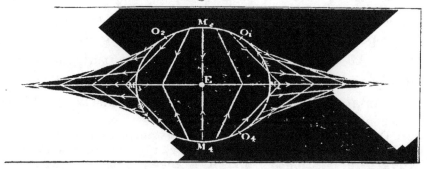

been indicated in any instance. The student will,
however, have no difficulty in interpreting the figure.
$M_1 M_2 M_3 M_4$ is the moon's orbit around the earth at E.
The sun is supposed to lie on the right in the prolongation of E A. At M_1 the perturbing force is
outwards towards the sun, and is represented in
magnitude and direction by the line M_1 A, which is
equal to twice E M_1. As the moon passes from M_1 to
O_1 the perturbing [force gradually becomes more and
more inclined to the line E A, but continues to act

outwards with respect to the orbit $M_1 M_2 M_3 M_4$. At O_1,[1] however, the perturbing force is for the moment tangential to the orbit, and after the moon has passed O_1, the force acts inwards. This continues until the moon has passed to O_2, a point corresponding in position to O_1 but on the left of M_2 E. At M_2 it is clear that the force is represented by the line M_2 E, and is simply radial. Also, in actual amount the perturbing force is less at M_2 than at any other point in the semicircle $M_1 M_2 M_3$. After passing O_2 the force is again exerted outwards, becoming wholly outwards at M_3, when it is represented by the line M_3 A′ equal to M_1 A, or to the diameter of the circle $M_1 M_2 M_3 M_4$. Passing from M_3 to M_4, and thence to M_1, the moon is subjected to corresponding perturbing forces, varying in the reverse way. At O_3 the force is wholly tangential, at M_4 it is wholly radial, and represented by the line M_4 E. At O_4 it is again wholly tangential ; and lastly, at M_1 the

---

[1] O_1 is determined by the circumstance, that when O_1 K is drawn square to E A (the student can pencil in the lines and letters here mentioned), and K L taken equal to twice E K, O_1 L is a tangent to the circle $M_1 M_2 M_3 M_4$. Since the square on the line E O_1 is equal to the rectangle under E K, E L, or to three times the square on E K, we obviously have the cosine of the angle O_1 E K equal to $\dfrac{1}{\sqrt{3}}$, whence $O_1 M_1$ is an arc of 54° 44′, and $O_2 M_3$, $M_3 O_3$, and $O_4 M_1$ are also arcs of 54° 44′. In Herschel's *Outlines of Astronomy* these arcs are given as 64° 14′, and the figure to art. 676 is correspondingly proportioned. But 54° 44′ is the correct value. Indeed it will be obvious in a moment that an arc of 60° would give a perturbing force lying within the tangent, since the tangent at the extremity of an arc of 60° clearly cuts the line E A at a distance from E four times as great as the distance of the foot of a perpendicular let fall from the same extremity.

F

force is again wholly radial, as at first, and represented
by the line M_1 A.

It will be very obvious that, on the whole, the perturbing action tends to diminish the earth's influence
on the moon, since the forces acting outwards are
greater in amount, and act over larger arcs than those
acting inwards. We see that M_1 A and M_3 A', the
maximum outward forces, are twice as great as M_2 E
and M_4 E, the maximum inward forces ; while the arcs
O_4 O_1 and O_2 O_3 each contain 109° 28', or in all nearly
219° out of 360°,—that is, more than three-fifths of the
complete circumference. Hence we infer that there is
a considerable balance of force exerted outwards.

Fig. 13.

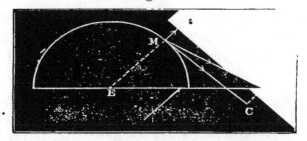

But it will be well to picture the radial forces
separately.

· Let M H, fig. 13, represent the disturbing force
on the moon at M, and draw E M B radially and M C
tangentially. Then complete the rectangle B C by
drawing the perpendiculars H B and H C. By the
well-known rule for the resolution of forces, the force
M H is equivalent to the two forces represented by
M B and M C, one radial, the other tangential. Simi-

larly, if we had commenced by considering the force
M′ H′, fig. 14, exerted on the moon at M′, we should
have found by a similar construction that the radial
and tangential forces at M′ are represented by the
lines M′ B′ and M′ C′; and so on, for all positions.

Fig. 14.

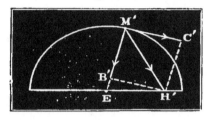

Leaving the tangential forces for subsequent consideration, let us suppose the above construction extended so as to give the radial forces exerted at points
all around the moon's orbit, and let us suppose these
forces separately represented. We should then have
the results pictured in fig. 15. The radial forces are

Fig. 15.

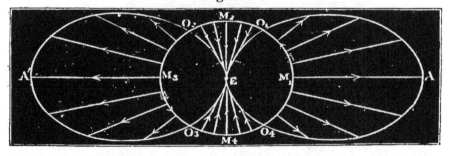

all exerted outwards from O_4 to O_1, and from O_2 to O_3,
while they are all exerted inwards from O_1 to O_2, and
from O_3 to O_4. We see that the former forces largely
exceed the latter.

The first great result, then, from the consideration of the sun's perturbing action, is this,—it tends to draw the moon on the whole outwards from the earth, reducing the earth's influence to a certain extent.

We can compare the actual amount of the radial force (or of the perturbing force generally) with the amount of the earth's attraction ; and it is important that we should do so in order that we may judge how the forces acting on the moon are related as respects magnitude.

For it will be remembered that the construction for obtaining fig. 12 is based on the supposition that the line from E to the sun represents the sun's direct attraction on the earth or moon. Now, the line from the earth to the sun is about 92,500,000 miles long ; while the line $M_1 A$ is equal to the diameter of the earth's orbit, or to 238,800 miles. So that the sun's maximum perturbing action on the moon is less than his direct action, in the proportion of 2,388 to 925,000, or is about one 387th part of the latter. But the earth's direct action on the moon is, as we have seen, equivalent to about 7-15ths of the sun's. Hence the sun's maximum perturbing influence is less than the earth's mean attraction on the moon, in the proportion of 15 to 7 × 387, or is about one-180th part of the latter. Thus the force pulling the moon at M_1 towards the sun, would be represented by a line 387 times as long as $M_1 A$, while the force pulling the moon towards E would be represented by a line 180 times as long as $M_1 A$. The relations for the perturbing forces exerted on the moon in other positions, as well for the whole forces as for their radial and tangential portions, are indicated by the proportions of the lines in figs. 12, 15, and 16. When the perturbing force has its least value, or when the moon is at M_2 or M_4, this force, now wholly radial, is about one-774th of the sun's direct action, and about one-362nd of the earth's.

But now we have to consider the circumstance that the earth's path around the sun is eccentric, and that thus the sun's perturbing influence on the moon necessarily varies in amount. It will be obvious that the perturbing forces must all be greater when the earth and her satellite are nearer to the sun. Let us inquire in what degree they will increase.

This question is readily answered. Fig. 12 indicates the magnitude of the perturbing forces when the line from the sun to E indicates the sun's direct action. Now to simplify matters let us take an illustrative case, in order to determine the law according to which the magnitude of the perturbing forces is affected. We have hitherto supposed the earth at her mean distance from the sun, or about 92,500,000 miles from him. Let us now take the case when she is in perihelion, or about 91,000,000 miles from him. The moon's distance, 238,800, is contained a smaller number of times in the smaller distance, in the proportion of 910 to 925; in other words, the perturbing force represented by M_1 A is a larger aliquot part of the sun's direct influence, in the proportion of 925 to 910. But the sun's direct influence is itself increased by the approach of the earth and her satellite, in the proportion of the squares of these numbers; or as $(925)^2$ to $(910)^2$. Hence the actual amount of the perturbing force is increased in the proportion of the cubes of these numbers, or as $(925)^3$ to $(910)^3$. Similarly, when the earth is in aphelion, or 93,000,000 miles from the sun, the sun's perturbing influence is less than when the earth is at her mean distance, in the proportion of $(910)^3$ to $(940)^3$.

There is, however, a simpler method, sufficiently accurate for our purposes, of indicating these relations. When we cube two numbers which are nearly equal, we triple the proportional difference (approximately). Thus, if we cube 100 and 101 (whose difference is 1-100th of the former), we obtain the numbers 1,000,000 and 1,030,301, which are to each other very nearly as 100 to 103 ; so that their difference is about 3-100ths of the former. Now the earth's greatest, mean, and least distances from the sun are approximately as the numbers 62, 61, and 60 ; and therefore the perturbing influences on the moon when the earth is in aphelion, at mean distance, and in perihelion, are respectively as the numbers 64, 61, and 58 (obtained by leaving the middle number 61 unaltered, and making the first and last differ three times as much as before from the middle number).

There is, then, an appreciable difference between the perturbing forces exerted by the sun when the earth is in perihelion, or at about the beginning of January, and when the earth is in aphelion, or at about the beginning of July. The earth's power over the moon is more considerably diminished in the former case than in the latter. Now the partial release of the moon from the earth's influence results in a slight increase of her mean distance and a lengthening of the moon's period of revolution (we refer of course to her sidereal revolution) around the earth. This will be evident when we consider that the earth's attraction is always tending, though the tendency may not actually operate, to reduce the moon's distance; so that any cause diminishing the total force towards the earth must enable the moon to resist this tendency more effectually than she otherwise would. In winter then, when the earth is near perihelion, the moon's mean distance and her period of revolution are somewhat in excess of the average; for the sun's releasing effect is then at a maximum. In summer, on the contrary, the earth being near aphelion, the moon's mean distance and her period of revolution are reduced slightly below their mean values; for the sun's releasing effect is then at a minimum. Thus the moon lags somewhat during the winter months, and regains her place by slightly hastening during the summer months. She is farthest behind her mean place, so far as this circumstance is concerned, in spring and autumn (at those epochs when she is at her mean distance), for it is at these times that the loss begins to change into gain, or *vice versâ*. The greatest possible amount of lagging accruing in spring is such that the moon is behind her mean place by about a third of her own diameter. In

autumn she gets in advance of her mean place by about
the same amount.

This peculiarity of the moon's motion is called the
annual equation, and was discovered by Tycho Brahé.

Associated with this variation is another of much
greater delicacy, and having a period of much greater
length. We have seen that the eccentricity of the
earth's orbit affects the amount of the sun's perturbing
influence, insomuch that this influence is sometimes
greater and sometimes less than when the earth is at
her mean distance. It might appear that as there is
thus an excess at one season and a defect at another,
the general result for the year would be the same as
though the earth travelled in a circular orbit at her
present mean distance from the sun. This, however, is
not the case. If we consider that, supposing the earth
to revolve always at her mean distance she would describe a circle having a diameter as great as the major
axis of her actual orbit, we see that the elliptical area
of her real path is less than that of the supposed circular orbit. Hence, on the whole, she is nearer to the
sun than if she described a circular orbit in a year
instead of her elliptical path. It is true that she moves
more slowly when in aphelion, and thus her virtual
yearly distance (so to speak) from the sun is increased ;
but this does not compensate for the actual reduction
of her orbit-area due to the eccentricity of her orbit.[1]
Hence the sun's perturbing influence on the moon is

---

[1] The reasoning by which this may be demonstrated corresponds
precisely with that in pp. 166, 167 of my treatise on *Saturn*, where

somewhat increased by the ellipticity of the earth's orbit. Now this ellipticity is subject to slow variation, due to the influences of planetary attraction. At present it is slowly diminishing. The earth's orbit is slowly becoming more and more nearly circular, without however any change (or any corresponding change) in the period of revolution. Thus the area swept out by the earth each year is slowly increasing, and the total of the sun's perturbing influence on the moon in each year is slowly diminishing. The moon then is somewhat less retarded year after year; so that in effect she travels somewhat more quickly year after year. This change is called the *secular acceleration of the moon's mean motion*; or rather, an acceleration which is partially accounted for by the above reasoning has received this name. As a matter of fact, the moon's mean motion is subject to an acceleration nearly twice as great as the change in the ellipticity of the terrestrial orbit will account for; and astronomers have been led to suspect that a portion of this acceleration may be only apparent and due to a real retardation of the earth's rotation, — that is, a slight increase in the sidereal day, the unit by which we measure astronomical time. With this circumstance, however, we are not at present concerned, save in so far as it relates to the history of that interesting cause of acceleration which has been described above. Halley had been led to suspect that

I show that a planet receives more heat during a complete revolution in an elliptical orbit, than it would receive in revolving round a circular orbit in the same period.

the moon had advanced somewhat farther in her orbit
than was consistent with the accounts of certain ancient
eclipses.[1] Further inquiries confirmed the suspicion.
The moon's advance was slight, it is true, but to the
astronomer it was as real as though it had taken place
under his very eyes. The theory of gravitation seemed
to give no account of this acceleration of the moon's
motion. At length, however, Laplace was led to turn
his attention to the variation of the earth's eccentricity
as a probable cause of the peculiarity. His calculation
of the effects due to this variation accorded very closely
with the observed amount of the acceleration. Yet,
although this agreement might have appeared con-

[1] I quote here some remarks on Halley's researches by the Rev. J. M.
Wilson, of Clifton, from a valuable paper contributed to the *Eagle*,
a magazine supported by members of St. John's College, Cambridge
(No. xxvi. vol. v.). 'Halley,' he says, 'seems to have been the
first who considered this question. With astonishing clearness he
seized the conditions of the question, saw that the knowledge of
the elements, on which the solution was to be founded, was as yet
incomplete, and saw also the probability that when the accurate
knowledge was obtained, it would appear that there was a peculiarity in the moon's motion entirely unforeseen by others, that it
was now moving faster and performing its revolution in a shorter
time than it did in past time. If the longitudes of Bagdad,
Antioch, and other places, were accurately known, "I could then,"
he says, "pronounce in what proportion the moon's motion does
accelerate; which that it does, I think I can demonstrate, and
shall (God willing) one day make it appear to the public." Newton
adds to his second edition of the *Principia* the words,—"Halleius
noster motum medium Lunæ, cum motu diurno terræ collatum,
paulatim accelerari primus omnium, quod sciam, deprehendit."'
I have given an account of the subject in the *Quarterly
Journal of Science* for October, 1866, in an essay entitled 'Prof.
Adams's Recent Discoveries,' and a more popular account appears
in my *Light Science for Leisure Hours*, in a paper called 'Our Chief
Timepiece losing Time.'

vincing, and although a portion of the acceleration is undoubtedly due to the cause in question, the inquiries of Professor Adams (confirmed by the researches of Delaunay and others, and now universally admitted) show that in reality only half the observed acceleration can be explained by the change in the earth's orbital eccentricity.

But it is to be noted that the variation itself is exceedingly small, as is also the discrepancy between observation and theory. We have seen that the *annual equation* causes the moon to be displaced by about one-third of its diameter in opposite directions in spring and autumn, the actual range of this oscillatory variation being therefore equal to about two-thirds of the moon's diameter. But the theoretical *secular acceleration*, though its effects are accumulative, and in geometrical progression, yet in a century would only cause the moon to be in advance of the place which she would have had, if the acceleration had not operated during the century, by one–300th part of her diameter; and the actual secular acceleration only causes the moon to gain about twice the distance, or about one-150th part of her diameter, in a century.[1]

We have next to consider one of the most important perturbations to which the moon is subjected so far as the rate of her motion in her orbit is concerned.

We have hitherto considered chiefly the radial part of the perturbing force. We must now discuss the

[1] In two hundred years the gain is four times as great, in three hundred years nine times as much, and so on. For the above illustration I am indebted to Mr. Wilson's paper mentioned in the preceding note.

variations in the tangential force. We have already seen how this force can be separated from the radial. force. Let us suppose the method applied to give a figure of the tangential forces corresponding to that already given (fig. 15) for the radial forces. To do this, we have to draw a number of lines obtained as M C and M′ A′ were obtained in figs. 13, 14. When this is done (and the reader is recommended not to be satisfied until he has effected the construction for himself independently), the force-lines are found to arrange themselves as shown in fig. 16. It will be

Fig. 16.

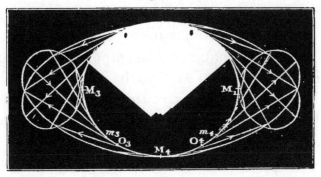

seen that each loop springs from one of the points M_1, M_2, M_3, M_4 (where the tangential force vanishes, and the radial forces have their unequal maxima), and bends round so as to end at another of those four points; and we see that at the four points m_1, m_2, m_3, m_4 (midway between the former, and not far from those where the radial force vanishes) the tangential force has its maximum value.[1]

[1] The tangential force attains its maximum midway between the points M_1, M_2, M_3, M_4, and not, as is sometimes stated, at the

Now as the moon is passing over the arc $M_1 M_2$, the tangential force, acting in the direction shown by the curves, is retardative, and most effectually so when the moon is in the middle of this arc, or at the point m_1. As the moon passes from M_2 to M_3, the tangential force is accelerative, and most effectually so when the moon is at the middle of the arc $M_2 M_3$, or at the point m_2. As the moon passes over the arc $M_3 M_4$, the tangential force is again retardative ; and it is again accelerative as the moon traverses the arc $M_4 M_1$, attaining its greatest value when the moon is at the middle of these respective arcs, or at m_3 and m_4.

Since, then, retardation ceases to act when the moon is at M_2, the moon is moving there with maximum velocity, so far as this cause of disturbance is concerned. In like manner the moon is moving with maximum velocity at M_3, with minimum velocity at M_4, and lastly with maximum velocity again at M_1. It will be clear, then, that near the points m_1, m_2, m_3, and m_4, the moon moves with mean velocity ; the arcs $m_4 m_1$ and $m_2 m_3$ are traversed with a velocity exceeding the mean ; and the arcs $m_1 m_2$ and $m_3 m_4$ with a velocity falling short of the mean. Thus at or near m_1 the moon ceases to gain, and therefore the amount by which she is in advance of her mean place has attained its maximum [1] when the moon is at or near m_1. Similarly, the

points where the radial force vanishes. It is obvious from fig. 13 that if the angle H E M $= \theta$, H B $= 3 \cos \theta \sin \theta = \frac{3}{2} \sin 2\theta$; and this expression has its greatest value when $\sin 2\theta = 1$, or $\theta = 45°$.

[1] It is singular how frequently the very simple principles on which the attainment of a maximum, mean, or minimum value

amount by which the moon is behind her mean place has attained its maximum when the moon is at or near m_y. At m_3 she is again in advance of her mean place by a maximum amount, and at m_4 she is again behind her mean place by a maximum amount.

This inequality of the moon's motion is called the *Variation*. It is so marked that at the points corresponding to m_1 and m_3 the moon is in advance of her mean place by an amount equal to about her own diameter, while at m_2 and m_4 she is by a similar amount behind her mean place. The range of the variation is thus equal to about twice the moon's diameter. The period of the variation is on the average half a lunation, since in that time the moon passes from her greatest retardation (due to this cause) to her greatest advance, and so back to her greatest retardation. We owe to Tycho Brahé the discovery of this inequality in the moon's motion.[1]

depend, are misunderstood; and how commonly the mistake is made of supposing that a maximum or minimum value is attained when the increasing or diminishing *cause* is most effective. It is precisely when an increasing cause is most effective that the *rate of increase* is greatest, and therefore the maximum value is then clearly not attained. And so of a minimum value; there can clearly be no minimum while the decreasing cause is still effective. It is when a cause neither tends to increase nor diminish,—that is, when it has a mean value,—that the maximum or minimum of effect is attained. Thus in spring the sun's daily elevation is increasing more rapidly than at any other time, and in autumn the daily elevation is diminishing most rapidly : but it is not at these seasons that the sun attains his maximum or minimum degree of elevation ; this happens in the summer and winter, when his daily elevation changes least.

[1] It will be evident that the ancients, who trusted chiefly to eclipses to determine the laws of the moon's motion, were pre-

And now, precisely as we had, after considering the *annual equation*, to discuss an associated but much smaller inequality, so there is an inequality associated with the variation, but much smaller in amount. It is, however, more interesting in many respects, precisely as the *secular acceleration* of the moon is a more interesting inequality than her *annual equation*.

We have hitherto not taken into account the circumstance that though the sun's distance enormously exceeds the radius of the moon's orbit, it is nevertheless not so great but that there is an appreciable relative difference between the moon's distance from the sun when in conjunction with him (or at the time of new moon), and when in opposition (or at the time of full moon). When the earth is at her mean distance from the sun (or 92,500,000 miles from him), the moon's distance from him when she is new is 92,738,800 miles, and when she is full it is only 92,261,200 miles,—so that these extreme distances are proportioned as the numbers 927,388 and 922,612, or, nearly enough for our purposes, they are as the numbers 201 and 200. Hence, by what has been already shown, the perturbing forces on the moon in these two positions are as the numbers 203 and 200. Thus the difference, though slight, is perceptible. Yet again, the points where lines drawn from the sun touch the moon's orbit are not quite coincident cluded from recognising the remarkable displacement due to the *variation*; since eclipses necessarily occur when the moon is on the line passing through the earth and sun, or when the moon is at M_1 or M_3, at which points the variation vanishes.

with the points M_2 and M_4 (fig. 12), but are slightly displaced from these positions towards M_1.   Here, again, the amount of either displacement, though slight, is appreciable.   It amounts, in fact, to an arc of about $8\frac{3}{4}$ minutes; so that the points in question divide the moon's orbit into two unequal arcs, whereof one, the farthest from the sun, exceeds a semicircle by $17\frac{1}{2}$ minutes, while the other falls short of a semicircle by the same amount,—the larger thus exceeding the smaller by $35'$, or more than half a degree.

It necessarily follows that the direct effect of the tangential force in increasing or diminishing the moon's mean motion, is not equal in the two halves $M_4\,M_1\,M_2$ and $M_2\,M_3\,M_4$ (fig. 12).   It is greater in the former semicircle, on the whole, than in the latter ; but the points where the tangential force vanishes lie outside the extremities of this latter semicircle. Thus the points where the variation attains its maximum value lie on the side of m_1 and m_4 *towards* M_1, and on the side of m_2 and m_3 *away* from M_3 ; and the amount of the maxima at the two former stations is greater than the amount at the two latter.   Moreover, when the earth is in perihelion these effects are greater, while when she is in aphelion they are less than when she is at her mean distance.   The maximum inequality thus produced, a variation of the ' variation ' as it were, amounts to about two minutes, or about the sixteenth part of the moon's apparent diameter.   It is called the *parallactic inequality*, because of its dependence on the sun's distance, which, as we know, is usually expressed by a reference to the solar parallax. And as the inequality depends on the sun's distance, so its observed amount obviously supplies a means of determining the sun's distance. It was, in fact, a determination of the sun's distance, deduced by Hansen from the observed amount of the moon's maximum parallactic inequality, which recently led astronomers to question a value of the distance, based on observations of Venus in transit, which had been for many years adopted in our text-books and national ephemerides.

Before concluding this sketch of the general effects resulting from the sun's perturbing action on the moon it is to be noticed that the tangential force affects the secular acceleration of the moon. It had long been held that only the radial force can really be effective in long intervals of time, because. the tangential force is self-compensating,—if not in each lunation,[1] yet at least in the course of many successive lunations. But as a matter of fact, inasmuch as the eccentricity of the earth's orbit is undergoing a continual though very gradual diminution, an element is introduced which renders this compensation incomplete,—not merely in many successive lunations or in many successive years, but in many successive centuries. So long as the eccentricity of the earth's orbit continues to diminish, there can in

---

[1] Of course, in a thorough analysis of the action of the tangential force, it has to be remembered that, apart from the ellipticity of the moon's orbit, and the consequent inequality of the sun's perturbing action in different quadrants as well as in different halves, the orbit is undergoing a process of continual change, even under the action of the tangential and radial forces themselves.

G

fact be no tendency to exact compensation so far as
this particular element is concerned.   Now this circumstance had not escaped Laplace when he discussed the
moon's secular acceleration ; but he was led to believe
that its effects would be insignificant.   Professor
Adams, however, in re-examining the whole subject,
made inquiry how far this view of the matter is justified.   The experience of past inquirers had shown
that no cause of variation, and particularly no cause
having effects cumulative for many successive years, can
safely be neglected.   Professor Adams remarked: ' In a
great problem of approximation, such as that presented
to us by the investigation of the moon's motion, experience shows that nothing is more easy than to
neglect, on account of their apparent insignificance,
considerations which ultimately prove to be of the
greatest importance.'

The further discussion of the moon's motions would
not be suitable to the pages of a popular work like the
present.

It was only the unique combination of powers
possessed by Newton that rendered it possible for him
to grapple with the problem of the moon's motions
in the first instance.   Even he would have failed
but for certain fortunate circumstances by which he
was assisted.   Since his day the problem has been
dealt with by the most acute mathematicians, the most
skilful observers.   Mathematical analysis has been
carried to an unhoped-for degree of perfection to
account for peculiarities of lunar motion revealed by

observation. Observation has been pushed to the utmost point of delicacy to detect peculiarities of lunar motion predicted by mathematical analysis. The history of the contest is adorned by the names of nearly all the leading observers and mathematicians of the last century and a half; a host of names so distinguished, that it becomes almost invidious to particularise any among them. In the whole history of the researches by which men have endeavoured to master the secrets of nature, no chapter is more encouraging than that which relates to the interpretation of the lunar motions.

CHAPTER III.

THE MOON'S CHANGES OF ASPECT, ROTATION, LIBRATION, ETC.

THE moon's motions in the heavens, as seen from the earth, are readily understood from what is known of her actual motions. I propose now to enter into a general consideration of these apparent motions of the moon, and of the varying aspect which she accordingly presents to us. It would be possible to fill a much larger volume than the present with the detailed discussion of these matters; nor would such a volume be wanting in interest, at least to those having mathematical tastes. I do not indeed know of any subject which a geometrician could better wish to examine. It is full of neat and interesting problems, and might worthily occupy many years of labour. But in this volume such researches would be out of place. We must be content with such a consideration of the subject as shall leave none of its salient features unexplained. In passing it may be remarked that even such a treatment of the moon's apparent motions has long been a desideratum, inasmuch as our text-books of astronomy have hitherto left these matters almost untouched.

In the first place, then, it is to be noticed that the moon completes the circuit of the heavens on the average in 27·322 days,—that is, in 27$^{d.}$ 7$^{h.}$ 43·7^{m}. If we watched her motion from the time when she was in conjunction with any given star until the next conjunction, and the next again, and so on, for many successive conjunctions, we should find that the mean interval is that just stated. This is called the *sidereal month*.

If, however, instead of taking a star, we took the point on the heavens where the ecliptic crosses to the north of the equator, we should not find the interval exactly the same as the sidereal month; because this point on the heavens is constantly, though slowly, moving backwards, or so as to *meet* the moon's motion. This point—called, as all know, ' the first point of Aries '—makes the complete circuit of the heavens in 25,868 years; and therefore in a sidereal month travels over a very minute arc indeed, less in fact than 4″. So that the difference between this new kind of month, called the *tropical month,* and the sidereal month, is very minute. The mean tropical month is necessarily slightly less than the sidereal. The latter is, with great exactness, 27·32166 days, the tropical month is 27·32156 days, or about 6⅓ seconds shorter.

Now let us in the first instance consider her motion as though it took place in the ecliptic, and uniformly, so that in fact we are supposing the moon to move apparently in the same course among the stars as the sun, only that instead of taking about 365¼ days in completing the circuit she takes about 27⅓ days.

Let E E', fig. 17, represent a part of the earth's path round the sun S, and let $M_1 M_2 M_3 M_4$ be the path of the moon, and suppose that the moon is at M_1 when the earth is at E. Then it is the time of 'new moon;' the moon lies towards the sun's place, and if she could be seen, would be at the same part of the

Fig. 17.

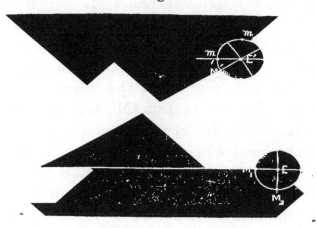

ecliptic, or in conjunction with the same star. Let E E' be the arc traversed by the earth in 27·322 days, or in a sidereal month. Then the moon has gone once round and is in conjunction with the same star,— in other words, the line E' m_1 directed towards the moon, is in the same direction as E S,—that is, E' m_1 is parallel to E S. But the moon has not come up to the line E' M' S, joining the sun and earth. Some time has still to elapse, therefore, before it is again new moon. In like manner, if the moon had been at M_2 when the earth was at E, it would have been the time of ' first quarter,'—she would be at m_2 when the earth was at E', —in other words, she would not yet have reached the place of ' first quarter.' And similarly, if it had been ' full moon,' ' third quarter,' or any other lunar epoch, when the earth was at E, the corresponding epoch would not have arrived when a sidereal month had elapsed.

We see then that the *lunation*, or the time in which the moon goes through her phases, is longer than the sidereal or than the tropical month. And it is very easy to calculate the exact length of the lunation, or, as it is called, the *synodical month*. In 27·322 days, the moon has not completed the whole cycle of her phases, but only the portion M' m_3 m_1 out of the whole cycle,—that is, she has completed the whole cycle, less the portion m_1 M'. Now, the angle m_1 E' M' is obviously the same as the angle E' S E ; hence the part wanting from the complete cycle bears to the whole cycle the same ratio that E E' bears to the complete orbit of the earth, or that 27·322 days bears to 365·242 days. The moon, then, in 27·322 days, completes only $\frac{337 \cdot 920}{365 \cdot 242}$ths of a lunation (the numerator being obtained by taking 27·322 from 365·242). So that a mean synodical month exceeds a mean sidereal month (or 27·322 days) in the same proportion that 365·242 exceeds 337·920. Increasing 27·322 in this proportion (a mere rule of three sum), we obtain 29·531,[1] which is the length of a lunation.

[1] More exact values are given in the tables.

The phases of the moon are explained in text-books of astronomy. But a few remarks on the subject may be useful.

Let M_1 M_2 M_3 . . . . fig. 18, represent the moon's

Fig. 18.

orbit, the sun being many times farther away than in the figure. The earth and moon are relatively much exaggerated in dimensions; and the moon is shown in eight equidistant positions, as though she performed a complete circuit while the earth remained at E. Now obviously, when the moon is at

Fig. 19.

| 1 | 2 | 3 | 4 | 5 | 6 | 7 | 8 | 9 |

M_1, her darkened side is turned towards the earth, and she cannot be seen. She is as at 1, fig. 19. As she advances towards M_2, the observer on the earth E, and supposed to be standing on the half of the earth shown

in the figure, sees the moon on the left of the sun,—
that is, towards the east,[1] and he would clearly see the
right or western side of the moon partly illuminated.
The case, so far as this illumination is concerned, is
exactly the same as though the moon at M_1 had turned
an eighth round on an axis upright to the plane of her
motion, in such a way as to bring into view the parts
beyond her eastern edge. Thus, the aspect of the moon
is as shown at 2, fig. 19. It is readily seen that when
she is at M_3, fig. 18, her aspect is as at 3, fig. 19; and
so on.

All this is as explained in the text-books. But
there are two points, even in this elementary matter,
which may need a word or two of explanation.

First, as to the position of the lunar crescent. We
see the moon in varying positions on the sky; and at
first sight there appears to be no definite relation
between her position and the position of her cusps or
horns. Indeed, this feature of her aspect has seemed so
changeful and capricious that it has even been regarded
as a weather-token. In reality, however, there is a
simple relation always fulfilled by the moon's cusps.
The line joining them is always at right angles to the
great circle passing through the sun and moon.[2] As

[1] The reader should here hold the plate so as to have E towards
him, and S and M_1 from him.

[2] This will perhaps seem obvious to most readers. The proof
of the proposition is comprehended in the following considerations:
—The circle bounding the illuminated half of the moon necessarily
has its plane at right angles to the line joining the centres of the
sun and moon; the circle bounding the moon's visible hemisphere
necessarily has its plane at right angles to the line joining the

the moon is always near the ecliptic, this amounts to saying that the line joining the cusps is always nearly at right angles to the ecliptic. It follows, of course, that as the angle at which the ecliptic is inclined to the horizon is variable, so the position of the line joining the cusps varies with respect to the horizon. As respects the gibbous moon (or moon more than half-full), these variations are not much noticed; but in the case of the crescent moon, generally observed rather near the horizon, they are very noteworthy. For instance, let the time of year be such that the part of the ecliptic near the western horizon, soon after sunset, is inclined at nearly the greatest possible angle to the horizon,—that is, let the season somewhat precede the vernal equinox, — the time as we know, when the zodiacal light is most conspicuous in the evening. Then, in our latitudes, the inclination of the ecliptic to the horizon is about sixty-two degrees, and supposing the moon on

Fig. 20.

the ecliptic, and *young*, as shown at M_1, in fig. 20, the line joining the cusps will only be inclined about twenty-eight degrees to the horizon. But next sup-

centres of the earth and moon: thus the intersection of these circles or the lunar cusps must lie on a line at right angles to the plane containing the three centres,—that is, to the plane of the great circle through the sun and moon.

pose that the moon at this time is at her greatest distance north of the ecliptic, or at M_2, five degrees from the position M_1, and about the same distance as in the former case from the sun.   Then the great-circle arc S M_2 from the sun to the moon is inclined ten or more degrees (according to the moon's age) to S M_1, and the line joining the cusps is, in this case, inclined less than 18° to the horizon. Indeed, when the moon is *very* young, the angle M_1 S M_2 is considerable : hence S M_2 makes a considerably larger angle with the horizon than S M_1, and the line joining the cusps is, as shown in the figure, much more nearly horizontal. A very young moon seen soon after sunset, under these circumstances, may have the line joining its cusps quite horizontal, or even have the northern cusp lower than the southern.[1]   Like considerations apply to the case of the old crescent moon,[2] before sunrise, soon after the autumnal equinox.

Next, however, suppose the western part of the ecliptic at its least inclination to the horizon, soon after sunset, or the time of year shortly before the autumnal equinox.   The state of things is that illustrated in fig. 21.   Then in our latitudes the inclination

[1] It is hardly necessary to say that the exact angles for any position can be quite readily calculated ; but the matter is not of such a nature as to require the introduction of such calculations here.   The student acquainted with the elements of spherical trigonometry may find interesting and not uninstructive occupation for a leisure hour or so in considering a few cases.   The angle M_2 S M_1 is more than 10° when the moon is less than one-eighth full, or halfway to the first quarter.

[2] The word crescent here means merely crescent-shaped, not crescent in the sense of increasing.

of the ecliptic to the horizon is about 15 degrees, and
supposing the moon on the ecliptic and *young*, as at
M_3, the line joining the cusps will be inclined about
75 degrees to the horizon. But suppose the moon, as
at M_4, at her greatest distance south of the ecliptic,
or five degrees from the position M_3, and about
the same distance from the sun, then the great
circle S M_4 from the sun to the moon is inclined
more than ten · degrees to S M_3 ; and the line

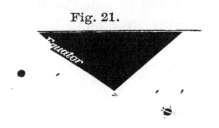

Fig. 21.

joining the cusps may
be much more nearly
upright than when the
moon is as at M_3. But
this line cannot be ac-
tually upright when the
sun is below the horizon,
for the line must always be square to the great circle
through the sun and moon, and, of course, when the
moon is above and the sun below the horizon, this
great circle is inclined to the horizon, and a line perpendicular to it is correspondingly inclined from the
vertical. Similar considerations apply to the case of
the old crescent moon before sunrise, soon after the
vernal equinox.

We see, from these extreme cases, that the line
joining the moon's cusps can have every inclination,
from being nearly vertical, to a horizontal position ; and
even that the northern cusp may be below the southern,
according to the season of the year and the moon's
position in her orbit. So that, to assert that there will

be such and such weather when the line joining the cusps is seen (for instance) nearly horizontal, the moon being new, is the same as asserting that there must be such and such weather at the time of new moon in February and March, if the moon is then nearly at her maximum distance from the ecliptic. And so with all such cases. If there were any value at all in such predictions, they would imply the strictly cyclic return of such and such weather.

Let us next consider the actual motions of the moon in the heavens at different times. We shall have, in so doing, to take into account the inclination of the moon's path to the ecliptic, as well as the eccentricity of the lunar orbit.

So long as we regard the moon as moving in the ecliptic, we can at once determine the nature of the moon's movements during any month of the year, by considering where the sun is placed on the ecliptic during that month. Thus in March the sun crosses the equator ascendingly. Hence, at the time of new moon, the moon is near the equator, and, like the sun, is about as many hours above as below the horizon. As the moon passes to the first quarter, she traverses the ascending part of the ecliptic, and at the time of first quarter is near the place occupied by the sun at the midsummer solstice. In other words (for we cannot too directly refer these motions to the stellar heavens), the moon is near the place where the constellations Taurus and Gemini meet together. Thus the first-quarter moon in spring is a long time above the horizon, and is high when in the south, like the sun in midsummer. She passes on to full, when she is again near the equator,—or rather when she is 'full' in March (which may be earlier than the date when she is at her first quarter) she is near the equator where the ecliptic crosses it, or in Virgo. So that the full moon in spring is about twelve hours above the horizon, and as high when due south as the sun in spring. The 'third-quarter moon' in March is, in like manner, nearly in the part of the ecliptic occupied by the sun in winter, or where the ecliptic crosses the equator in Sagittarius. She is therefore but a short time above the horizon, and low down when due south, like the winter sun. And it is easily seen how at intermediate phases she occupies intermediate positions.

By similar reasoning, we find that in midsummer— (i) the new moon is in Taurus or Gemini,[1] and long above the horizon ; (ii) the first-quarter moon is in Virgo, and about twelve hours above the horizon ; (iii) the full moon in Sagittarius, and a short time above the horizon ; (iv) the third-quarter moon in Pisces, and about twelve hours above the horizon. In mid-autumn—(i) the new moon is in Virgo, and about twelve hours above the horizon ; (ii) the first-quarter moon in Scorpio or Sagittarius, and only a short time above the horizon ; (iii) the full moon in Pisces, and about twelve hours above the horizon ; (iv) the three-quarter moon in Taurus or Gemini, and

[1] The reference throughout is to the *constellations*, not to the *signs*.

a long time above the horizon. And lastly, in mid-winter—(i) the new moon is in Scorpio or Sagittarius, and only a short time above the horizon ; (ii) the first-quarter moon in Pisces; and about twelve hours above the horizon ; (iii) the full moon in Taurus or Gemini, and a long time above the horizon ; (iv) the third-quarter moon in Virgo, and about twelve hours above the horizon.

The student will find no difficulty whatever in extending these considerations to other months, or in applying much more exact considerations to special cases. For he will notice that what has just been stated presents only the rougher features of the matter. But nothing can be easier than to apply the first rough corrections for such an inquiry. Supposing, for example, that we wish to know generally what will be the moon's diurnal path (that is, her course round the heavens during the twenty-four hours) when she is at her first quarter on the 10th of April : we know that on the 10th of April the sun is some twenty degrees past the vernal equinox, which he had crossed on or about the 20th of March ; the moon at her first quarter is 90° farther forward, or some twenty degrees past the place of the summer solstice ; corresponding to a position on the ecliptic, about equidistant from the two stars κ and δ Geminorum. Her course above the horizon will correspond to the sun's course about twenty-one days after the summer solstice,—that is, on or about July 11th. Similarly any other case may be dealt with.

Before passing from this part of our subject we may here conveniently consider the phenomena of the *harvest moon* and of the *hunter's moon*.

If the moon moved in the equator, she would rise later night after night by a nearly constant interval; or, in other words, the actual number of hours between successive risings (or settings) would be constant. But as she moves on a path considerably

Fig. 22.

inclined to the equator, this does not happen with her any more than it does with the sun; moreover, as she moves much more rapidly along the equator than the sun does, the difference is much more perceptible. If we consider two extreme cases we shall see the reason of this. Let H H', fig. 22, be a portion of the eastern horizon, E the true east point, E Q the equator; and let us suppose that when the moon rises on a certain night she is on the equator at E. She is then carried by the diurnal motion along E Q to her culmination in the south, and so to her setting place in the west. Now· if her orbital motion were on the equator, she would be on the next night at the same hour at a point such as m on the equator (E m being an arc of about 12° 12′), and would be carried by the diurnal motion to E, where she would rise about 50½ minutes later than on the former day (and about 13° in advance of her former place). But her actual motion is nearly on the ecliptic; and when she was at E on the first day the ecliptic must have been in one of the two positions e E or e' E. (In other words, E must be the point where the ecliptic crosses the equator, either descendingly or ascendingly.[1]) Now, in the former case, the moon on the second night will be as at M, and will be carried by the diurnal motion to the point h on the horizon; in the latter she will be as at M′, and will be carried to the point h'; and obviously M h is a much longer arc than M′ h'. In fact, if K E K′ be part of the equinoctial colure (or circle square to the equator through the equinoctial point E), the two arcs M K and M′ K′ are obviously equal,[2] and we see that M h exceeds, while M′ h' falls short of, the common length of those equal arcs by the very appreciable equal arcs K h and K′ h'. Thus the hour of rising in the former case will be later than in the latter, by the time corresponding to twice the diurnal arc K h or K′ h', as well as by

[1] The direction in which we follow the ecliptic is contrary to that of the diurnal motion, because the sun's annual motion in the ecliptic is from west to east.

[2] They are also each very nearly equal to E m.

H

a not inconsiderable increment of time due to the fact
that the moon is all the while moving on her orbit, and
moves farther, of course, the longer her rising is delayed.
The hour of rising will in both cases be later than the
hour at which the moon rose on the preceding night
(at least in our latitude, and everywhere save in very
high latitudes), but the difference will be much greater
in one case than in the other.

Now these are the extreme cases: the ecliptic can
never cross the horizon at a greater angle than e E H$'$,
or at a less angle than e' E H$'$. Accordingly—still
assuming that the moon moves in the ecliptic—we shall
have the greatest possible difference between the hours
of rising when the moon is on the ecliptic placed as at
e E M, and the least possible difference when she is on
the ecliptic placed as at e' E M$'$; and if the moon is 'full'
or nearly so, when in one or other of these positions, the
peculiarity will be very noteworthy. In one case we
shall have a remarkable, retardation in the hours of
rising on successive days, and in the other as remarkably small a difference. Now the full moon is in or
near the former position in spring, for then the new
moon is, with the sun, at or near the ascending node of
the ecliptic, and therefore the full moon at or near the
descending node. Accordingly in spring the difference
between the hours at which the full moon rises on successive nights is considerable. It amounts, in fact, on
the average, in our latitudes to about an hour and
twenty minutes,[1] the mean interval being only about

[1] There is a table in Ferguson's *Astronomy* which seems to

$50\frac{1}{2}$ minutes.   And the full moon is near the ascending
node of the ecliptic in autumn, for then the new moon
is, with the sun, at or near the descending node of the
ecliptic.   Accordingly, in autumn, the difference between the hours at which the full moon rises on successive nights is small.   It amounts, in fact, on the
average, in our latitudes to rather more than twenty
minutes (or about half an hour less than the mean
interval).

But the inclination of the moon's orbit and the
moon's variable motion due to the eccentricity of her
orbit cause these results to be considerably modified.
We can at once consider this feature (proposing presently to discuss more particularly the moon's motion
on her inclined eccentric orbit).   Let us suppose that
when at E, fig. 22, the moon is crossing the equator
ascendingly, or towards M', and is also at the rising
node of her orbit.   Then, instead of following the
course E M', she will travel along such a course as is
shown by the dotted line E 1, or will be yet nearer

imply differently, since he gets 1 h. 16 m. as the greatest possible
difference between the hours of successive rising or setting of the
moon, when the inclination of her orbit to the ecliptic is taken into
account ; and this value has been carefully reproduced in our text-
books of astronomy.   But it should be noticed that Ferguson did
not compute the values in this table, but only estimated the values
' as near as could be done from a common globe, on which the
moon's orbit was delineated with a black-lead pencil,' and he was
not successful even in his application of this very rough method,
by which, or by a simple method of projection, it may readily be
shown that the maximum difference is greater and the minimum
difference less than Ferguson supposed.   If the eccentricity of the
moon's orbit and her consequently variable motion be taken into
account, a yet greater difference results.

than M′ to the horizon at the end of the twenty-four
hours; in other words, the interval between successive
risings at this season will be yet more shortened than
we have found it to be on the assumption that the
moon moves on the ecliptic.   In like manner, if when
at E, and crossing the equator descendingly, the moon
is at her descending node (which will obviously correspond to the period when she crosses the equator ascendingly while near her ascending node), then, instead of
following the course E M, she will follow the course
E 4, or will be yet farther than M from the horizon at
the end of the twenty-four hours; in other words, the
interval between successive risings will be yet further
lengthened than we have found it to be on the assumption that the moon moved in the ecliptic.   On the
contrary, if the moon, when crossing the ecliptic ascendingly, is at her descending node (so following the
course E 2), while when crossing the ecliptic descendingly she is at her ascending node (so following the
course E 3), the intervals between successive risings and
settings will be less markedly· affected than on the
assumption that the moon moves in the ecliptic.   These
are the extreme cases either way.   It is readily seen,
however, that the position of the moon as to the perigee
and apogee of her orbit must also have an effect, since
her motion from E will be greater or less according as
she is nearer or farther from her perigee, and the interval between successive risings will be diminished or
increased respectively.

Taking all these considerations into account, it is

found that instead of the moon rising about twenty
minutes later night after night for several successive
days at the time of harvest moon, she at times rises
only nine or ten minutes later on successive nights;
while at other times, at the same season, the difference
exceeds half an hour. As regards the maximum difference between the hours of rising of the full moon in
spring, it varies from about an hour and ten minutes to
about an hour and a half.

It is to be noticed that in every lunation corresponding variations occur, because the moon necessarily passes through Pisces and Aries, and through
Virgo and Libra in each lunation. But it is only in
spring that the full moon is in Libra and Virgo, and
in autumn that the full moon is in Pisces and Aries.
The autumn phenomena are the more important, since
they cause the nights to be almost completely moonlit for
four or five days in succession. We have, at and near
the time of full moon in September, the moon rising
not far on either side of six in the evening; and
though the hour of setting varies considerably, yet
this is obviously a matter of small importance, since
the moon sets in the morning hours. The operations
of harvesting can thus be continued far on into the
night, or all night if need be. This relates, however
(at least in England), to the full moon preceding the
middle of September, for harvesting operations are
nearly always completed throughout England before
that time. The full moon following September, which
partakes to about an equal degree with that preceding

the autumnal equinox in the peculiarity we have been dealing with, is sometimes called the *hunter's moon*.

.In latitudes higher than ours the phenomena of the *harvest moon* and *hunter's moon* are more marked, because the angle H E M′ (fig. 22) grows smaller and smaller as the arctic circle is approached.   At the arctic circle this angle vanishes, and the moon, when moving parallel to the ecliptic, rises night after night (for a time in each lunation) at the same sidereal time, or nearly four minutes earlier on successive nights. However, into such peculiarities as these we need not here enter, because the subject would thus become an exceedingly wide one, while in reality there is little importance in the relations thus involved, since in the arctic regions there are no harvesters to be benefited, nor is hunting there pursued in the night hours.

But we must now take into account the circumstance that the moon moves on an orbit somewhat inclined to the ecliptic.   It will, in the first place, be manifest that if the *position* [1] of the plane in which

---

[1] I use this word to indicate not the actual place of the plane in question, but the manner in which it is posed in space. Thus the position of the earth's equator-plane would, according to this usage of the word, be described as identical (neglecting precession) throughout the year, the position of the earth's orbit-plane identical year after year as the sun moves onward with his family of dependent orbs through space, the position of the plane of the Saturnian rings identical throughout the Saturnian year, and so on. A discussion occurred a few years ago, in the pages of a weekly journal, as to the proper word to indicate this particular relation, and I advocated then the use of the word ' position ' as on the whole the most suitable. The question is one to which my attention has been particu-

the moon travels were invariable, she would cross the ecliptic at the two fixed points which would be her nodes. During any single revolution of the moon this is not far from the actual case ; so that we may say, without gross error, that in a sidereal month the moon is twice on the ecliptic, and twice at her greatest distance north and south of the ecliptic, that is, about 5° 9′ (on the average) north and south of that circle Viewing the matter in this way for the moment, let us inquire in what way the moon's range north and south of the equator, and her motions generally, as seen from the earth, are affected, according as her nodes lie in different parts of the ecliptic.

Let S E N W (fig. 23) represent the plane of the horizon, N being the north point, and S P N the visible celestial sphere.   Let E Æ W Æ′ be the celestial equator, the arrow on this circle showing the direction

larly drawn, because it has chanced that repeatedly in my writings I have had to deal with this feature ; and I have found no word so readily understood in this particular sense as the word ‘position.’ At the same time I must admit, first, that the word is not wholly free from objection ; and secondly, that several mathematicians, to whose opinion I feel bound to attach great weight, are opposed to its use in this sense. Unfortunately they suggest no other term. It appears to me that the objections to the use of the word ‘position’ in the sense in question are precisely parallel to those which may be urged against the word ‘direction’ as applied to lines. I find, moreover, that Herschel, Grant, and other writers, use the word ‘position’ as I have done, being apparently forced so to use it for want of any better word. Accordingly I retain the use of the word, and would suggest, as the best remedy against its defects, that writers should carefully avoid the use of the word to indicate *place*, adopting instead the word *situation*. I give, then, this definition :—Planes are said to have the same *position* when lines normal to them have the same *direction*.

of the diurnal motion, and let W e E e' be the ecliptic,
the arrow showing the direction of the sun's annual
motion.   The student will understand of course that
the ecliptic is only placed for convenience of drawing
in such a position as to cross the equator on the horizon
at E and W.   Twice in each day it occupies that
position, as it is carried round by the diurnal motion,
and once in each day it is in the exact position in-

Fig. 23.

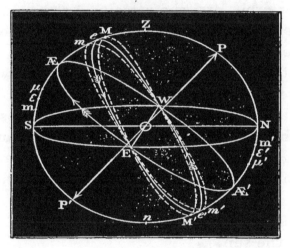

dicated in fig. 23 ; that is, with its ascending node (or
the first point of Aries) just setting in the west.

Now let us suppose that the rising node of the
moon's orbit is at W, the place of the vernal equinox.
Then W M E M' is the moon's orbit, e M and e' M'
are arcs of about 5° 9' ; and we see that the range of
the moon north and south of the equator exceeds the
range of the ecliptic (that is, of the sun) by these equal
arcs.   In other words, the moon when at M is about

28° 36′ north of the equator, instead of being only about 23° 27′ north, as she would be if she moved on the ecliptic, while when at M′ she is about 28° 36′ south of the equator : she moves throughout the sidereal month as the sun moves throughout the sidereal year, passing alternately north and south of the equator, but with a greater range, due to the greater inclination of her orbit. Accordingly, she remains a longer time above the horizon when at any given stage of the northern half of her orbit, and she remains a shorter time above the horizon when at any given stage of the southern half of her orbit, than she would be if she moved on the ecliptic. She also passes higher than the sun above the horizon when at her greatest northerly range, attaining at this time (in our latitudes) a height of more than 66°, as at M, instead of less than 61° ; and she is correspondingly nearer the horizon in southing when at her greatest southerly range from the equator, attaining in fact a southerly elevation of less than 10°, as at m, instead of more than 15°, as is the case with the sun.

Next let us suppose that the descending node of the moon's orbit is at W (fig. 23), the place of the vernal equinox ; then W m E m′ is the moon's orbit ; e m and e m′ are arcs of about 5° 9′ ; and we see that the range of the moon north and south of the ecliptic is less than the range of the sun by these equal arcs. Hence the moon when at m is about 18° 18′ north of the equator instead of 23° 27′, and she is about 18° 18′ south of the equator when at m′.

Thus she has a smaller range than the sun north and
south of the equator. She never attains a greater
elevation above the southern horizon than about 56°,
as at m; but, on the other hand, her least elevation
when due south exceeds 20°, as at μ (the sun's greatest
and least southerly elevations, as at e and ε, being respectively about 61° and about 15°).

Fig. 24.

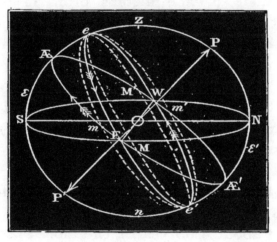

Thirdly, let the rising node of the moon's orbit be
near e, the place of the summer solstice (fig. 24); then
e M e' M' is the moon's orbit, which crosses the equator
at two points, M and M', in advance of the equinoctial
points W and E.[1] We see that its greatest range from

---

[1] These points and the points m and m' are about $12\frac{1}{2}$ degrees
from the points E and W, being determined by the relation that
they are points on the equator about 5° 9' north of the ecliptic.
If great nicety were required in the above explanation, we should
have to take into account the fact that the moon's orbit has not
exactly its mean inclination to the equator when the nodes are on
the solstitial colure; for the angle e M Æ is not equal to the angle

the ecliptic is attained nearly at the points e and e′, and is therefore appreciably equal to the sun's range. The circumstances of the moon's motion must therefore resemble very closely those of the sun's, the chief difference resulting from the fact that the nodes of the moon's orbit on the equator are some twelve or thirteen degrees in advance of the equinoctial points.

Lastly, similar considerations apply when the descending node of the moon's orbit is near e, the moon's path being in this case e m e′ m′, and its nodes on the equator some twelve or thirteen degrees behind the equinoctial points.

Now let it be noticed that the moon's orbit passes through the complete cycle of changes (of which the above four cases are the *quarter*-changes) in about 18·6 years, the lunar node moving on the whole backwards on the ecliptic. Thus, if such a cycle of years begin with the moon's orbit in the position W M E M′ (fig. 23), then in about a fourth of the cycle (that is, in about 4·65 years), the moon's orbit is in or near the position e′ m′ e m (fig. 24), the node having moved backwards from W to near e′, or one quarter of a revolution. One fourth of the cycle later—that is, about 9·3 years from the beginning of the cycle,—the moon's orbit is in or near the position E m′ W m (fig. 23), the node having moved still backwards from e′ to near E. Yet another fourth of the cycle later, or

e E Æ, the mean inclination in question. But considerations of this kind need not detain us in a general explanation such as that we are now upon.

about 13·95 years from its commencement, the moon's
orbit is in or near the position e M e′ M′ (fig. 24), the
rising node having shifted backwards from E to near e ;
and lastly, at the end of the complete cycle of 18·6
years, the moon's orbit is in or near its original
position.

It is obvious that since, on the whole, the lunar
nodes thus regrede, or, as it were, meet the advancing
moon, she must cross her nodes at intervals somewhat
shorter than a sidereal month. In fact, supposing
her to start from her rising node at the beginning
of a sidereal month of 27·322 days, then at the end
she has returned to the part of the ecliptic she had
occupied at the beginning, while the node has regreded
on the average by that amount which is due to a
period of 27·322 days. This amount is easily calculated, since the node regredes through the complete
circuit of the ecliptic in 6793·391 days: it is rather
less than 1° 27′. So that, estimating her motion with
reference to her rising node, the moon completes a circuit, and nearly a degree and a half *over*, in 27·322
days ; hence she completes a nodal circuit in a period
less than 27·322 in the proportion very nearly of 360 to
$361\frac{1}{2}$.[1] This period, called the *nodical* month, amounts

[1] Or another and more exact way of viewing the matter is as
follows :—The moon advances at a mean rate of $\frac{360}{27\cdot322}$ degrees per
day, the node regredes at a mean rate of $\frac{360}{6793\cdot39}$ degrees per day.
Thus the diurnal advance of the moon with respect to the node is
the sum of these two quantities, and we have only to calculate how
often this sum is contained in 360 degrees to find the exact number
of days in a mean nodical month. This number is obviously the
reciprocal of $\frac{1}{27\cdot322} + \frac{1}{6793\cdot39}$. This method is clearly the correct

to 27·212 days.   It follows that the mean interval between successive passages of the lunar nodes is about
13½ days.   Accordingly, the moon must always be
twice at a node in every lunar month of 29½ days, and
may be three times at a node; since, if she is at a
node within the first 2·3 days from new moon, she is
again at a node within 15·9 days from new moon, and
yet again within 29·5 days,—that is, before the next
new moon.

The effects of the eccentricity of the lunar orbit are
too obvious to need any special discussion.   The moon
moves more quickly (in miles per hour) when in
perigee than when in apogee, in the proportion of
about 19 to 17 on the average; but as she is nearer
in the same degree when in perigee, her apparent
rate of motion along her orbit is yet further increased,
and in the same degree, so that her motion in her
orbit is greater when she is in perigee than when she
is in apogee, in about the proportion of the square of
19 to the square of 17, or about as 5 to 4.   (We note,
in passing, that 19 to 17 is about the ratio in which
the moon's apparent linear dimensions are greater when
she is in perigee than when she is in apogee, while 5 to
4 is the apparent ratio in which her disc when she is in

method to pursue in all such cases.   The rule may be thus expressed:—Let P P′ be the periods in which two objects—which
may be planets, nodes, perigee-points, or others—make a circuit
of the same celestial circle, P′ being greater than P: then the
interval between successive conjunctions is the reciprocal of $\frac{1}{P} - \frac{1}{P'}$,
if the objects move in the same direction, and the reciprocal of
$\frac{1}{P} + \frac{1}{P'}$ if they move in different directions.

perigee exceeds her disc when she is in apogee.)   As
the eccentricity of her orbit is variable, its mean value
being about 0·055, while its greatest and least values
are about 0·066 and 0·044, there is a different range in
her rates of real and apparent motion, according to
the amount of eccentricity when she is in perigee or
apogee respectively.   The actual maximum rate of the
moon's motion is attained when she is in perigee and
her eccentricity has its maximum value 0·066, while
the actual minimum is attained when she is in apogee
at such a time.   The ratio between her real motions,
under these circumstances, is that of 1,066 to 934, or
about 8 to 7 ; the ratio between her apparent motions
in her orbit being rather greater than 13 to 10.

These variations are sufficiently great to modify in a
remarkable degree the movements of the moon when
considered with reference to the change from day to
day in her apparent place in the heavens, and therefore in her apparent course from horizon to horizon.
We saw that this must be so when we inquired into
the phenomenon called the harvest moon.   It is manifest also that all the circumstances of eclipses, solar as
well as lunar, must be importantly modified by the
remarkable variations which take place in the moon's
distance from the earth, and in her real and apparent
motions.   The eccentricity of the moon's orbit also
produces very interesting effects in relation to her
librations.   If the perigee and apogee always held a
fixed position with respect to the nodes of the lunar
orbit, the peculiarities thus arising would be less re-

markable; but the continual shifting of the relative positions of the nodes and apses (as the perigee and apogee are called) causes a continual variation, as we shall see hereafter, in the circumstances of the lunar librations.

Speaking generally, it may be said that the lunar perigee advances at such a mean rate as to make a complete circuit in about 3232·575 days. Accordingly, applying considerations resembling those applied to her motion with respect to her nodes, we see that the period of her motion from perigee to perigee must exceed a sidereal month. Its actual length is found to be about 27·555 days. This is the mean *anomalistic* month; [1] it exceeds the mean nodical month by rather more than the third part of a day; or more exactly by 0·342 of a day.

The actual motion of the perigee and apogee with respect to the nodes is very variable. The apses are sometimes advancing rapidly, while at others they are almost as rapidly receding,—and they advance on the whole or recede on the whole for several successive months; and the node itself, though on the whole receding in every lunation, yet sometimes advances slowly for several successive days. Thus the perigee and rising node are sometimes moving the same way, at others in opposite ways; they may be both advancing or both receding, or the perigee may be advancing and

[1] The actual interval between the moon's passages of her perigee varies during the course of a year from about 25 days to about 28½ days.

the apogee receding, or the perigee receding and the apogee advancing. However, so far as the mean advance of the perigee from the node is concerned, the case is sufficiently simple ; for the perigee advances so as to complete a revolution on the average in 3232·575 days, or 8·8505 years, while the node recedes so as to complete a revolution on the average in 18·5997 years. Thus the mean annual advance of the perigee is $\frac{1}{8\cdot8505}$ of a revolution, while the mean annual regression of the node is $\frac{1}{18\cdot5997}$ of a revolution. Adding these together, we find the mean motion of the perigee with respect to the node equal to $\frac{1}{5\cdot997}$ of a revolution.[1] In other words, the mean interval between successive conjunctions of the perigee and rising node is very nearly six years, falling short of six years in fact by but about three thousandths of a year, or almost exactly $1\frac{1}{10}$ days.[2] The mean interval between successive conjunctions of the apses and nodes (without regard to the distinction between apogee and perigee, rising node and descending node) is three years, wanting only about half a day,—or, more exactly, wanting 13 h. 18·5 m.

We are now in a position to discuss the effects of the moon's rotation.

If the moon as she went round the earth turned several times round upon an axis nearly square to the

[1] The agreement of the figures in the denominator of this fraction with the last four in the fraction representing the motion of the node is of course a merely accidental coincidence.

[2] The mean interval between successive conjunctions of the perigee and the rising node is 2190·343 days, and in six years there are 2191·452 days ; so that the mean difference is 1·109 days.

level of her path, she would present every part of her surface several times successively towards the earth, precisely as the earth turns every part of her surface towards the sun in the course of a year. On the other hand, if the moon did not *turn* round at all as she went round the earth, we should see in turn every part of her surface, since at opposite sides of the earth she

Fig. 25.

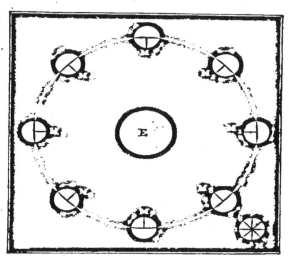

would necessarily present two opposite faces towards the earth. Since as a matter of fact it may be said (as a first rough account of the moon's appearance) that she turns always the same face towards the earth, it follows that she must turn *once* on an axis nearly square to the level of her path as she performs one complete circuit.

This is shown again in fig. 25, where we see that if the middle point of the disc of the moving globe is the

I

same real point on this globe, as it travels through the positions M_1, M_2, M_3, M_4 . . . . to M_8, this globe must have turned in the manner shown at M, fig. 25, the radii in which to the points 1, 2, 3, 4, &c., are respectively parallel to the radii to M_1, M_2, M_3, M_4, &c., all of which are directed upon the central orb E.

But it may occur to some readers that in the nature of things if a body were set without rotation travelling round a central globe, it would as it went round turn itself *also*, as if upon an axis, and so keep always the same face directed towards the central globe. For example, if a rod extending from E, and rigidly attached to M_1, carried that globe round E in the manner indicated, then the face A would remain constantly turned towards E : may it not be, it might be asked, that as the globe moved under gravity round E the same thing would happen?

Now it is mathematically demonstrable that the attraction of E can have no effect whatever in causing the direction of the line A M to *change* as the body (supposed to be spherical) [1] circles around E. But the considerations on which such a demonstration would be based are by no means so obvious as is commonly supposed. We shall not, therefore, present them here, but proceed at once to mention two experimental proofs of the fact in question. The first experiment is very simple. Let a tolerably heavy ball be suspended by a

---

[1] If the body be not spherical, forces tending to produce rotation come into play ; but if the body has even only a roughly globular form, such forces are altogether too small to produce any appreciable amount of rotation during a single revolution.

long fine cord.   Let it be left hanging until all signs
of twisting have passed away ; then, having placed a
mark upon the ball about midway between the top and
bottom, cause it to swing in a circle, communicating
this motion by means of the string held at a point high
above the ball, so that no rotational movement can be
imparted.   It will be found that the mark continues
always to be directed towards the same point of the
compass, *not* turning so as always to bear in the same
direction with respect to the centre of motion.   The
second was suggested by Galileo, who pointed out that
if a body be set to float in a basin of water, and this
basin be held out at arm's length while the holder turns
round, it will be found that the floating body does not
partake in the turning motion ; so that the side turned
towards the holder of the basin at the beginning is
turned directly away from him when he has made half
a turn.   It is, however, by no means easy to carry out
this experiment in a satisfactory manner, the most
striking phenomenon under ordinary conditions being
the spilling of three-fourths of the water, or there-
abouts.

Fig. 26.

But a very effective experiment for those who feel
doubts respecting the moon's rotation may be conducted as follows:—Let A B (fig. 26) be a flat wooden
bar of any convenient dimensions (according to the

circumstances under which the experiment is to be
conducted). Let fig. 27 present a side view of the
same bar, which, it will be observed, is arranged to run
on casters at A and B, and to turn on a pivot at C.
At A let a small circle and arrow be marked on the bar;
at C and B let small basins of water be placed, in which
let small wooden rods float,—or preferably, let the rods
float in half-filled saucers, themselves floating in the
basins. If now the experimenter wait until the water
is still, the floating rods being central and parallel to
the arrow at A, and if he then gently turn the wooden

Fig. 27.

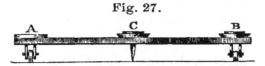

bar round on its pivot at C, the casters rolling on a
smooth table or floor, he will see that the rods floating
at B and C both retain a direction almost wholly unchanged throughout the motion ; and thus while continuing parallel to each other and also to any line on
the table or floor to which they were parallel in the
first instance, they no longer continue parallel to the
arrow at A, whose direction changes throughout the
motion. The slight change of position they undergo
is obviously referable to friction between the water and
the basins and saucers. Of course the basin C is not
essential in this experiment, nor the fixed arrow at A.
If the basin B were simply carried round the end A as
a centre, a similar result would follow. But it is interesting to show that so far as the rotation of the water

within the basin is concerned, the condition of the basin
B is exactly the same as that of a basin at C turning
simply on a pivot immediately beneath it.

Another experiment may be tried with the same
apparatus. The water in C and B may, without much
trouble, be set rotating at the same rate. If this be
done, and then the rod be carried round at the same
rate, so that the floating rod in C retains an unchanged position with respect to the bar A B or to
the arrow at A, it will be found that the water in B
behaves precisely as the moon's globe behaves (so far
at least as the general relation we are dealing with is
concerned), turning always the same portion towards
the centre C. Thus we learn that it is only by an
additional rotational movement that such a relation
can be preserved.

The moon, then, turns once upon her axis as she
completes the circuit of her orbit. Yet it is not
strictly the case that the moon turns always the same
face towards the earth. We see somewhat more than
one-half of the moon's surface. Let us inquire how
this is brought about.

In the first place, the moon's axis is not at right
angles to the plane of the path in which she travels
round the earth. (Let it be noticed, in passing, that
it is the inclination of the moon's axis to this plane,
and not to the plane of the ecliptic, which affects her
appearance as seen from the earth. This will appear
obvious as we proceed.)

The moon's equator-plane is inclined 1° 30′ 11″ to

the plane of the ecliptic, and is always so placed that
when the moon is at the ascending or descending
node of her orbit the equator-plane is turned edge-
wise towards the earth, and is inclined descendingly
or ascendingly (respectively) to the ecliptic. Since the
average inclination of the moon's orbit to the ecliptic is
nearly 5° 9′, it follows that the angle at which the
moon's equator-plane is thus inclined has a mean value

Fig. 28.

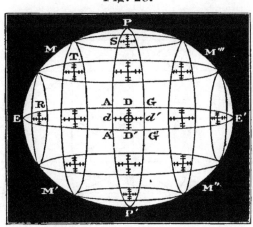

of about 6° 39′; but this angle varies as the inclination
of the moon's orbit varies, and is sometimes as great as
6° 44′,[1] sometimes as small as 6° 34′.

Now the effect of this inclination of the moon's axis
to the plane of her orbit about the earth corresponds

[1] I find commonly 6° 47′ set as the value of this angle. This
seems to be obtained by adding the moon's maximum orbit inclination 5° 17′ to the inclination of her axis to the ecliptic. But the
moon is always near a node when her orbit attains its maximum
inclination, whereas the maximum opening due to her inclination is
attained when she is farthest from her nodes.

precisely to the seasonal variations of the earth's presentation towards the sun.   The point O, the mean
centre of the lunar disc M M″, fig. 28, passes alternately
north and south of the moon's equator, or, which is the
same thing, the middle point of the visible half of the
equator passes alternately south and north of the centre
of the disc.   The range of this oscillation for the mean
centre of the disc is shown by the vertical line D O D′,
E D E′ and E D′ E′ representing the moon's equator

Fig. 29.

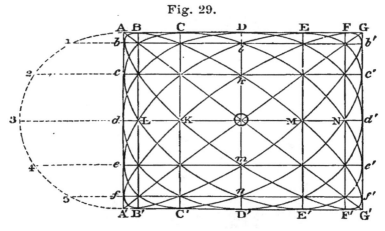

as most bowed upwards and downwards through the
effect of inclination.   The other vertical dotted lines,
as at S, T, R, &c., represent the corresponding oscillations due to the moon's inclination for other parts of
the lunar disc.   The dots represent the position of the
centre at twelve equal intervals of time throughout a
nodical month or at intervals of about $2\frac{1}{4}$ days ; it is
easily seen from very simple geometrical considerations
that all these vertical short lines are divided in the
same manner as the lines A A′ and D O D′ of fig. 29,

where the points of division on A A' are obtained by drawing perpendiculars to A A' from points dividing the semicircular arc A 3 A' into six equal parts.

But next let us take into consideration the effect of the want of perfect accordance between the moon's motions of revolution and rotation. She rotates uniformly on her axis, or very nearly so, while she moves with varying velocity round the earth. But fig. 25 shows that, for the same face always to be seen, there should be perfect agreement between the motions of rotation and revolution. When the eccentricity of the moon's orbit has its mean value, the moon falls alternately about 6° 17' 19''·04 in advance of and behind her mean place (which she has when in perigee and apogee). But when the eccentricity has its maximum value, the angle $P E M_2$ or $P' E M_4$ amounts to 7° 20', and owing to lunar perturbations it may be increased to so much as 7° 45'.[1]

The effect of the want of accordance between the moon's rotation and revolution is to sway the lunar meridian across the mean central point of the disc through precisely the angular amount by which the moon is in advance of or behind her mean place. The short horizontal cross-lines of fig. 28 indicate the range of the oscillations of various points of the lunar disc, on account of the cause we are considering. The law of

[1] This is the result of my own calculations. I find 7° 53' and 7° 55' set by different authorities as the greatest value of the angle in question. It appears to me that the circumstance has been overlooked that the moon's orbit never has its maximum eccentricity when the moon is at her mean distance.

the oscillating motion, determining the division of
these horizontal lines as in the figure, is the same as
that for the vertical lines. So that d O d' in fig. 29,
which represents d O d' of fig. 28 on an enlarged scale,
is divided at L, K, O, M, and N, similarly to D O D'
in the points l, k, O, m, and n. P d P' and P d' P', in
fig. 28, represent the extreme position of the mean
central meridian east and west of the mean centre.

It is readily seen that as the two oscillations along
the vertical and horizontal short lines of the lunar disc
(fig. 28) take place together, the mean centre and every

Fig. 30.   Fig. 31.   Fig. 32.

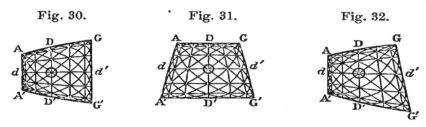

other point on the disc will usually describe an oval
curve resulting from the composition of the two motions.
If the displacement of the mean centre vanishes for
both oscillations simultaneously, the combined oscillations of the mean centre will be along one or other of
the lines A O G' and A' O G (fig. 29). If one displacement attains its maximum value when the other vanishes,
and *vice versâ*, the oscillations will be in the ellipse
D d' D' d. In intermediate circumstances one or other
of such intermediate ellipses as are shown in fig. 29
will be followed by the mean centre. Figs. 30, 31, and
32 show the corresponding curves for points of the
moon's disc near R, S, and T of fig. 28. As the mean

nodical month is slightly shorter than the mean anomalistic month, it follows that the libration curves traced by the mean centre and other points of the moon's disc change constantly in form, passing from a straight line as A O G′ when the rising node and perigee coincide, to the curve b′ B′ f F, thence to the curve c′ C′ e E, and to the curve d′ D′ d D, at which time the rising node is 90° behind the perigee. Still changing in the same direction (on the whole) the curve changes to e′ E′ c C, to f′ F′ b B, and to G′ O A, when the rising node coincides with the apogee ; thence to F′ f′ B b, to E′ e′ C c, and to D′ d′ D d, when the rising node is 90° in advance of the perigee ; and so to C′ c′ E e, to B′ b′ F f, and to G O A′, when rising node and perigee coincide again as at first. The last six curves are the same as the first, but traced out the reverse way, and entered on in reverse order. The total time occupied by all these changes, the interval between successive coincidences of rising node and perigee, is almost exactly six years. As the rising node is not always retrograding nor the perigee always advancing, though they move in these directions respectively on the whole, the actual changes are exceedingly complicated. In fact, it may be truly said that the librating motion of the moon's centre (or of any other point on the moon's disc) involves implicitly the whole theory of the moon's motions.

Such are the chief features of the lunar librations in latitude and longitude. It remains that we should consider what is the actual extent of the moon's surface

which these librations bring into view in addition to
that which is seen when the mean centre is at the actual
centre of the lunar disc. In making the inquiry we
must take into account another libration, called the
diurnal libration, which depends on the circumstance
that, owing to the earth's rotation, the place of the
observer is shifted with respect to the line joining the
centres of the earth and moon. This form of libration might very well be made the subject of a separate
investigation, which would, however, be more tedious
than profitable, because the extent and nature of the
diurnal libration vary in different latitudes and at
different seasons. On this point I shall content myself
with remarking that if we imagine an observer placed
at the centre of the moon's visible disc, a line drawn
from him to any station on the earth would be carried
by the earth's rotation along a latitude parallel, and the
angle which it made at any moment with a line joining
the centres of the earth and moon would correspond to
the *diurnal* displacement of the moon's centre, as seen
from the station at that moment. This consideration,
combined with what will hereafter be stated respecting
the aspect of the earth as seen from the moon, will
suffice to show the exact nature of the diurnal libration at any given station, and at any season. Here,
however, all that is necessary to be noticed is that,
since the earth's radius, as supposed to be seen from
the moon, subtends nearly a degree when the moon is
at her mean distance, and more than a degree when
the moon is in perigee, we may obviously add an arc

of about a degree on the moon's surface to any libratory displacement in any direction whatever, estimated
for the centre of the earth, if we wish to determine
the maximum displacement in that direction *for any
part of the earth.* For, if we suppose an observer on
the moon to shift his place, in any direction, by one
lunar degree (corresponding to a distance of nearly
twenty miles), he would see the earth's centre shifted
one degree on the heavens ; and therefore the point on
the heavens formerly occupied by the earth's centre
would now be occupied by a point on or very close
to the circumference of the earth's disc. Therefore,
when we have determined the fringe of extra surface
brought into view by the moon's maximum librations,
we can widen this fringe all round by a breadth of
about one degree. We must not indeed widen it
everywhere by a breadth of $1° 1' 24''$, the maximum
apparent semidiameter of the earth as seen from the
moon, simply because this apparent semidiameter is
only presented when the moon is in perigee, while the
moon attains her greatest total libration, as well as her
greatest libration in longitude, only when she is at her
mean distance. We may, however, employ even this
maximum value of the horizontal parallax when the
moon has her maximum libration in latitude, since
there is nothing to prevent her from attaining this
libration when she is at her nearest to the earth. These
considerations, however, are unimportant, compared
with those depending on the moon's librations in longitude and latitude, simply because the diurnal libration

—or, as it may more fitly be termed, the parallactic libration—attains its maximum only when the moon is on the horizon, and therefore very ill-placed for telescopic observation.

In considering the actual extent of the moon's surface which her librations carry into and out of view alternately, we need not trouble ourselves about the varying nature of the combined libration. It might seem, at first sight, as though certain parts of the moon would only be brought into view when the libration in latitude attains its maximum value,—that is, when the libration in longitude vanishes ; and *vice versâ*. But as a matter of fact, if we consider the four cases where the total libration has its absolute maximum value— viz. when the mean centre is at the four points A, G, A', and G' (fig. 29)—we take into account every portion of the moon's surface which libration can possibly bring into view.

So that all we have to ascertain is the area of the space on the sphere corresponding to the four lunes brought into view at these extreme librations. This is easily effected,[1] and we learn that the area thus brought

---

[1] We know the maximum breadth of the four lunes. It is easily shown that the total area brought into view by libration bears to the whole sphere the ratio—

$$2 \ (7° \ 45' \ + \ 6° \ 44') : 360°$$
$$= \quad 14° \ 29' : 180$$
$$= \quad 869 \quad : 10800.$$

Thus the total area brought into view by libration bears to a hemisphere the ratio of about 100 to 621. (Arago makes the ratio 1 to 7, though using 10° 24' as the absolute maximum of libration. It is not easy to understand how an error crept into his treatment of a problem

into view by libration is between one-twelfth and one-thirteenth of the whole area of the moon, or nearly one-sixth part of the hemisphere turned away from the earth when the moon is at her state of mean libration. Of course a precisely equal portion of the hemisphere turned towards us during mean libration is carried out of view by the lunar librations.

If we add to each of these areas a fringe about 1° wide, due to the diurnal libration—a fringe which we may call the parallactic fringe, since it is brought into view through the same cause which produces the lunar parallax,—we shall find that the total brought into view is almost exactly one-eleventh part of the whole surface of the moon. A similar area is carried out of view: so that the whole region thus swayed out of and into view amounts to $\frac{2}{11}$ths of the moon's surface.

so simple.) The proportion of the part of this hemisphere never seen to the whole hemisphere is therefore about 521 to 621; or if we represent the whole sphere by 1, the area of the part absolutely invisible will be represented by 0·4198. (Klein, in his *Sonnensystem*, gives 0·4243, which is nearer to the truth than the value resulting from Arago's estimate, namely, 0·4286, yet still considerably in error, particularly as Klein also names the value 10° 24′ for the maximum libration.)

If, however, we take into account the effects of the diurnal libration, it can readily be shown that the portion of the moon which is never seen under any circumstances bears to the area of the whole moon almost exactly the proportion which 148 bears to 360, or 37 to 90,—that is, it is equal to 0·4111 of the whole area. The part which can be carried out of view or into view by the libration, including the parallactic libration, amounts to $\frac{8}{45}$ths of the whole surface, or $\frac{1}{5\frac{5}{8}}$ (= 0·17) if the whole area is represented by unity.

The above numerical results have been carefully tested, and can be relied on as strictly accurate. It is easy for the reader to reexamine them, however.

In fig. 33 a side view of the moon is given.   The figure is self-explanatory ; but it is to be observed that m M *m* and m' M' *m'* are arcs of 20° 32', corresponding to the absolute maximum libratory swayings, A O G'

Fig. 33.

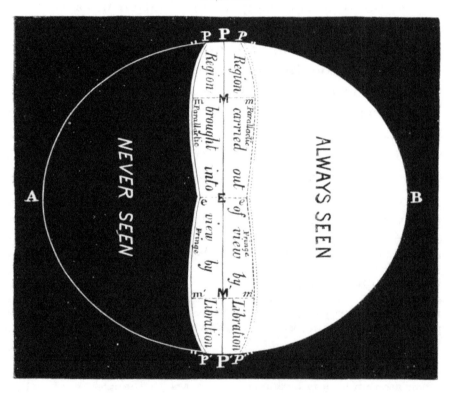

and A' O G of fig. 28 ; p P *p* is an arc of 13° 28', corresponding to the maximum libratory swaying in latitude (D O D' of fig. 28) ; and e E *e* is an arc of 15° 30', corresponding to the maximum swaying in longitude (*d* O *d'* of fig. 28).

It must always be remembered, however, that

although such regions as p E p' (fig. 33) are brought
into view by libration, they are always seen very much
foreshortened, not as presented in fig. 33.

This chapter would be incomplete without some
reference to what has been called the physical libration
of the moon.

We have assumed throughout the preceding pages
that the moon rotates with perfect uniformity on her
axis while revolving around the earth. This, however,
is not strictly the case. In the first place it is manifest that since the moon's mean sidereal revolution
is undergoing at present a process of diminution,
owing to what is termed her secular acceleration, her
rotation must either undergo a corresponding acceleration, or she would in the course of time so turn
round with respect to the earth that the regions now
unseen would be revealed to terrestrial observers. She
would, in fact, thus have turned round by the time
when, owing to her acceleration, she had gained half a
revolution. It has been shown, however, by Laplace,
that the attractions to which she is subject suffice to
prevent such a change, and that her rate of rotation
changes *pari passu* with her rate of revolution. It
must, therefore, be to this slight extent variable. A
similar remark applies to all secular perturbations
affecting the moon's motions. So that it is impossible
that the further side of the moon should ever be turned
towards the earth unless under the action of some
extraneous influence, as the shock of a mass comparable
with her own.

But a real libration much more considerable in amount, and possibly recognisable by observation, must affect the moon's rotation. Newton was the first to point out, that if the moon was originally in a fluid state, the earth's attraction would draw her into the form of a spheroid, the longer axis of which, when produced, would pass through the earth's centre. 'Comparing this phenomenon,' says Professor Grant, 'with the tidal spheroid occasioned by the action of the moon upon the earth, he found that the diameter of the lunar spheroid which is directed towards the earth would exceed the diameter at right angles to it by 186 feet. He discovered in this elongation of the moon the cause why she always turns the same side towards the earth, for he remarked that in any other position the action of the earth would not maintain her in equilibrium, but would constantly draw her back, until the elongated axis coincided in direction with the line joining the earth and moon. Now in consequence of the inequalities of the moon in longitude, the elongated axis would not always be directed exactly to the earth. Newton therefore concluded that a real libration of the moon would ensue in consequence of which the elongated axis would oscillate perpetually on each side of its mean place.'

Lagrange, in dealing with this relation, noticed further what had apparently escaped Newton's attention, that, owing to the moon's rotation on her polar axis, her globe must be, to some slight degree, compressed

K

in the direction of this axis. 'Lagrange,' says Professor Grant, 'found that both effects were of the same order, and that the moon would, in reality, acquire the form of an ellipsoid, the greatest axis being directed towards the earth, and the least being perpendicular to the plane of the equator. The greatest and the mean axes will both lie in the last-mentioned plane.'

Proceeding to consider the effect of the earth's attraction upon the rotating moon, Lagrange found that the mean rotation would be affected by a series of changes corresponding to those affecting the moon's mean motion round the earth. In effect, all the perturbations affecting the moon's motion of revolution would, as it were, be reflected, or represented in miniature, in these variations of her motion of rotation.

While dealing with this matter Lagrange noted a circumstance to which Newton had not referred, though, as Professor Grant well remarks, it is a natural corollary to Newton's reasoning. He showed that it was not necessary to suppose that the motions of revolution and rotation were equal in the beginning. If the moon's true rotation once took place in a period not absolutely coincident with that of her revolution, the attraction of the earth would have sufficed to force the rotation-period into *mean* coincidence with the period of revolution. The rotation would in that case, however, no longer be strictly uniform, apart from the real libration we have hitherto considered. The moon would librate on either side of her mean position, independently of her variable motion in her orbit. This libration would depend, like the other, on the circumstance that the orb of the moon must be somewhat elongated in the direction of the line joining the centres of the earth and moon.

Now the form of real libration last mentioned has not been observationally recognised ; but the real libration, theoretically predicted by Newton, and confirmed by the analytical researches of Lagrange, has been detected by observers. I have said that in this libration every feature of the moon's motions is reflected. Now it might seem, at first sight, that this libration would be most noticeable as depending on the moon's varying motion in a single revolution, since she may be so much as 7° 45′ before or behind her mean place. But, as a matter of fact, the extent of the real libration depends much more on the length of time during which the earth's action is exerted, than on the actual displacement of the moon's longer axis from its mean position. Accordingly, the lunar irregularity called the annual equation, although, as we have seen, it only affects the earth's place by a small amount at the maximum, yet, as its period is a long one, enables the earth to affect the mean rotation-rate more effectually than do any of the other lunar perturbations. ‘Bouvard and Nicollet undertook,’ says Professor Grant, ‘a series of careful observations of the moon's librations in longitude, at the Royal Observatory of Paris. The

" Connaissance des Temps " for 1822 contains a beautiful paper by Nicollet, in which he submitted these observations, amounting in number to 174, to a searching
discussion.   The only sensible inequality was that corresponding to the *annual equation*.   It appeared by
observation to have a maximum value equal to 4' 45".
The results at which he arrives relative to the ratios
of the axes do not accord with the generally admitted
opinion respecting the primitive condition of the moon.
He found, in fact, that the difference between the least
and greatest axes was greater than it would be on the
supposition that the moon was originally a fluid mass.'
It would, however, be rash to base any opinion respecting the latter hypothesis upon observations so very
delicate in their nature.

It is important to notice that the ellipsoidal form
of the moon is not only demonstrated by the existence
of a recognisable real libration, but also by the con-
tinuance of that singular relation between the position
of the moon's equator and orbit referred to at p. 118.
It is manifest that since the *position* of the plane of
the orbit is continually shifting, this plane would
depart from coincidence with the plane of the moon's
equator, unless some extraneous force acted to preserve
the coincidence.   If the moon were a perfect sphere,
the earth would have no grasp upon her, so to speak,
whereby to maintain the observed relation between the
equator-plane and the orbit-plane.   But Lagrange has
shown that the action of the earth on an ellipsoidal
moon would constantly maintain the coincidence.   As

the coincidence is maintained, we must conclude that the moon is an ellipsoid, and not a sphere.

It need hardly be said that no instrumental means at present in our possession could show the ellipticity of the lunar disc. The ellipsoidal figure of the moon remains none the less, however, a demonstrated fact.

CHAPTER IV.

STUDY OF THE MOON'S SURFACE.

ALTHOUGH the study of the moon's surface can scarcely be said to have been fairly commenced before the invention of the telescope, yet in very early ages men began to form opinions respecting the moon based on the appearances presented on her disc.   Doubtless the ancient Chaldæan, Chinese, Indian, Egyptian, and Persian astronomers theorised about the moon's physical constitution; but of their views no record has reached us.   We know only that they studied the moon's movements so carefully as to recognise the principal features of her orbital motion, but what ideas they formed as to the condition of her surface we do not know.

The earliest recorded opinion as to the moon's condition is the theory of Thales (B.C. 640), that a portion of the moon's lustre is inherent.   He recognised the faint light from the illuminated part of the moon's globe at the time of new moon, or rather at the time before and after new moon, when the illuminated portion forms a narrow crescent; and it was also known to him that the moon does not disappear wholly when totally eclipsed. He therefore inferred that she shines in part by native light. It is somewhat singular that he did not perceive the remarkable contrast which exists between the two kinds of light which he regarded as belonging to the moon. The deep ruddy colour of the totally eclipsed moon differs so completely from the ashy pale light of ' the old moon in the new moon's arms,' that one can hardly understand how both could be referred to one and the same cause. Nevertheless, there have not been wanting those who, in comparatively recent times, have maintained a similar theory.

Anaxagoras (B.C. 500) was the next of the ancient philosophers who theorised respecting the moon. We learn from Diogenes Laertius that Anaxagoras regarded the moon as an inhabited world, and taught that the varieties of tint perceived on her surface are due to mountains and valleys. He held—and was ridiculed for holding—the opinion that the moon may be as large as the Peloponnesus.

Some of the Pythagorean philosophers, on the contrary, taught that the moon is altogether unlike the earth. They regarded her as a smooth, crystalline body, having the power of reflecting light like a mirror; and they supposed the spots upon her disc to be the reflection of the oceans and continents of our earth. But others believed the moon to be an inhabited world like the earth, and since daylight on the moon continues for about fifteen terrestrial days, they concluded somewhat boldly that the creatures inhabiting the moon must be fifteen times as large as corresponding terrestrial beings.   Heraclitus supposed the moon to be of the same nature as the sun, but darker, because involved in the denser part of the earth-surrounding ether.   Origenes also maintaining the moon to be a self-luminous body, considered her surface to be uneven, and regarded the dark spots as the shadows of the regions lying higher.

Passing over many less distinguished names, we come to Aristotle, who adopted the theory that the light and dark regions in the moon are the reflected images of the continents and oceans of our own earth. It is worthy of notice that the maintenance of this opinion indicates either complete ignorance or a very remarkable forgetfulness respecting the laws of reflection on the one hand, and those relative motions of the moon and earth on the other hand respecting which even the Ptolemaists held accurate ideas. Whether the earth is fixed or in motion, whether she rotates or the heavens rotate around her, it is certain that her continents and seas are presented in a continually varying manner towards the moon.   It is obvious, then, that if the moon were a mirror reflecting the features of the earth, the moon's aspect must necessarily change from hour to hour, and from day to day.   Yet nothing is more certain, even to those who only study the moon with the unaided eye, than that her aspect, so far as the spots on her disc are concerned, remains very nearly constant.   Her phases cause a greater or less portion of her spotted disc to be visible to the observer on earth, but the part which is seen belongs always to one and the same face.

The Stoics maintained for the most part that the moon is a mixture of fire, earth, and air, but spherical, like the earth and sun.

Lastly—for it would be idle to devote any considerable portion of our space to the vague fancies which the ancients formed respecting the moon,—we find that Plutarch strenuously supported the views which Anaxagoras had maintained six hundred years earlier. He even recognised the indications of mountains in the moon, in the irregularities of the lunar terminator, noting that the lunar mountains would necessarily throw vast shadows, precisely as Mount Athos, at the time of the summer solstice, cast a shadow towards evening which reached across the Thracian sea as far as the market-place of Myrina, in Lemnos, a distance of eighty-seven miles.

But it was only after the invention of the telescope that just ideas began to be formed as to the condition of the moon's surface.

In May, 1609, Galileo directed towards the moon the first telescope of his own construction. His first observations showed him that the moon's surface is covered with irregularities; but it was not until he applied his largest telescope—magnifying only thirty times—that he recognised the true conformation of the lunar surface. He found that the lunar mountains are for the most part circular in shape, forming rings around depressed regions, and in some respects resembling the mountain-chains which surround Bohemia. He could perceive bright points of light separated by dark spaces from the terminator of the crescent or gibbous moon, and he recognised the fact that these points are the tops of mountains, illuminated by sunlight, while the surrounding valleys are in darkness. He traced at once the analogy between this circumstance and terrestrial phenomena. Those who have watched the rising of the sun from the summit of a lofty mountain know that when the summit of the mountain is in the full glory of sunlight, the sides of the mountain are still in shadow, and that the neighbouring valleys are plunged in a yet deeper gloom. Corresponding appearances are seen when the sun is setting. Long before the mountain tops are darkened, the level country around is shadowed over, and the obscurity of night has already settled over ravines and passes. The only difference which Galileo perceived in the phenomena of sunrise and sunset on the lunar mountains and what is observed on our earth, was that no half-lights could be seen, nothing but the full blaze of sunlight on the mountain-tops and intense blackness in the valleys. Here was the first indication of a circumstance of which I shall presently have to speak at greater length,—the absence of any lunar atmosphere, or at least the extreme tenuity of whatever air there may be on the moon. For it is readily seen that the faint light which illuminates the valleys of a mountain region, while as yet only the mountain tops are in sunlight, comes from the sky, and the light of the sky is due to the existence of an atmosphere.

The reader will find illustrations of the illumination of lunar mountain tops in the accompanying photographs of the moon near her first and third quarters.

Galileo perceived that in the phenomenon here described he possessed the means of measuring the altitude of the lunar mountains. Without entering into details, it may be remarked that in the case of a mountain standing alone on a wide plain the distance of the peak, when just touched by the light, from the boundary of light and darkness on the plain, depends obviously on the height of the mountain. For, in fact, if a person is on the summit of the mountain at the moment he will see the sun on the horizon, and the point on his horizon where he sees the sun is in reality a point on the plain where also the run is rising at the moment: the distance of this point, or of the observer's horizon, depends on the height of the mountain, as is shown in all our text-books of astronomy. Hence, if this distance is known, the height of the mountain can be determined, and what is true of a mountain on our earth is true, with certain changes as to details, for a mountain on the moon. Now it was in Galileo's power to estimate the apparent distance of a lunar mountain peak in sunlight from the neighbouring terminator, and to determine thence the real distance in miles. This done, he could estimate the height of the mountain, always supposing that the mountain was isolated and the surrounding region fairly level. Proceeding on this assumption, Galileo was led to the conclusion that several of the lunar mountains are nearly five miles in height.

It will be obvious, however, from a study of the moon at her quarters, that this method cannot be depended upon, alone, to give trustworthy results; and this will be yet more manifest to any who will examine the moon, when not full, with a telescope of even moderate power. It is seen that as a rule not only are the lunar mountains not isolated, but the surrounding regions are so uneven as to be thrown into light or shadow, confusedly intermixed, when the sun is low down—that is, when they lie near the terminator. There is no means of judging exactly where the mean terminator lies—that is, where the boundary between light and darkness would lie if the moon were a smooth orb. Accordingly very little reliance could be placed on the measurements of Galileo, or on any estimate of the height of a lunar mountain not based on a long and careful study of the region surrounding the mountain.

It is worthy of notice, in passing, that the recognition of lunar mountains by Galileo was regarded by some of his contemporaries as a grave offence against the Aristotelian philosophy. Even those who admitted that his telescope showed objects which appeared like mountains, maintained that in reality the surface of the moon is smooth. Over the irregularities perceived by Galileo, they argued, there exists a transparent or crystalline shell, filling up the cavities and having an outer surface perfectly smooth, as Aristotle taught.   To this argument Galileo gave an answer precisely equal in value to the objection.   ' Let them be careful,' he replied ; ' for if they provoke me too far, I will erect on their crystalline shell invisible crystalline mountains, ten times as high as any I have yet described.'

Galileo was the first to recognise the great number of craters which exist on certain parts of the moon's surface.   He compared the craters in the south-western quadrant of the moon (see the accompanying lunar chart) to the ' eyes ' in a peacock's tail.

Galileo's chart of the moon, though creditable to him considering his imperfect telescopic means, has very little value except as a curiosity.   A similar remark applies to the drawings by Scheiner, Schirlaus, and others.

At this early stage of lunar research the darker portions of the moon's surface were considered to be seas, the brighter parts being looked upon as land regions.   Thus we find Kepler saying, ' Do maculas esse maria, do lucidas esse terras.'   Galileo himself seems to have been better satisfied with his recognition of mountains and valleys on the moon than with the supposed distinction between land and sea regions. It is worthy of notice that in Milton's brief references to the Florentine astronomer, based undoubtedly on the poet's recollection of his interviews with Galileo (see the ' Areopagitica '), there is no mention of seas.

Thus in Book I. of 'Paradise Lost' Milton compares
the shield of Satan to—

> ' The moon, whose orb
> Through optic glass the Tuscan artist views
> At evening, from the top of Fesolé,
> Or in Val d' Arno, to descry new lands,
> Rivers, or mountains, on her spotty globe.'

Again, in the fifth book, Raphael sees the earth—

> ' As when by night the glass
> Of Galileo, less assured, observes
> Imagined lands and regions in the moon.'

It is difficult to suppose that Milton would not have
said ' oceans' instead of ' regions' if Galileo had entertained the opinion that the dark lunar regions are seas.

Hevelius, who next made any considerable advance
in the study of the moon's surface, adopted Kepler's
opinion as to the distinction between the dark and
bright regions of the moon. He constructed a chart
which contained more detail and was more correct
than Galileo's, and adopted a system of nomenclature
indicating his belief in the existence of analogies
between lunar and terrestrial regions. Thus we find
in his list of names—mountains, deserts, marshes,
seas, lakes, islands, bays, promontories, and straits.
In some cases he named these from their imagined
resemblance to terrestrial regions; in others he indicated their appearance as seen in his telescope. Thus,
the great crater now called Copernicus was by Hevelius
called Mount Etna; while the dark enclosed surface
called Plato was named by Hevelius ' the greater
black lake.' The chart by Hevelius was necessarily

imperfect compared with those now in existence. The telescopic power he employed was very little greater than that used by Galileo ; and he had to trust, like Galileo, to mere estimation of the proportions of the different lunar regions, not possessing even the roughest appliances for micrometrical measurement.

We owe to Hevelius the recognition of the most important of the lunar librations. Galileo had detected the libration in latitude, and had shown that there must also be a small diurnal libration (see last chapter). Hevelius perceived that spots near the eastern and western edge of the lunar disc were sometimes farther on the disc than at others. He not only showed that this is due to the libration in longitude, but was able to prove that this libration depends on the varying motion of the moon and her (appreciably) uniform rotation.

Hevelius's ' Selenographia,' which contains his chart (engraved on metal by himself), appeared in 1647. At this time Peyresl and Gassendi were engaged in the construction of a lunar chart; but when they heard that Hevelius had completed such a chart, they ceased from their labour, having drawn only one sheet of their chart.

Father Riccioli, of Bologna, published in 1651 a much less valuable chart than that of Hevelius. He adopted a new system of nomenclature, replacing the terrestrial names of Hevelius by the names of astronomers and philosophers. Mädler says, indeed, that Riccioli's work would have been forgotten had he not been led by vanity to find a place for his own name on the moon, an arrangement only to be achieved by displacing all the names used by Hevelius, at the risk of causing perplexity and confusion to later astronomers. The charge is rather a serious one.

Riccioli's estimates of the altitude of the lunar mountains were altogether unsatisfactory.

Dominic Cassini constructed a chart of the moon 12 Paris feet in diameter, but not showing many details. So far as the method of construction was concerned, this map should have been an important improvement on its predecessors. The places of the chief lunar spots were determined by measurement, the other spots were placed by eye-estimates corrected for the effects of libration. In 1680 Cassini constructed a chart 20 Paris inches in diameter, respecting which Mädler remarks that it surpassed that of Hevelius in fulness of detail but not in correctness. All the copies of this chart were soon sold, and Mädler considers it likely that the chart was unknown in Germany until a new edition was published by Lalande in 1787.

The first really reliable chart of the moon was constructed by Tobias Mayer. During a lunar eclipse in the year 1748, Mayer wished to note the passage of the earth's shadow over the principal lunar features, and he recognised the want of an exact chart of the moon. It would appear from Lichtenberg's account that Mayer proposed to himself the construction of a chart on a large scale, showing the places of the chief lunar spots determined micrometrically. This plan he was prevented from carrying out by a pressure of other engagements. A small chart, however ($7\frac{1}{2}$ Paris inches in diameter), was found among his papers, and was published at Göttingen in 1775, thirteen years after his death, among his ' Opera Inedita,' and remained until 1824 the only trustworthy map of our satellite.

Schröter of Lilienthal studied the moon with great care and patience, using first a 7-feet reflector, then one of 18 feet, and lastly one of 27 feet in focal length. The labours of Schröter as a selenographist were not altogether successful, because of his want of skill in delineating what he saw. Beer and Mädler consider that the accuracy of Schröter's work was further affected by his desire to recognise signs of change in the moon. But Webb says respecting Schröter's ' Selenographische Fragmente,' ' I have never closed the simple and candid record of his most zealous labours with any feeling approaching to contempt' (somewhat guarded praise, by the way), and he adds that possibly Beer and Mädler were not themselves free from a prepossession opposite to that which they condemned in Schröter.

The work of Lohrmann must be regarded as the first really scientific attempt to delineate the moon's surface in detail. Lohrmann was a land-surveyor of Dresden. He planned the construction of a lunar chart on a large scale in 25 sections, and in 1824 the first four sections were published. But failing sight compelled him to desist from his arduous attempt.

L

In 1838 he published an excellent general chart of the moon 15¼ inches in diameter.[1]

MM. Beer and Mädler began their selenographic work in 1830, and their 3-feet chart, together with their fine work on the moon,[2] appeared in 1837. The telescope employed by them was only four inches in diameter, and the chart does not show every feature which can be recognised with a telescope of that aperture. Yet the amount of detail is remarkable, and the labour actually bestowed upon the work will appear incredible to those who are unfamiliar with the telescopic aspect of the moon. In 'Der Mond,' Beer and Mädler give their measurements of the positions of no less than 919 lunar spots, and 1,095 determinations of the height of lunar mountains.[3] The map which accompanies the present work has been reduced from Mr. Webb's,—itself reduced from the large chart by MM. Beer and Mädler. Mr. Webb's map is valuable as the work of one who is himself so skilful a student of the moon's surface. The following is Mr. Webb's modest account of a map which has long been recognised as a very useful contribution to selenography :—' It professes to be merely a guide to such of the more interesting features as common telescopes

---

[1] Lohrmann died in 1840.

[2] 'Der Mond, nach seinen kosmischen und individuellen Verhältnissen.'

[3] The heights are given in toises, a toise being about 6·3946 English feet. The highest mountain of all is very appropriately named Newton, and, according to the measures of Beer and Mädler, its summit is 3,727 toises, or about 23,800 feet, above the level of the floor of the crater.

will reach. It has been carefully reduced from the " Mappa Selenographica " of Beer and Mädler, omitting an immense amount of detail accumulated by their diligent perseverance, which would only serve to perplex the learner. Selection was difficult in such a crowd. On the whole, it seemed best to include every object distinguished by an *independent name* ; many of little interest thus creep in, and many sufficiently remarkable ones drop out ; but the line must have been drawn somewhere, and perhaps would have been nowhere better chosen for the student. Other spots, however, have been admitted, from their conspicuousness, to which Beer and Mädler have given only a *subordinate* name ; minuter details come in, in places, for ready identification ; elsewhere larger objects are passed by, as less useful for the purpose of the map.'

Two lists of 400 of the lunar objects shown in the map—first, in the order of the number; and secondly, in alphabetical order—will be found at the end of this volume.

I may add that in the year 1869 I carefully examined every object included in Webb's map, with a telescope $2\frac{1}{4}$ inches in aperture, using low powers, and satisfied myself that the map fulfils in every respect the object aimed at by its designer.

And here, in passing, I may remark that I cannot indicate a more pleasing occupation for the possessor of a telescope of that size (or any larger size up to four inches) than to go over the moon's disc, examining each object *seriatim*, and carefully comparing what is seen with the appearance shown in the photographs. In particular, it is a most useful and instructive exercise to observe the varying appearance of particular objects as they come into sunlight, as sunlight grows fuller upon them, and afterwards as sunlight passes away from them, until at length they are in darkness. The most convenient objects to select for this purpose (though it need hardly be said that the true lunarian astronomer will not be content with observing these only) are those which lie near the terminator of the moon rather early during her first quarter, for these will be again on the terminator rather early in the third quarter. Thus they can be observed first in the early evening, and then later and later, until, when the terminator is just leaving them, they must be observed after midnight, but not very late ; whereas those objects which are first reached by the advancing terminator during the moon's second quarter are left by the receding terminator during the fourth quarter, and to be well studied at this time must be observed in the early morning hours. Those students of astronomy, however, who are ready to observe at any hour of the night from twilight to dawn, can study any part of the moon from sunrise to sunset at that part. It will be obvious that thoroughly to examine any spot on the moon, it must be observed during many lunations. Apart from the circumstance that unfavourable weather breaks the continuity of the observations, the interval of many hours necessarily elapsing between successive observations suffices to render the study of any spot during any single lunation imperfect. This is especially the case with objects near the eastern and western limbs, because the moon must be nearly new (either before or after conjunction with the sun) when sunrise or sunset occurs at such points, and the moon can only be observed a short time in the morning when she is approaching conjunction, and a short time in the evening soon after conjunction. But even for other parts of the moon the difficulty exists. An observer may watch the progress of sunrise at any spot near the terminator of the half-moon, hour after hour, for several hours in succession; but he must be interrupted for a much longer period, after the moon has approached too near the horizon for useful study, until she is again at a fair elevation. Now in the interval—say sixteen or seventeen hours—sunrise or sunset at the spot will have made great progress, notwithstanding the great length of the lunar day. For sixteen hours on the moon (about a forty-fourth part of the lunar day) correspond to more than half an hour on the earth, and we know that in every part of the earth the sun's place on the heavens alters considerably in half an hour. In fact, in sixteen hours, the sun, as seen from the moon, changes his place by about eight degrees, and this most importantly affects the position and dimensions of the shadows thrown by any lunar heights, especially near the time of sunrise and sunset. It is further to be considered that the circumstances under which a lunar spot is studied vary markedly during the progress of a lunation.

The labours of Schmidt, of Athens, must be regarded as altogether the most important contribution yet made to selenography. The observations on which the construction of his chart has been based were commenced in 1839, and in 1865 Schmidt began to combine these observations together into chart-form. He proposed at that time to have a chart with a diameter of 6 Paris feet, and divided into four quadrants, like Mädler's chart. The telescope employed for reviewing the observations was the refractor of the Athens Observatory, having an aperture of 6 Paris inches. In April, 1868, the work had progressed so far that Schmidt was able to form an opinion as to the probable value of a chart completed on the adopted plan. He was dissatisfied with the result. The work was not exact enough nor sufficiently delicate in drawing for his purposes. He determined therefore to begin the charting afresh. Retaining the original diameter of 6 Paris feet, he divided the chart into 25 sections, adopting Lohrmann's arrangement. Each section forming a much smaller map than the former quadrants, it was possible to adopt a much finer and more exact method of drawing. He began this work in April, 1868, and it was published in 1879. There were difficulties on the score of expense, but after some delay these were surmounted. After Schmidt had given the labours of a life, or the best part of a life, to a scientific work of such great difficulty, and with results so valuable, it

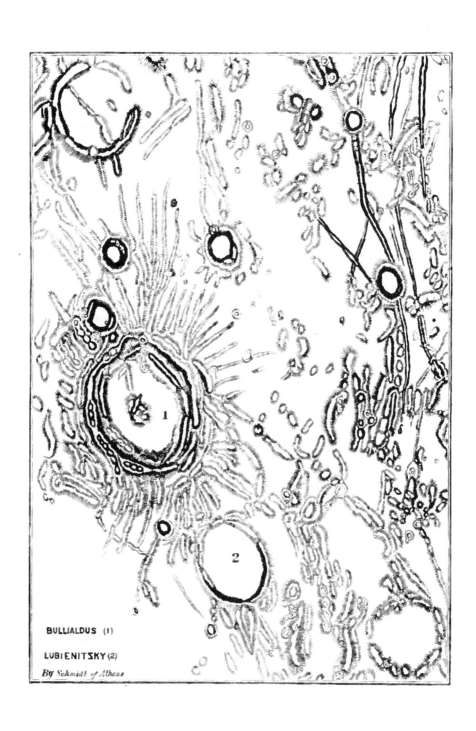

BULLIALDUS (1)

LUBIENITSKY (2)

By Schmidt of Athens

would have been discreditable to science if the work had not been published in a way securing him a just reward for his untiring exertions.

The map of Bullialdus and Lubienitzky, Plate I., affords an idea of Schmidt's method of delineation. It has been reduced, however, considerably from the original. The reader should seek out Bullialdus in Mr. Webb's map (it is numbered 213, and is in the third quadrant). The comparison of the two maps will afford an excellent idea of the plan on which Schmidt has carried out his processes of charting.

The application of photography to the moon, closely associated with the subject of lunar charts, has next to be considered.

So early as 1840 Arago dwelt on the possibility that the moon might be persuaded to take her own portrait,—speaking of the hope that instead of those long and wearisome labours by which men had hitherto sought to chart the moon, a few minutes might suffice to bring her image on Daguerre's prepared plates. However, in the very year when Arago made this remark, Dr. Draper, of New York, had succeeded in photographing the moon. The following history of photographic work on the moon is abridged from a chapter on the subject contributed by Mr. Brothers to Chambers' 'Handbook of Descriptive Astronomy':—

'It appears from a paper by Professor H. Draper, of New York, published in April, 1864, that in the year 1840 his father, Dr. J. W. Draper, was the first who succeeded in photographing the moon. Dr.

Draper states that at the time named (1840) "it was generally supposed the moon's light contained no actinic rays, and was entirely without effect on the sensitive silver compounds used in daguerreotyping." With a telescope of 5 inches aperture Dr. Draper obtained pictures on silver plates, and presented them to the Lyceum of Natural History of New York. Daguerre is stated to have made an unsuccessful attempt to photograph the moon, but I have been unable to ascertain when this experiment was made.

'Bond's photographs of the moon were made in 1850. The telescope used by him was the Cambridge (U.S.) refractor of 15 inches aperture, which gave an image of the moon at the focus of the object-glass 2 inches in diameter. Daguerreotypes and pictures on glass mounted for the stereoscope were thus obtained, and some of them were shown at the Great Exhibition of 1851, in London.

'Between the years 1850 and 1857, we find Secchi in Rome, and Bertch and Arnauld in France, and in England Phillips, Hartnup, Crookes, De la Rue, Fry and Huggins, appearing as astronomical photographers. To these may be added the name of Dancer, of Manchester, who in February, 1852, made some negatives of the moon with a 4¼-inch object-glass. They were small, but of such excellence that they would bear examination under the microscope with a 3-inch objective, and they are believed to be the first ever taken in this country. Baxendell and

Williamson, also of Manchester, were engaged about the same time in producing photographs of the moon.

'The first detailed account of experiments in celestial photography which I have met with is by Professor Phillips, who read a paper on the subject at the meeting of the British Association at Hull in 1853. In it he says: "If photography can ever succeed in portraying as much of the moon as the eye can see and discriminate, we shall be able to leave to future times monuments by which the secular changes of the moon's physical aspect may be determined. And if this be impracticable—if the utmost success of the photographer should only produce a picture of the larger features of the moon, this will be a gift of the highest value, since it will be a basis, an accurate and practical foundation of the minuter details, which, with such aid, the artist may confidently sketch." The pictures of the moon taken by Professor Phillips were made with a $6\frac{1}{4}$-inch refractor, by Cooke, of $1\frac{1}{4}$ feet focus; this produced a negative of $1\frac{1}{4}$ inch diameter in 30 seconds. Professor Phillips does not enter very minutely into the photographic part of the subject, but he gives some very useful details of calculations as to what may be expected to be seen in photographs taken with such a splendid instrument as that of Lord Rosse. It is assumed that an image of the moon may be obtained *direct* of 12 inches diameter, and this, when again magnified sufficiently, would show " black bands 12 yards across." What may be done remains to be seen, but up to the present time these anticipations have not been realised.

'We have next, from the pen of Crookes, a paper communicated to the Royal Society of London in December, 1856, but which was not read before that Society until February in the following year. Mr. Crookes appears to have obtained good results as early as 1855, and, assisted by a grant from the Donation Fund of the Royal Society, he was enabled to give attention to the subject during the greater part of the year following. The details of the process employed are given with much minuteness. The telescope used was the equatorial refractor at the Liverpool Observatory, of 8 inches aperture and $12\frac{1}{2}$ feet focal length, which produced an image of the moon 1-35 inch diameter. *The body of a small camera* was fixed in the place of the eye-piece, so that the image of the moon was received in the usual way on the ground glass. The chemical focus of the object-glass was found to be $\frac{8}{10}$ths of an inch beyond the optical focus, being over-corrected for the actinic rays. Although a good clock movement, driven by water-power, was applied to the telescope, it was found necessary to follow the moon's motion by means of the slow-motion handles attached to the right ascension and declination circles, and this was effected by using an eye-piece with a power of 200 on the finder, keeping the cross-wires steadily on one spot. With this instrument Hartnup had taken a large number of negatives, but owing to the long exposure required he was not successful; but with more suitable collodion and chemical solutions, and although the temperature of the Observatory was below the freezing-point, Mr. Crookes obtained dense negatives in about 4 seconds. Crookes afterwards enlarged his negatives 20 diameters, and he expresses his opinion that the magnifying should be conducted simultaneously with the photography by having a proper arrangement of lenses, so as to throw an enlarged image of the moon at once on the collodion plate ; and he states that the want of light could be no objection, as an exposure of from 2 to 10 *minutes* would not be " too severe a tax upon a steady and skilful hand and eye."

' In an appendix to his paper Mr. Crookes gives some particulars as to the time required to obtain negatives of the moon with different telescopes, from which it appears that the time varied from 6 minutes to 6 seconds. The different results named must, I conclude, have been caused not so much by the differences in the instruments as in the various processes employed, and in the manipulation. I must observe, also, that it is not stated whether all the experiments were tried upon the *full* moon—a point materially affecting the time.

' In 1858 De la Rue read an important paper before the Royal Astronomical Society, from which it appears that the light of the moon is from 2 to 3 times brighter than that of Jupiter,[1] while its actinic power

---

[1] Theoretically the light of the moon should be nearly 27 times as bright as Jupiter's, since Jupiter is $5\frac{1}{5}$ times farther from the sun.

.is only as 6 to 5, or 6 to 4.   On Dec. 7, 1857, Jupiter
was photographed in 5 seconds and Saturn in 1 minute,
and on another occasion the moon and Saturn were
photographed in 15 seconds just after an occultation of
the planet.

‘ The report of the Council of the Royal Astronomical Society for 1858 contains the following remarks :
—“A very curious result, since to some extent confirmed by Professor Secchi, has been pointed out by De
la Rue, namely, that those portions of the moon's surface which are illumined by a very oblique ray from the
sun possess so little photogenic power that, although
to the eye they appear as bright as other portions of the
moon illumined by a more direct ray, the latter will
produce the effect called by photographers ‘solarisation’
before the former (the obliquely illumined portions)
can produce the faintest image.”   And the report also
suggests that the moon may have a comparatively dense
atmosphere, and that there may be vegetation on those
parts called seas.

‘ At the meeting of the British Association at Aber-
deen, in 1859, De la Rue read a very valuable paper on
Celestial Photography.   An abstract of it was published
at the time in the “British Journal of Photography,”
and in August and September of the following year
further details of this gentleman's method of working
were given in the same journal.   The processes and
machinery employed are so minutely described that it
is unnecessary here to say more than that he commenced his experiments about the end of 1852, and that

he used a reflecting telescope [1] of his own manufacture of 13 inches aperture and 10 feet focal length, which gives a negative of the moon averaging about $\frac{1}{10}$th of an inch in diameter. The photographs were at first taken at the side of the tube after the image had been twice reflected. This was afterwards altered so as to allow the image to pass direct to the collodion plate, but the advantage gained by this method was not so satisfactory as was expected. In taking pictures at the side of the tube, *a small camera box* was fixed in the place of the eye-piece, and at the back a small compound microscope was attached, so that the edge of a broad wire was always kept in contact with one of the craters on the moon's surface, the image being seen through the collodion film at the same time with the wire in the focus of the microscope. This ingenious contrivance, in the absence of a driving-clock, was found to be very effectual, and some very sharp and beautiful negatives were thus obtained. De la Rue afterwards applied a clockwork motion to the telescope, and his negatives taken with the same instrument are as yet the best ever obtained in this country.

'Nearly a quarter of a century has elapsed since the moon was first photographed in America, and a good deal has been done since on that side of the Atlantic. To an American we are indebted for the best pictures of our satellite yet produced, and it is difficult to

---

[1] 'The advantage of the reflecting over the refracting telescope is very great, owing to the coincidence of the visual and actinic foci ; but it will presently appear that the refractor can be made to equal, if not excel, the work of the reflector.'

conceive that anything superior can ever be obtained ; and yet with the fact before us that De la Rue's are better than any others taken in this country, so it may prove that even the marvellous pictures of Mr. Rutherfurd may be surpassed.

'Mr. Rutherfurd appears, from a paper in Silliman's "American Journal of Science " for May, 1865, to have begun his work in lunar photography in 1858, with an equatorial of $11\frac{1}{4}$ inches aperture and 14 feet focal length, and corrected in the usual way for the visual focus only. The actinic focus was found to be $\frac{7}{10}$ths of an inch longer than the visual. The instrument gave pictures of the moon, and of the stars down to the fifth magnitude, satisfactory when compared with what had previously been done, but not sufficiently so to satisfy Mr. Rutherfurd, who, after trying to correct for the photographic ray by working with combinations of lenses inserted in the tube between the object-glass and sensitive plate, commenced some experiments in 1861 with a silvered mirror of 13 inches diameter, which was mounted in a frame strapped to the tube of the refractor. Mr. Rutherfurd enumerates several objections to the reflector for this kind of work, but admits the advantage of the coincidence of foci. The reflector was abandoned for a refractor specially constructed, of the same size as the first one, and nearly of the same focal length, but corrected only for the chemical rays. The glass was completed in December, 1864, but it was not until March 6 of the following year that a sufficiently clear atmosphere occurred, and on that night

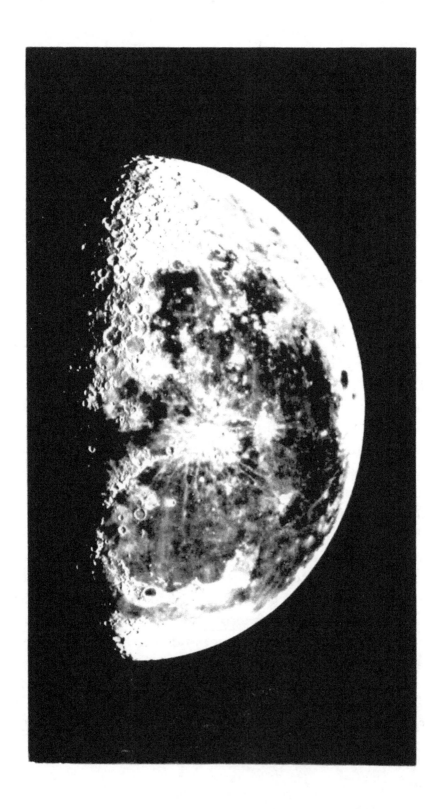

the negative was taken from which the prints were made. '

Mr. Brothers has himself taken many photographs of the moon with great success, though using a telescope (refracting) only five inches in aperture. The convenience and simplicity of the arrangements he employed will be recognised when it is mentioned that on the evening of the partial eclipse of the moon, Oct. 4, 1865, he succeeded, 'with the help of two assistants, in taking no less than 20 negatives, though the telescope was several times disturbed to oblige friends who desired to see the progress of the eclipse through the instrument.'

Before passing to the description of the general results which have followed from the telescopic observation of the moon, as well as from processes of charting and photographing, it will be well to discuss the observations which have been made on the moon's light— viz. first on the total quantity of light which she reflects, when full, towards the earth ; secondly, on the varying proportion of light so reflected when she is at her phases ; and thirdly, on the different light-reflecting qualities of different portions of her surface.

The consideration of the total quantity of light reflected by the moon implies in reality the question what degree of *whiteness* she possesses. For a perfectly white object [1] would reflect all the light it received,

---

[1] There is no such thing as perfect whiteness in nature (referring to opaque objects). Even new-fallen snow does not reflect so much as four-fifths of the incident light. The following table (resulting from the observations of Zöllner) is useful for purposes

but a coloured object reflects only a portion, while a perfectly black object would reflect none. An object of many colours—and the moon unquestionably is such an object—may be said to tend (as a whole) towards blackness or whiteness, according as it reflects less or more of the light which shines upon it.

Let us first consider the comparison between the moon's light and the sun's, according to the best observations hitherto made :—

The observations of Bouguer assigned to the moon a total brightness equal to one 300,000th part of the sun's. The method he employed was the direct comparison between sunlight and candlelight, and between moonlight and candlelight. Wollaston also took candlelight as the means of comparison, but determined the relative brightness of the sources of light by the method of equalising the shadows. He obtained the result that

of comparison, the total light incident on a surface being represented by unity :—

Snow just fallen reflects	. . . . .	0·783
White paper	„	0·700
White sandstone	„	0·237
Clay marl	„	0·156
Quartz porphyry	„	0·108
Moist soil	„	0·079
Dark grey syenite	„	0·078

These objects shine by diffused reflected light. For light regularly reflected the following table is useful :—

Mercury reflects	. . . . .	0·648
Speculum metal reflects	. . . .	0·535
Glass reflects	. . . . .	0·040
Obsidian „	. . . . .	0·032
Water „	. . . . .	0·021

the moon's light is but one 801,070th part of the
sun's.

We owe, however, to Zöllner the most satisfactory
determination of the moon's total brightness. He
employed two distinct methods. In one he determined
the illumination by comparing surface-brightness; in
the other he obtained point-like images of the sun and
moon for comparison with corresponding images of
candle-flames. The results obtained by these two
methods were in close agreement,—according to one,
the light of the full moon is one 618,000th part of the
sun's light, while, according to the other, the proportion is as 1 to 619,000.

It would be easy to determine from this result the
exact proportion of the incident light which the
moon's surface, regarded as a whole, is capable of reflecting, if the moon were a smooth but unpolished
sphere; for we know exactly what proportion of the
sun's light the moon intercepts, and it is also known
that a smooth half-sphere, seen under full illumination,
reflects two-thirds of the light which a flat round disc
of the same diameter would reflect. But the problem
is complicated in the present instance by the uneven-
ness of the moon's surface, which causes the light to
fall upon various parts of the lunar surface at angles
very different from those in the case of a smooth
sphere. In fact, it is perfectly manifest, from the
aspect of the full moon, that we have to deal with a
case very different from that of a smooth, or, as it is
called, *mat* surface. For such a surface, seen as a

M

disc under full solar illumination, would be brightest at the centre, and shade off gradually to the edge; whereas it is patent to observation that the disc of the full moon is as bright near the edge as near the centre.[1] Before we can undertake the inquiry, therefore, into the moon's average brightness, we must endeavour to ascertain what effect should be ascribed to the inequalities upon her surface.

This has been accomplished by Zöllner in a sufficiently satisfactory manner, by comparing the total quantity of the moon's light at her various phases, with what would be obtained if the moon were a smooth sphere. It is obvious that as the different parts of the moon's disc, when she is full, do not shine with the brightness due to a smooth surface, we might expect to find her total brightness at any given phase markedly different from the value estimated for the case of a smooth sphere. This Zöllner found to be the case. The 'full' moon is far brighter by comparison with the gibbous moon (especially when little more than half full), than would be the case if she were smooth. The considerations on which Zöllner based his interpretation of this peculiarity are not suited

[1] It is necessary to exercise some caution, however, in adopting a result of this kind, since the eye is very readily deceived. We see the full moon on a dark background, and this certainly tends to add to the apparent brightness of the edge of the disc. As a case illustrating this effect of contrast, it may be mentioned that Jupiter appears to the eye to be brighter near the edge than near the middle of the disc, and yet when his disc is examined with a graduated darkening glass, it is found to be brighter near the middle than near the edge.

to these pages, involving analytical considerations of some complexity. The result, therefore, is all that need here be stated. Zöllner's conclusion is, that the average slope of the lunar inequalities amounts to about 52 degrees.[1] Be it noticed, that this result is in no degree affected by observations of the apparent slope of lunar mountains and craters, because irregu-

[1] The following table will show how closely the results obtained by Zöllner agreed with the empirical formula which he deduced from his estimate of the mean slope of the lunar irregularities. The first column gives the distance of the moon from full, the distance being regarded as positive when the observation was made after the time of full moon, and as negative when the observation preceded full moon :—

Arc from Moon's place to point opposite the Sun	Theoretical Brightness Full Moon's as 100.		Observed Brightness Zöllner
	Moon regarded as smooth	By Zöllner's formula	
+ 1°	99·98	98·60	98·60
5	99·63	92·79	87·20
8	99·06	88·41	92·19
11	98·24	84·04	88·76
− 13	97·57	81·21	82·60
+ 19	94·93	72·29	68·41
24	92·13	65·15	71·38
27	90·18	61·00	57·90
− 27	90·18	61·00	63·47
+ 28	89·50	59·60	56·15
− 28	89·50	59·60	57·00
+ 23	85·82	52·90	48·60
− 39	80·87	45·00	41·70
+ 40	80·04	43·70	47·10
41	77·78	42·50	43·95
− 42	76·27	41·40	38·00
+ 46	74·61	36·70	36·10
− 52	68·87	27·63	29·11
+ 58	62·91	24·30	27·10
− 62	58·89	20·60	20·40
− 69	51·82	15·20	14·60

larities much smaller than any which the telescope can
detect would suffice to explain the observed variations
of brilliancy.   If the whole surface of the moon were
covered with conical hills only a foot, or even only an
inch in height, the same general result would be
produced as though there were mountains of the same
form a mile, or several miles, in height.

It appears from this result, that the brightness of
the full moon is considerably greater than it would
be if the moon were a smooth sphere; and, in fact,
Zöllner would seem to regard the brightness of the
full moon as very nearly equal to that of a flat disc of
equal diameter.   I do not enter here into a calculation
of the quantity of light which such a disc would reflect;
but the following result may be accepted as sufficiently
near the truth.   A perfectly white disc of the same
diameter as the moon's, and under direct solar illumination, would have a total brightness equal to about
one 92,600th part of the sun's.   Now we have seen
that the actual quantity received from the moon is
about one 618,000th part of the sun's light; and
taking into account the smaller mean disc of the
moon, as compared with the sun, we find that the
moon's light is rather more than one-sixth part of
that of a disc of perfect whiteness, under direct solar
illumination, and looking as large as the moon's disc.
Zöllner, from his estimate of the mean irregularity of
the moon's surface, deduces a result so near to this as
to imply what I have just stated,—viz. that he regards
the brightness of the full moon as not much less than

that of a flat disc of equal size, and having a surface of the same average reflective power. For he sets the light of the full moon at rather less than a sixth part of that which it would have if the moon were made of a perfectly white substance. The exact proportion assigned by him is that of 1,736 to 10,000. This is what, following Lambert, he calls the *albedo*, or whiteness of the moon, and he justly remarks that, considering her whole brightness, she must be regarded as more nearly black than white. Nevertheless, he adds that from his estimates of the moon's brighter parts he is satisfied that their whiteness can be compared with that of the whitest of terrestrial substances.[1]

It is worthy of notice that Sir John Herschel had already in a far simpler way deduced a result closely agreeing with Zöllner's. It will be seen from the table in the note at p. 160 that white sandstone reflects about 0·237 of the incident light; and it may be inferred from other values in that table that weathered sandstone rock would have an *albedo* of about 0·150. Now Herschel remarks that the actual illumination of the lunar surface is not much superior to that of weathered sandstone rock in full sunshine. 'I have frequently,' he proceeds, 'compared the moon setting behind the grey perpendicular façade of the Table Mountain, illuminated by the sun just risen in the opposite quarter of the horizon, when it has been scarcely distinguishable in brightness from the rock

[1] His words are : 'Dass der Mond an seinen helleren und hellsten Stellen aus einem Stoffe besteht, der, auf die Erde gebracht, zu dem weissesten der uns bekannten Körper gezählt werden würde.'

in contact with it.   The sun and moon being nearly at
equal altitudes, and the atmosphere perfectly free from
cloud or vapour, its effect is alike on both luminaries.'[1]

A difficulty will present itself to most readers on a
first view of Zöllner's result.   The full moon, taken as
a whole, seems white when high above the horizon on
a dark clear night ; and it appears quite impossible to
regard her as more nearly black than white.   Again,
as another form of the same difficulty, it appears
obvious to anyone who regards ordinary sandstone or
any substance of like reflective power in full daylight,
that the brightness of the substance is markedly inferior
to that of the full moon at midnight.   Herein is illustrated one of those effects of contrast which are so
deceptive in all questions of relative brightness.   We
see the full moon on a dark background, and with no
other object comparable with her in brightness, and
the eye accordingly overestimates her light,—a comparison is made between her real but not obvious
darkness, and the very obvious and much greater
darkness of the sky, and thus the idea of whiteness is
suggested.   On the contrary, when we look at stone
or rock illuminated by full sunlight, objects as brightly,

---

[1] It is to be noted, however, that the *illumination* of the sandstone would be reduced by atmospheric absorption, which would
not happen, of course, with the moon. The effect of atmospheric
absorption in reducing the apparent brightness of the moon thus
fully illuminated, and of the sandstone thus not quite fully illuminated, would not be equal, because the sandstone was seen
through only a portion of the atmospheric strata interposed
between the eye and the moon. Hence would result a near
approach to equalisation so far as atmospheric effects are concerned.

or even more brightly, illuminated are all around, and the eye accordingly estimates fairly, or perhaps even underestimates, the whiteness of the illuminated rock.[1]

Returning to Zöllner's remark that the brightest parts of the moon are comparable in whiteness with the whitest terrestrial substances, it follows obviously that the darker portions of the moon are very much less bright than the average. Thus the bright summit of Aristarchus, whose reflective power is so great that as seen on the dark part of the moon (when therefore only illuminated by earth-light) it has been mistaken for a volcano in eruption, has probably a reflective power nearly equal to that of new-fallen snow, or 0·783, which exceeds the average whiteness of the moon about $4\frac{1}{2}$

---

[1] Amongst hundreds of illustrations of the effect of contrast in deceiving the eye in such cases (a subject of the utmost importance in astronomical observations) may be mentioned our estimate of the brightness of the old moon in the new moon's arms. Nothing can be more certain than that in reality the light of the old moon in this case is due to illumination by the earth, and at a moderate computation this illumination exceeds full moonlight twelve times. (The only doubtful point is the average light-reflecting quality of the earth's surface, which I am here assuming to be rather less than that of the moon's surface.) Now we know how bright a landscape appears when bathed in full moonlight, and we can infer that under twelve times that amount of light the brightness would be very considerable. Assuredly an object as large in appearance as the moon would under such light appear very conspicuous, and *white*. Yet the old moon in the new moon's arms, though illuminated to this degree, can scarcely be perceived at all until twilight has made some progress. The light of the early evening sky is quite sufficient to render the considerable light of the old moon quite imperceptible. To this may be added the fact that the disc of the moon during total eclipses, although it appears so dark to the eye, is nevertheless illuminated by nearly full earth-light, and certainly with ten times the lustre of a terrestrial landscape under full moonlight.

times. And we may assume that the dark floor of Plato and the yet darker Grimaldi are as far below the average of brightness. But even dark-grey syenite, the lowest in reflective power of all the substances in Zöllner's table (see note, p. 160), reflects 0·078 of the incident light, which indicates a whiteness nearly half the average whiteness of the moon's surface. We may safely assume that the darkest parts of the moon are darker than this.

A question of much greater difficulty is suggested by observations which appear to indicate changes in the brightness of certain lunar regions. Some observations of this kind are referred to in a subsequent chapter. At present I shall merely remark that such observations do not appear to have been hitherto made in such a way as to afford convincing evidence that change takes place with the progress of the lunar day. In particular, it seems to me that the readiness with which the eye may be deceived by the effect of contrast has not been duly taken into account. Therefore, while recognising, in the observations directed to the recognition of tint-changes or colour-changes, a possible means of advancing in a very marked manner our knowledge of the moon's condition, I find myself at present unable to regard as demonstrated any of the phenomena which are described by those who have made researches in this department of selenography.

In considering the general results of the telescopic scrutiny of the moon, it is well to remember the circumstances under which such scrutiny has been made.

The highest power yet applied to the moon (a power of about six-thousand) brings her, so to speak, to a distance of forty miles,—a distance far too great for objects of moderate size to become visible. Many of my readers have probably seen Mont Blanc from the neighbourhood of Geneva, a distance of about forty miles. At this distance the proportions of vast snow-covered hills and rocks are dwarfed almost to nothingness, extensive glaciers are quite imperceptible, and any attempt to recognise the presence of living creatures or of their dwellings (with the unaided eye) is utterly useless.

But even this comparison does not present the full extent of the difficulties attending the examination of the moon's surface with our highest powers. The circumstances under which such powers are applied are such as to render the view much less perfect than the mere value of the magnifying power employed might seem to imply. We view celestial objects through tubes placed at the bottom of a vast aërial ocean, never at rest through any portion of its depth ; and the atmospheric undulations which even the naked eye is able to detect are magnified just in proportion to the power employed.

These undulations are the bane of the telescopist. What could be done with telescopes, if it were not for these obstructions to perfect vision, may be gathered from the results of Professor Smyth's observations from the summit of Teneriffe. Raised here above the densest

and most disturbed strata, he found the powers of his
telescope increased to a marvellous extent.   Stars which
he had looked for in vain with the same instrument in
Edinburgh now shone with admirable distinctness and
brilliancy.   Those delicate stipplings of the discs of
Jupiter and Saturn, which require in England the
powers of the largest telescopes, were clearly seen in
the excellent but small telescope he employed in his
researches.   It is probably not too much to say that
even if the Rosse telescope were perfect in defining
power, which unfortunately is very far indeed from
being the case, yet on account of atmospheric disturbance, instead of reducing the moon's distance to forty
miles, it would in fact not be really effective enough
to reduce that distance to less than 150 miles.

Accordingly, though we recognise in the grey plains
or seas on the moon the appearance of smoothness, it is
very far from being certain that these regions may not
in reality be covered with irregularities of very considerable slope.   They probably resemble sea-bottoms,
or they may be analogous to deserts and prairies on
our own earth, yet be considerably uneven.   The uniformity of curvature which marks their surfaces as a
whole affords an argument in favour of their having once
been in a liquid condition ; but that their solidification
should have resulted in a smooth surface is far from
being certain.   On the contrary, it seems not unlikely
that the true surface may be marked with corrugations,
or crystalline formations, or other uniform unevennesses,
if one may so speak.

It is a noteworthy circumstance that the lunar plains do not form portions of the same sphere, some lying deeper than others,—that is, belonging to a sphere of smaller radius.

Again, it is to be remembered that the mountain-chains on the moon are seen under circumstances which enable us to recognise none but the boldest features of these formations. It is as unsafe to theorise as to their geological or selenological conformation, as it would be to speculate on the structure of a mountain-range on earth which had only been seen from a distance of two or three hundred miles. The following description by Mr. Webb must be read with this consideration carefully held in remembrance :—
' The mountain-chains,' he remarks, ' are of very various kind : some are of vast continuous height and extent, some flattened into plateaux intersected by ravines, some rough with crowds of hillocks, some sharpened into detached and precipitous peaks. The common feature of the mountain-chains on the earth— a greater steepness along one side—is very perceptible here, as though the strata had been tilted in a similar manner. Detached masses and solitary pyramids are scattered here and there upon the plains, frequently of a height and abruptness paralleled only in the most craggy regions of the earth. Every gradation of cliff and ridge and hillock succeeds ; among them a large number of narrow banks ' (that is, of banks which look narrow at the enormous distance from which they are seen), ' of slight elevation but surprising length, extending

for vast distances through level surfaces: these so frequently form lines of communication between more important objects, uniting distant craters or mountains, and crowned at intervals by insulated hills, that Schröter formerly, and Beer and Mädler in modern times, have ascribed them to the horizontal working of an elastic force, which, when it reached a weaker portion of the surface, issued forth in a vertical upheaval or explosion. The fact of the communication,' he justly adds, ' is more obvious than the probability of the explanation.'

But although, as will be manifest from the photographs which illustrate this work, the lunar mountainranges form by no means an unimportant feature of the moon's surface, the crateriform mountains must be regarded as the more characteristic feature. If we adopt Mallet's theory of the formation of surfaceirregularities on a planet, we must assume that the intermediate stage between the formation of great elevated and depressed regions corresponding to our continents and oceans, and the epoch of volcanic activity, lasted but a relatively short time. If the crateriform mountains were due to volcanic action, then either that action was more widespread and intense than on the earth, or else the records of such action on our earth have disappeared. The considerations thus suggested are discussed in a subsequent chapter. Here I shall consider only the classification of the crateriform mountains. They may be conveniently divided, after Webb, into walled or bul-

warked plains, ring mountains, craters, and saucer-
shaped depressions or pits. 'The second and third,'
he remarks, 'differ chiefly in size; but the first have
a character of their own, in the perfect resemblance of
their interiors to the grey plains, as though they had
been originally deeper, but filled in subsequently with
the same material, many of them in fact bearing
evident marks of having been broken down and overflowed from the outside. Their colour is often suggestive of some kind of vegetation, though it is difficult
to reconcile this with the apparent deficiency of air and
water. It has been ingeniously suggested that a shallow
stratum of carbonic acid gas, the frequent product of
volcanoes and long surviving their activity (for instance,
among the ancient craters of Auvergne, where it exists
in great quantity), may in such situations support the
life of some kind of plants; and the idea deserves to
be borne in mind in studying the changes of relative
brightness in some of these spots. The deeper are
usually the more concave craters; but the bottom is
often flat, sometimes convex, and frequently shows
subsequent disturbance in ridges, hillocks, minute
craters, or more generally, as the last effect of eruption,
central hills of various heights, but seldom attaining
that of the wall, or even, according to Schmidt, the
external level. The ring is usually steepest within, as
in terrestrial craters, and many times built up in vast
terraces, frequently lying, Schmidt says, in pairs divided
by narrow ravines. Nasmyth refers these—not very
probably— to successively decreasing explosions; in

other cases he more reasonably ascribes them to the slipping down of materials upheaved too steeply to stand, and undermined by lava at their base, leaving visible breaches in the wall above. They would be well explained on the supposition of fluctuating levels in a molten surface. Small transverse ridges occasionally descend from the ring, chiefly on the outside ; great peaks often spring up like towers upon the wall ; gateways at times break through the rampart, and in some cases are multiplied till the remaining piers of wall resemble the stones of a huge megalithic circle.'

The accompanying picture of Copernicus, by Nasmyth (Plate II.), aptly illustrates the appearance of large craters when seen with powerful telescopes. I give Mr. Webb's description of the crater in full, as showing his method of dealing with lunar details, in the useful work to which I have already invited the reader's attention. ' Copernicus,' he says, ' is one of the grandest craters, 56 m. in diameter. It has a central mountain (2,400 feet in height, according to Schmidt), two of whose six heads are conspicuous ; and a noble ring composed not only of terraces, but distinct heights separated by ravines ; the summit, a narrow ridge, not quite circular, rises 11,000 feet above the bottom, the height of Etna, after which Hevel named it. Schmidt gives it nearly 12,800 feet, with a peak of 13,500 feet, west ; and an inclination in some places of 60°. Piazzi Smyth observed remarkable resemblances between the interior conchoidal cliffs and those of the

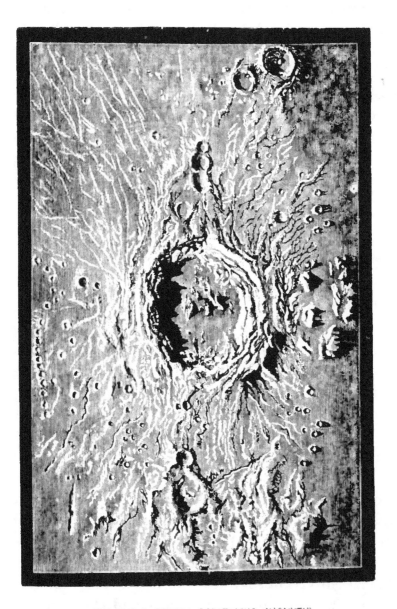

THE LUNAR CRATER COPERNICUS (NASMYTH)

great crater of Teneriffe. A mass of ridges leans
upon the wall, partly concentric, partly radiating : the
latter are compared to lava. The whole is beautifully, though anonymously, figured in Sir J. Herschel's
" Outlines of Astronomy." There is also a large drawing
by Secchi ; but this grand object requires, and would
well reward, still closer study. It comes into sight a
day or two after the first quarter. Vertical illumination brings out a singular cloud of white streaks related
to it as a centre. It is then very brilliant, and the
ring sometimes resembles a string of pearls. Beer and
Mädler once counted more than fifty specks.' It is
manifestly the crest of a large raised region.

Schmidt's map of Bullialdus and the neighbourhood
(Plate I.) also well illustrates the nature of the lunar
crateriform mountains of various dimensions. But yet
further insight into the characteristics of the more
disturbed and uneven portions of the moon's surface
will be obtained from the study of Plate III., which
represents a very rough and volcanic portion of the
moon's surface, as modelled from telescopic observations by Mr. Nasmyth. The engraving was taken
from a photograph of the original model, furnished to
Sir J. Herschel by Mr. Nasmyth ; and I am indebted
to Messrs. Longmans for permission to use this admirable engraving in the present work.

'A succession of eruptions may be constantly
traced,' Mr. Webb remarks, 'in the repeated en-
croachment of rings on each other, where, as Schmidt
says, the ejected materials seem to have been disturbed

before they had time to harden, and the largest are thus pointed out as the oldest craters, and the gradual decay of the explosive force, like that of many terrestrial volcanoes, becomes unquestionable. The peculiar whiteness of the smaller craters may indicate something analogous to the difference between the earlier and later lavas of the earth, or to the decomposition caused, as at Teneriffe, by acid vapours in the grey levels. We thus perhaps obtain an indication of the superficial character of their colouring.'

The lunar valleys include formations as remarkable as the long banks described above,—viz. the *clefts*, or *rilles*, furrows extending with perfect straightness for long distances, and changing in direction (if at all) suddenly, thereafter continuing their course in a straight line. These were first noticed by Schröter, and a few were discovered by Gruithuisen and Lohrmann; but Beer and Mädler added greatly to the known number, which was raised by their labours to 150. Schmidt has discovered nearly 300 more. Mr. Webb makes the following remarks on the rilles :—' These most singular furrows pass chiefly through levels, intersect craters (proving a more recent date), reappear beyond obstructing mountains, as though carried through by a tunnel, and commence and terminate with little reference to any conspicuous feature of the neighbourhood. The idea of artificial formation is negatived by their magnitude (Schmidt gives them 18 to 92 miles long, $\frac{1}{2}$ to $2\frac{4}{10}$ miles broad): they have been more probably referred to cracks in a shrinking

H Adlard

A portion of the Moons surface, from a model by M.ʳ Nasmyth.

London. Longmans & Co

surface. The observations of Kunowsky, confirmed by 'Mädler at Dorpat, seem in some instances to point to a less intelligible origin in rows of minute contiguous craters ; but a more rigorous scrutiny with the highest optical aid is yet required.'

A feature which is well seen in the illustrative photographs is the existence of radiating streaks from certain craters. The most remarkable system of rays is that which has the great crater Tycho as its centre. This system can be recognised over a very large proportion of the visible hemisphere, and doubtless extends on the south (that is, the uppermost part of the picture) far upon the unseen hemisphere. The photograph of the moon in her third quarter exhibits the radiating bright streaks from Copernicus, Kepler, and Aristarchus ; and other less striking systems can be recognised in the two views of the moon. The telescope shows others. ' In some cases,' Webb remarks, ' the streaks proceed from a circular grey border surrounding the crater ; in others they cross irregularly at its centre. They pass alike over mountain and valley, and even through the rings and cavities of craters, and seem to defy all scrutiny.' Nichol makes the following suggestive comments on this peculiarity, though in quoting his remarks I would not be understood to imply assent to them in all respects :—' They consist of broad brilliant bands (seen in their proper splendour only when the moon is full) issuing from all sides of the crater, and stretching to various distances from their origin,—one of them can be traced along a reach of 1,700 miles.

N

There are several *defining* characteristics of these
bands. *First,* It is only when the moon is full
that we see them in their entire clearness. They may
be traced, although very faintly, when the moon is not
full ; their splendour at full moon is very great.
This cannot wholly be attributed to the effect of
direct instead of oblique light, because at the edges
of the moon's apparent disc, on which the solar ray
falls very obliquely at full moon, their brilliancy is
the same. No rational explanation whatever has
been proposed regarding this remarkable peculiarity.
Secondly, The light thrown towards us by the rays
from Tycho is of the same kind as that reflected from
the edge and centre of the crater itself; so that the
matter of which they are composed had probably the
same origin as those other portions of Tycho. *Thirdly,*
These rays pass onward in thorough disregard of the
general contour of the moon's surface ; nowhere being
turned from their predetermined course by valley,
crater, or mountain ridge. Now, this critical fact
quite discredits the hypothesis that they are akin to
lava, or that they are merely superficial. A stream
of lava spreads out on meeting a valley or low-land,
and forms a lake ; nor can it ever overpass a mountain
barrier. The question remains then, are these rays
composed of matter that has been shot up from the
interior of the moon? It may seem incredible that
we can solve this problem by virtually digging pits
of vast depth down through those singular bands, and
thus ascertaining practically that the matter composing

them certainly descends towards the interior of our satellite, and that in all probability it has been forced up from that interior. The telescope, which in this instance is our *labourer*, has discovered numerous small craters of varying depth in the midst of many of the rays, and it reveals the fact, that these small craters, however deep, do not penetrate through the matter we are examining, inasmuch as there comes from their bases always the same kind of light that characterises the ray. There is one remarkable case in point. A large crater named Saussure, not far from Tycho, lies directly in the line of a ray, and of course appears to interrupt it; but at the bottom of Saussure, notwithstanding the great depth of that crater, the ray from Tycho may be traced. Nay, there is reason to believe that in favourable circumstances the same ray might be seen rising *up the sides* of Saussure, just as a vein of trap or of volcanic rock pierces the sedimentary strata upon earth. What, then, can we make of such phenomena? Are not our terrestrial trap dykes or veins their fitting similitudes? Piercing the other rocks, as if shot up from below these singular veins pass onward across valley and over mountain; their direction *their own*—independent for the most part of the rocks they have cut; they appear, too, in *systems*, some limited in magnitude and evidently radiating from a known source; others of vast extent, and usually considered parallel, but probably owing their apparent parallelism to the fact that we trace them only through a brief portion of their course. Accept this analogy,—and none other appears within reach,—and the rays or bright lines of the moon assume an import quite unexpected,—they become *indices to those successive dislocations that constitute epochs in the progress of our satellite.*'

Elsewhere Nichol shows in what sense he uses these words : where any system of radiations is intersected by another, it is manifest that the earlier formation will have its radiations broken at the places of intersection. Thus Nichol assigns as the result of the telescopic scrutiny of the radiations from Copernicus, Aristarchus, and Kepler, that the three systems were formed in the order in which they are here named. He also assigns to the radiations from Tycho (manifestly with good reason) a great antiquity. 'Another indication,' he proceeds, 'furnished by the rays demands notice. Reflect on the course, as to *continuous visibility,* of any stream of lava or any trap dyke upon the surface of the earth. No lava current from Etna could be traced to any great distance by a spectator in the moon, however powerful his telescope ; and it would be the same with regard to those lines or dykes of trap, even supposing them endowed with an excessive power to reflect light. The reason is that they soon enter forest regions, and are concealed there, or become overspread by grass or other vegetable carpetings. But not even a lichen stains the brightness of the bands issuing from Tycho ; they preserve, not their visibility merely, but one invariable brightness through their entire courses. The inference is but too clear; and we are glad to find a refuge from it, in the certainty that arrangements must be different on the other side of our satellite. The existence of a rocky desert, devoid of life or living thing, of the extent of even one lunar hemisphere, is startling enough.'

Nasmyth is of opinion that the radiations 'are cracks divergent from a central region of explosion, and filled up with molten matter from beneath.' But Webb objects that this theory is irreconcilable with the fact that the radiations seldom, if ever, cause any deviation in the superficial level. 'Trap dykes on the earth are indeed apt to assume the form of the surface, but the chances against so general and exact a restoration of level all along such multiplied and most irregular lines of explosion, would be incalculable; many of the rays are also far too long and broad for this supposition, or for that of Beer and Mädler, that they may be stains arising from highly heated subterranean vapour on its way to the point of its escape.' It appears to me impossible to refer these phenomena to any general cause but the reaction of the moon's interior overcoming the tension of the crust; and to this degree Nasmyth's theory seems correct; but it appears manifest also, that the crust cannot have been fractured in the ordinary sense of the word. Since, however, it results from Mallet's investigations that the tension of the crust is called into play in the earlier stages of contraction, and its power to resist pressure in the later stages,—in other words, since the crust at first contracts faster than the nucleus, and afterwards not so fast as the nucleus,—we may assume that the radiating systems were formed in so early an era that the crust was plastic. And it seems reasonable to conclude that the outflowing matter would retain its liquid condition long enough (the crust itself being intensely hot) to spread widely, a circumstance which would account at once for the breadth of many of the rays, and for the restoration of level to such a degree that no shadows are thrown. It appears probable also, that not only (which is manifest) were those craters formed later which are seen around and upon the radiations, but that the central crater itself acquired its actual form long after the epoch when the rays were formed. In the chapter on the moon's physical condition, considerations will be dealt with which bear upon this point. At the moment I need only remind the reader that the processes of cooling must have proceeded much more rapidly in the moon's case than in the earth's, and that this circumstance serves to account for phenomena indicative of a widely extended bursting of the lunar crust. I am disposed to believe, moreover, that although the radiating systems are manifestly not contemporaneous, they were all formed during a period of no great duration—possibly, indeed, not lasting for more than a few years, if so long.

The following peculiarities of arrangement mentioned by Mr. Webb should be carefully noted in connection with the considerations dealt with in Chapter VI.:—'The remarkable tendency to circular forms, even where explosive action seems not to have been concerned, as in the bays of the so-called seas, is very obvious; and so are the horizontal lines of communication. The gigantic craters, or walled plains, often affect a meridional arrangement: three huge rows of this kind are very conspicuous near the centre, and the east and west limbs. A tendency to parallel direction has often a curious influence on the position of smaller objects: in many regions these chiefly point to the same quarter, usually north and south, or north-east and south-west; thus in one vicinity (between G, L, and M in the map of the moon), Beer and Mädler speak of thirty objects following a parallel arrangement for one turned any other way; even small craters entangled in such general pressures (as round L) have been squeezed into an oval form, and the effect is like that of an oblique strain upon the pattern of a loosely woven fabric: an instance (near 27, 28 on the map) of double parallelism, like that of a net, is mentioned, with crossing lines from south-south-west and south-east. Local repetitions frequently occur; one region (between 290 and 292) is characterised by exaggerated central hills of craters; another (A) is without them; in another (185) the walls themselves fail. Incomplete rings are much more common towards the north than the south pole; the defect is usually in the north, seldom in the west part of the circle; sometimes a cluster of craters are all breached on the same side (near 23, 32). Two similar craters often lie north and south of each other, and near them is frequently a corresponding duplicate.

Two large craters occasionally lie north and south, of greatly resembling character—the southern usually three-fourths of the northern in size—from 18 to 36 miles apart, and connected by ridges pointing in a south-west direction (20, 19 ; 78, 77 ; 83, 84 ; 102, 103 ; 208, 207, 204 ; 239, 242 ; 261, 260 ; 260, 263 ; 340, 345). Several of these arrangements are the more remarkable as we know of nothing similar on the earth.'

But, interesting as these observations may be, it has not been for such discoveries as these that astronomers have examined the lunar surface. The examination of mere peculiarities of physical condition is, after all, but barren labour, if it lead to no discovery of physical condition. The principal charm of astronomy, as indeed of all observational science, lies in the study of change,—of progress, development, and decay, and specially of systematic variations taking place in regularly recurring cycles. The rings of Saturn, for instance, have been regarded with a new interest, since the younger Struve first started the theory of their gradual change of figure. The snowy poles of Mars, in like manner, have been examined with much more attention and interest by modern astronomers than they were by Cassini or Maraldi, precisely because they are now recognised as snow-covered regions, increasing in the Martial winter and diminishing in the Martial summer. In this relation the moon has been a most disappointing object of astronomical observation. For two centuries and a half, her face has been scanned with the closest possible scrutiny: her features have been portrayed in elaborate maps ; many an astronomer has given a large portion of his life to the work of examining craters, plains, mountains, and valleys for the signs of change ; but hitherto no certain evidence—or rather no evidence save of the most doubtful character—has been afforded that the moon is other than ' a dead and useless waste of extinct volcanoes.'

Early telescopic observations of the moon were conducted with the confident expectation that the moon would be found to be an inhabited world, and that much would soon be learned of the appearance and manners of the Lunarians. With each increase of telescopic power a new examination was conducted, and it was only when the elder Herschel's great reflector had been applied in vain to the search, that men began to look on the examination as nearly hopeless. Herschel himself, who was too well acquainted, however, with the real difficulties of the question to share the hopes of the inexperienced, was strongly of opinion that the moon is - inhabited. After describing the relations, physical and seasonal, prevailing on the lunar surface, he adds, ' there only seems wanting, in order to complete the analogy, that it should be inhabited like the earth.'

When Sir John Herschel conveyed a powerful reflector to Cape Town, the hope was renewed that something might yet be learned of the lunar inhabitants, through observations conducted in the pure skies of the southern hemisphere. So confidently was this hope entertained and expressed, that the opportunity seemed

a good one to some American wits to play off a hoax
on those who were anxiously awaiting the result of Sir
John's observations.   Accordingly an elaborate account
was prepared of a series of discoveries respecting the
appearance and behaviour of certain strange and not
very well-conducted creatures inhabiting the moon.
(See my 'Myths and Marvels of Astronomy.')   The
readiness with which the story was believed showed how
prevalent was the opinion that the moon is inhabited.

Lord Rosse's giant reflector has been applied, as we
have said, to the examination of the moon's surface,
without any results differing in character from those
already obtained.

The considerations discussed at p. 169 are sufficient
to show that it is not only hopeless to look on the
moon's surface for the presence of living creatures, but
even to look for constructions erected by such supposed
inhabitants of the moon, unless these works were far
greater than the largest yet constructed by man.   Large
cities, indeed, might be visible, but not separate edifices ;
nor could variations in the dimensions of cities be easily
detected.   It has been argued, indeed, that since gravitation, which gives weight to living creatures as well as
to the objects around them, is so much less at the
moon's surface than at the earth's, lunar inhabitants
might, without being cumbrous or unwieldy, be very
much larger than the races subsisting on our earth ;
they might also easily erect buildings far exceeding in
magnitude the noblest works of man.   Nor is the argument wholly fanciful.   A man of average strength and

agility placed on the lunar surface (and supposed to preserve his usual powers under the somewhat inconvenient circumstances in which he would there find himself) could easily spring four or five times his own height, and could lift with ease a mass which, on the earth, would weigh half a ton. Thus it would not only be possible for a race of Lunarians, equal in strength to terrestrial races, to erect buildings much larger than those erected by man, but it would be *necessary* to the stability of lunar dwellings that they should be built on a massive and stupendous scale. Further, it would be convenient that the Lunarians, by increased dimensions and more solid proportions, should lose a portion of the superabundant agility above indicated. Thus we have at once the necessity and the power for the erection of edifices far exceeding those erected by man.

But having thus shown that lunar structures might very possibly be of such vast dimensions as to become visible in our ·largest telescopes, it remains only to add, that no object that could, with the slightest appearance of probability, be ascribed to the labours of intelligent creatures, has ever been detected on the moon's surface.

Failing the discovery of living creatures, or of their works, it was hoped that at least the telescope might reveal the progress of natural processes taking place on a sufficiently important scale. There can hardly be a doubt that our earth, examined from the moon's distance, would exhibit (in telescopes of considerable power) a variety of interesting changes. It would be easy to trace the slow alternate increase and diminution of the polar snow-caps. The vast llanos, savannahs, and prairies would exhibit with the changing seasons very easily distinguishable changes of colour ; the occasional covering of large districts by heavy snowfalls would also be a readily recognisable phenomenon.

Now the moon's surface exhibits distinctly marked *varieties* of colour. We see regions of the purest white —regions which one would be apt to speak of as *snow-covered*, if one could conceive the possibility that snow should have fallen where (now, at least) there is neither air nor water. Then there are the so-called seas, grey or neutral-tinted regions, differing from the former not merely in colour and in tone, but in the photographic quality of the light they reflect towards the earth. Some of the seas exhibit a greenish tint, as the Sea of Serenity and the Sea of Humours. Where there is a central mountain within a circular depression, the surrounding plain is generally of a bluish steel-grey colour. The region called the Marsh of Sleep exhibits a pale red tint, a colour seen also near the Hercynian mountains, within a circumvallation called Lichtenburg.

But although there are varieties, there has never yet been detected any *variation* of colour. Nothing has been seen which could be ascribed, with any appearance of probability, to the effects of seasonal change.

Failing evidence of the existence of living creatures, or of processes of vegetation, there only remains one form of variation to be looked for: I refer to changes such as, on our own earth, are produced by volcanic eruptions or by earthquakes.

It is evident, in the first place, that the inquiry must be one of extreme delicacy.   Indeed, if the volcanic changes taking place on the moon were no greater than those observed on our own earth, it would be almost hopeless to seek for traces of their occurrence. The light proceeding from a burning mountain could never be detected at the moon's distance.   It would also be extremely difficult to detect such small new craters as have been formed on our earth.   It is the overspreading of extensive tracts with the materials ejected from volcanoes that would form the most readily detected feature of change.   There have been instances in which, for many miles around a volcano, the country has been covered with ashes, and there can be little doubt that the change of appearance thus produced might be detected even at the moon's distance.   There have also been cases in which, during an earthquake, the features of an extensive region have been entirely altered.   Instances such as these, however, are so few and far between, that if we supposed the moon's surface correspondingly altered, the chances would be great against the detection of any change.

Assuming the probable, or, at least, the possible, existence of active volcanoes upon the moon, it remains to be seen how the operation of such volcanoes is to be detected from our earth.   The colours seen in different parts of the moon's surface are little marked, and grey or neutral-tinted regions are so prevalent that it would be very difficult to note the change of colour produced by the downfall, over large tracts, of matter ejected from erupting volcanoes. Differences of elevation produced by such downfall would afford a much more favourable object of examination.

One of the earliest to record the supposed occurrence of volcanic action upon the moon was the elder Herschel. He observed luminous appearances, which he attributed to the presence of active volcanoes on the dark part of the moon's disc. The cause of these (which had been noticed also, but less satisfactorily, by Bianchini and Short) has now been shown to be the greater brilliancy of the light reflected under particular circumstances from our own earth upon the moon.

Prof. Shaler, of Harvard College, gives the following interesting evidence respecting the degree of illumination of the 'old moon in the new moon's arms':— 'With the 15-inch Merz of the observatory of this university it is possible, under favourable conditions, to see all the principal features of the topography on the dark region illuminated only by this earth-shine. In the course of some years of study upon the geology, if we may so call it, of the moon, I have had several opportunities of seeing under these conditions all the great features of the dark surface shine out with amazing distinctness. The curious point, however, is that the eye is not enabled to recognise the craters by light and shade, for the light is too feeble for that, besides being too vertical for such a result; but the relief is solely due to the difference in the light-reflecting

power of the various features of the topography.   Whatever becomes very brilliant under the vertical illumination of the full moon (the edges and floors of many
craters, certain isolated hills, and the radiating bands
of light) shines out with a singular, distinctness when
lit by our earth's light.   This is important, inasmuch
as it shows pretty conclusively that the difference in
the brightness of various parts of the surface of the
moon is not due to the effects of the heating of the
surface during the long lunar day, but is dependent
upon difference in the light-reflecting power.   There
are several degrees of brightness observable in the
different objects which shine out by the earth-light.
In this climate there are not over three or four nights
in the year when the moon can be caught in favourable
conditions for this observation.   The moon should not
be over twenty-four hours old (the newer the better),
and the region near the horizon should be reasonably clear.   Under these conditions I have twice
been able to recognise nearly all the craters on the
dark part over 15 miles in diameter, and probably
one-half the bands, which show with a power of 100
when the moon is full.   That this partial illumination
of the dark part of the moon is in no way connected
with the action of an atmosphere, is clearly shown by
the fact that the light is evenly distributed over the
whole surface, and does not diminish as we go away
from the part which is lit by direct sunlight, as it should
do if an atmosphere were in question.   It will be noticed
that this fact probably explains the greater part of the

perplexing statements concerning the illumination of certain craters before the terminator came to them. It certainly accounts for the volcanic activity which has so often been supposed to be manifested by Aristarchus. Under the illumination of the earth-light this is by far the brightest object on the dark part of the moon's face, and is visible much longer and with poorer glasses than any other object there.'

Schröter, who devoted a large part of his time to the study of the moon, imagined that he had detected signs of change, which, singularly enough, he seems to have been disposed to attribute rather to changes in a lunar atmosphere of small extent than to volcanic action. He was not able to assert positively, however, that appreciable changes had taken place. One observation of his, however, deserves special notice, as will presently appear. In November, 1788, he noted that the place of the crater Linnæus, in the Sea of Serenity, was occupied by a dark spot, instead of appearing, as usual, somewhat brighter than the neighbouring regions. Assuming that he made no mistake, we have evidence here of activity in this particular crater.

Since the time of Schröter, other observers have been led to suspect the occurrence of change. Mr. Webb pointed out in 1865 eight noteworthy instances. Several of these seem easily explained by the well-known effects of difference in telescopic powers, observational skill, keenness of vision, and the like; but there are one or two which seem to deserve a closer scrutiny :—

On February 8, 1862, the south-south-west slope of

Copernicus was seen to be studded with a number of minute craters not seen in Beer ánd Mädler's map. These seemed to form a continuation of a region crowded with craters between Copernicus and Eratosthenes. And it is singular that this last-named region exhibits a honeycomb appearance, which would seem not to have existed in Schröter's time, since it is not recorded in his maps, and could hardly have escaped his persevering scrutiny.

Another instance of supposed change is well worthy of attention, as showing the difficulty of the whole subject. There is a ring-mountain, called Mersenius, which has attracted the close attention of lunar observers, in consequence of its *convex* interior—a very uncommon feature. This bubble-like convexity is represented by Schröter, and also by Beer and Mädler, as perfectly smooth. Not only is this the case, but we have distinct evidence that Beer and Mädler paid particular attention to this spot. Now, in 1836, only a year or two after the publication of Beer and Mädler's map, Mr. Webb detected a minute crater on the summit of the convexity within Mersenius; he also saw several delicate markings, resembling long irregular ravines, 'formed by the dropping-in of part of an inflated and hollow crust.' Here one would feel satisfied that a change had taken place, were it not that in Lohrmann's map a minute crater had already been inserted on the convexity in question, while from the dates (1822 and 1836) between which Lohrmann constructed his map, the probability is that the crater had been observed by

o

him at or before the time when Beer and Mädler failed
to detect its existence.

I have already referred to Schröter's observations
of the crater Linné on the Sea of Serenity. Whether
Schröter had been deceived or not, when he asserted
that a dark spot hid the place of this crater in 1788,
it is certain that during the last half-century the crater
had been distinctly visible. When the sun is high
upon Linné, it appears as a small bright spot, but
when the spot is near the terminator, the crater has
been recognisable through the appearance of a shadow
within and without its wall. Now, in October, 1866,
Schmidt observed that the crater Linné had disappeared. When the spot was close to the terminator no
shadow could be seen, as usual, either within or outside
the crater. In November he again looked in vain for
Linné.

It is to be noted that the crater is no insignificant
formation, but fully five and a half miles wide, and
very deep. It is, in fact, one of the largest craters
within the Sea of Serenity; (H in Webb's map, where
Linné is numbered 74).

The crater is represented in Riccioli's map (published in 1653). We have seen, also, that in 1788
Schröter recorded the appearance of a dark spot,
instead of a crater, in Linné's place. Lohrmann, in
1823, observed Linné to be one of the brightest spots
on the whole surface of the moon. His map shows
Linné as a distinct crater, and he describes it as more
than one (German) mile in diameter, very deep, and

visible in every illumination. In Beer and Mädler's map the crater is also distinctly noted ; they measured its position no less than seven times ; and they describe it as very deep and ,very bright. In photographs by De la Rue and Rutherfurd, Linné appears as a very bright spot : but singularly enough, we have also photographs taken during the month in which Schmidt looked in vain for the crater, and in these photographs (taken by Mr. Buckingham, of Walworth) Linné, though discernible as a light spot, has scarcely one-third of the brilliancy observed in De la Rue's and Rutherfurd's photographs, taken between the years 1858 and 1865.

Mr. Webb, one of our most careful observers, examined the Mare Serenitatis on December 13, 1866, for confirmation or disproof of Schmidt's views. The following is extracted from his notes of this observation :—' About one-third of the way from a marked high mountain on the northern shore of the Sea of Serenity, is a minute darkish-looking crater. This I presume to be Linné, *as I can trace no crater anywhere else. At some little distance south-east, there is an ill-defined whitishness on the floor of the sea.*' When Mr. Webb tested the results of his observations by means of a lunar map, he found that the first-named crater was not Linné, and that the ' ill-defined whitishness ' occupied the exact spot on which Linné is depicted. Subsequent observations fully confirmed the existence of this spot, which, singularly enough, is found, on careful measurement, to be twice as large as the crater whose place it conceals.

Many other observers who carefully examined Linné agreed in confirming the results of Schmidt's observation. One of the most satisfactory observations of Linné was effected by Father Secchi at Rome. On the evening of February 10, 1867, he watched Linné as it entered into the sun's light, and on the 11th he renewed his observations. In place of the large crater figured in lunar maps, he could just detect, with the powerful instrumental means at his command, a very small crater, smaller even than those craters which have received no names. 'There is no doubt,' he said, 'that a change has occurred.' Schmidt, it may be mentioned, independently detected the small crater described by Secchi.

The evidence thus far was as follows :—Where there used to be a ring-mountain surrounding a deep crater—so that, under suitable illuminations, the shadow of the mountain could be seen within and without the crater—no shadow could be traced ; a space, considerably larger than that originally surrounded by the ring-mountain, appeared somewhat brighter than the neighbouring parts of the Sea of Serenity ; in very powerful telescopes a minute black spot could be seen in place of the original wide and deep crater. It seemed clear, then, first, that there had not been a mere eruption of ashes filling up the crater, because then we should still see the shadow of the ring-mountain. Nor could the whole region have sunk, because then a large shadow would appear when the spot was near the terminator. The ring-mountain had not been destroyed, because its fragments and their shadows would remain visible. The only explanation available, therefore, appeared to be this,—that a mass of matter had been poured into the crater from below, and had overflowed the barrier formed by the ring-mountain, so as to cover the steep outer sides of the ring. Instead, therefore, of an outer declivity which could throw a shadow, there appeared to be an inclination sloping so gradually that no shadow could be detected, the whole surface thus covered with erupted matter shining with the same sort of light, so that a spot was seen somewhat lighter than the Sea of Serenity, and larger than the original crater.

Not only did the above explanation account for all the observed appearances, · but it corresponded to phenomena of eruption presented on our own earth. Mud volcanoes (or *Salsen*), as distinguished from volcanoes proper, present a very close analogy to the process of change just described. 'Mud volcanoes,' says Humboldt, 'continue in a state of repose for centuries. When they burst forth, they are accompanied by earthquakes, subterranean thunder, the elevation of a whole district, and (for a short time) by the eruption of lofty flames. After the first forcible outburst, mud volcanoes present to us the picture of an incessant but feeble activity.'

Yet subsequent observations have not confirmed the interpretation thus placed on the apparent changes in Linné. It has been shown by several observers, and notably by Mr. Browning in 1867, that Linné changes remarkably in aspect in a very short space of time, under changing solar illumination; and the inference would seem to be, that the supposed changes have been merely optical. Many observers of experience still retain the opinion, however, that there has been a real change in this region.

In Chapter VI. reasons are suggested for believing that, owing to the changes of temperature of the moon's surface, as the long lunar day and night succeed each other, gradual processes of change must take place in the surface contour.

The history of the inquiries which have been made as to the actual heating of the moon's surface during the lunar day is full of interest, but in this place I must be content with a brief account of the matter.

There are two ways in which the moon's surface sends out heat towards the earth. First, a portion of the sun's heat must necessarily be reflected precisely as the sun's light is reflected. But the moon's surface must also be heated by the sun's rays, and this heat is radiated into space. Thus at and near the time of full moon, the moon's surface is reflecting sun-heat towards us, and it is also giving out the heat which it has itself acquired under the sun's rays. Now the distinction between these two forms of heat is recognisable by instrumental means. The reflected heat is of the same quality as direct solar heat, and accordingly passes readily, like sun-heat, through absorbing media, such as glass, moist air, and others, which have the power of preventing the passage of heat which is merely radiated from bodies not so far heated as to become highly luminous.[1] We see this illustrated in our greenhouses. The sun's heat passes freely through the glass (at least only a small proportion is prevented from passing), but the warmed interior of the greenhouse does not part thus freely with its heat, the glass preventing the heat from passing away. Accordingly, when evening comes on, the interior of the greenhouse becomes considerably warmer than the surrounding air. In like manner, the heat reflected by the moon will pass freely through glass, while the heat which she radiates will not so pass ; and in this circumstance we recognise the means of comparing the quantity of heat which the moon reflects and radiates, and thus of determining the degree to which the moon's surface is actually heated at any given time.

The first inquiries made into this subject did not, however, deal with relations so delicate as these. ' Probably,' says the anonymous writer of a fine essay on the subject in ' Fraser's Magazine ' for January, 1870, ' the old observers had exaggerated notions of the moon's warmth and thought they could measure it by an ordinary thermometer. This was the tool employed

---

[1] We may state the matter thus : the shorter heat-waves pass through the media in question, the longer heat-waves are absorbed. From researches by Dr. Draper, it may be inferred that heat is produced, not merely or chiefly by waves from the red end and beyond the red end of the spectrum, but by waves from all parts of the visible spectrum and from beyond both ends of the spectrum. His researches, as also those of Sorby of Sheffield, demonstrate also that chemical action is produced by æther-waves of all orders of length.

by one Tschirnausen, who condensed the moon-light by means of burning glasses, in hope of getting measurable warmth, somewhere about the year 1699. Of course he got nothing. The famous La Hire followed suit some half a dozen years after, using a three-foot burning mirror and the most delicate thermometer then known; he, too, could obtain no indication, though his mirror condensed the light, and any heat with it, some 300 times; that is to say, the quantity of light falling upon the reflector was concentrated upon a spot one-three-hundredth of its area. After these failures, a century elapsed, and then Howard, and subsequently Prevost, attempted to gain direct evidence of lunar caloric, but since they had only expansion thermometers at their command, their results were valueless; for one, from some accidental circumstance, brought out a temperature obviously too high, while the other found negative heat!'

The much more effective heat-measuring instrument called the thermopile, was first brought into action by Melloni. Space does not permit me to describe here at length the nature of this instrument, for a full description of which I would refer the reader to Prof. Tyndall's 'Heat considered as a Mode of Motion.' Suffice it to say that the heat to be measured is suffered to fall on the place of junction of plates of bismuth and antimony, and that the electric current thus established is measured by the movement of a delicately poised magnetic needle. Melloni 'concentrated the lunar rays' (says the account from which

I have already quoted) 'by means of a metallic mirror, upon the face of his thermopile, in the hope of seeing the needle swing in the direction indicating heat; but it turned the opposite way, proving that the anterior and exposed surface of the pile was colder than its posterior face. Here was an anomaly. Did the moon, then, shed cold? No, the reverse action was due to the frigorific effect of a clear sky: the pile cooled more rapidly on one side than on the other, and a current was generated by this disturbance of the thermal equilibrium; a current, however, of opposite character to that which would have been produced if the moon had rendered the exposed face of the pile warmer than that which was turned away from the sky. Melloni's experiments were made about the year 1831.

'Two or three years after this the late Professor Forbes set about some investigations upon the polarisation of heat, which involved the use of a very sensitive thermopile, and he was tempted to repeat Melloni's moon-test, with the substitution of a lens for a mirror as a condensor: The diameter of this lens was 30 inches, and its focus about 40 inches; of course it was of the polygonal construction familiar to lighthouse-keepers and their visitors, the grinding of a thirty-inch lens of continuous surface not having been contemplated in those days. Allowing for possible losses from surface-reflection or absorption by the glass, it was estimated that the lunar light and heat would be concentrated three thousand times. One fine night in 1834, near the time of full moon, the lens and thermopile were put to the test. First the condensed beam of moon-rays was allowed to fall upon the pile and then it was screened by an interposed board. The exposures and screenings were repeated many times; but Professor Forbes was always disappointed with the effect, for it was nearly *nil*. There was a suspicion of movement in the galvanometer needle, but the amplitude of the swing was microscopic, possibly not greater than a quarter of a degree. Assuming that this deflection may have resulted, Professor Forbes subsequently proceeded to estimate the amount of heat that it represented. By exposing his pile and a thermometer to one and the same source of artificial heat, he was enabled to institute a comparison between the indications of each, and when he had done this and made all allowances for the condensing power of his lens, he concluded that the warming effect of the full moon upon our lower atmosphere was only equal to about the two hundred thousandth part of a centigrade degree!

'From what has since been learned, it appears strange that, with such a condensing power, such an insignificant result should have come out; but there was one point to which Forbes does not appear to have given the consideration it demanded. The sky was covered, he tells us, with a thin haze. Here was the secret, no doubt, of his comparative failure: this haze entirely cut off the little heat the moon had to give. When Melloni, using a similar lens, repeated his experiments under the pure sky of Naples, he saw his galvanometer swerve three or four degrees whenever the moon's condensed light fell upon the pile ; from which he concluded that the moon gave warmth by no means insignificant, though he did not take the pains to infer the actual degree upon any known scale.

'This last essay of Melloni's was made in 1846. Ten years elapsed before it was repeated, and then Professor Piazzi Smyth, who was about to test the advantages of a lofty astronomical station by carrying instruments to the summit of Teneriffe, placed this subject upon his programme, thinking reasonably, that in higher regions of the atmosphere he might catch some of the warmth that is intercepted in its passage through these to the earth. He furnished himself with a pile and thermomultiplier, as the sensitive galvanometer has been termed ; but he used no lens, contenting himself with a polished metal cone in front of the pile to collect and reflect the lunar heat upon its face. There was no mistaking the effect at this elevation of 10,000 feet : when the cone was turned towards the moon, the needle swung towards the heat side of the scale through a perceptible angle, and when it was turned towards the sky opposite to the moon, the needle returned to zero. By repeating this alternation of exposures an average deflection was obtained which was free from the effects of slight disturbing causes. Then it became of interest to learn what this average deflection meant in terms of any terrestrial source of warmth, and Professor Smyth found that it was equivalent to one seventeenth part of that which his warm hand produced when it was held three feet from the pile, or about twice that of a Price's candle fifteen feet distant.   He left as an afterwork the conversion of this warmth into its equivalent on a known scale.   The translation was quite recently made in France by M. Marié-Davy, and the result showed that the moon-heat experienced upon the mountain-top amounted to 750 millionths of a centigrade degree.

'We come now to touch upon the recent more con-clusive experiments of the Earl of Rosse.   When we look back upon the old trials, it is easy to see that the instruments employed, sensitive as they were, were yet not sufficiently so for the purpose.   It seems that the want of delicacy was not in the thermopiles that con-verted the heat into weak electric currents, but in the galvanometers by which the weak currents were sought to be measured.   Now these were formed of ordinary magnetic needles, poised upon points or turning upon pivots, the motion of the needle in each case being impeded to some extent by friction at its bearings. Then again, upon small, that is, short needles, feeble deflections are with difficulty seen, and those caused by the weak currents generated by moon heat were, per-haps, too small to be seen at all.   But it will be re-membered that the requirements of sub-Atlantic tele-graphy brought about the invention of an exceedingly delicate galvanometer, in which the needle is suspended by a hair, and its most minute deflections are rendered visible by a small mirror which reflects a beam from an adjacent lamp on to a distant scale, so that an almost imperceptible twist of the needle causes a large dis-

placement of the reflected light-spot.   Here, then, was
an indicator capable of rendering visible the most feeble
of electric currents generated in a thermopile.   It was
not invented long before it was turned to use by the
astronomers.   The Earl of Rosse was the first to test
its capabilities upon the moon.

'Lord Rosse, using a reflecting telescope of three
feet aperture, set about measuring the lunar warmth,
with a view to estimating, first, what proportion of it
comes from the interior of the moon itself, and is not
due to solar heating; second, that which falls from the
sun upon the lunar surface, and is then reflected to us;
and third, that which falling from the sun upon the
moon, is first absorbed by the latter and then radiated
from it.   We need not follow the instrumental details
of the processes employed for the various determinations; suffice it for us to know that the moon-heat was
clearly felt, and that the quantity of warmth varied
with the phase of the moon—greatest at the time of
full and least towards the period of new.   From this it
was evident that little or no heat pertains to the moon
per se; that our satellite has no proper or internal heat
of its own, or at least that it does not radiate any such
into space; if it did, there would probably have been
found evidence of a continuity of warming, independent
of the change of phase.   Of the heat which came with
the light only a small portion would pass through a
glass screen in front of the pile; from this it was
evident that the greater part of the whole consisted of
heat-rays of low refrangibility; from which Lord Rosse

concludes that the major portion of the lunar warmth does consist of that solar heat which has first been absorbed by the moon and then radiated from it.

'By the aid of a vessel containing hot water, subtending the same angle at his pile as the reflector employed to condense the moon's light and heat, he was enabled to judge of the actual temperature which the lunar surface must have to produce the effect that it does; and this was found to be about 500 degrees of Fahrenheit's scale. In this result we have a striking verification of a philosophical deduction reasoned out by Sir John Herschel, many years ago, that " the surface of the full moon exposed to us must necessarily be very much heated, possibly to a degree much exceeding that of boiling water." [1]

'Lord Rosse's conclusion that the heat increases with the extent of illumination has been confirmed by Marié-Davy, who has even measured the actual warmth day by day of a semi-lunation, and given the results in parts of the centigrade scale. He finds that the moon at first quarter warms the lower air by 17 millionths of a single degree, and that a regular increase takes place

[1] These observations have recently been renewed under more favourable conditions. The result has been to show that a larger proportion of the moon's heat than had been supposed is reflected sun-heat. The difference in the radiation from the full moon and from the new indicates, according to these later observations, a difference of about 200 degrees in temperature. Moreover, during a partial eclipse of the moon on November 14, 1872, it was found that 'the heat and light diminished nearly, if not quite, proportionally, the minimum for both occurring at or very near the middle of the eclipse, when they were reduced to about half their amounts before and after contact with the penumbra.'

till about the time of full moon, when the calorific effect reaches 94 millionths of a degree ! These insignificant figures refer only to the heat which can penetrate our atmosphere. The greater part of the whole lunar caloric must be absorbed in the high aërial regions.' [1]

Mr. Langley of the Alleghany observatory, near Pittsburg, has recently attempted to measure the moon's temperature with the very delicate instrument called the bolometer. The results he has obtained, according to which the moon's surface is colder than ice at the time of lunar midday, must be regarded, I fear, as showing only that the instrument he has used is unsuitable (perhaps too delicate) for this particular research. For they are inconsistent with physical possibilities.

Here I must conclude my brief and necessarily imperfect sketch of the researches which have been made into the aspect and condition of the moon's surface. But after all, no course of reading can prove so instructive or interesting as a thorough study of the moon's surface with a telescope, even though the telescope be of moderate power ; and I cannot better close this chapter than by earnestly recommending every student of astronomy to survey the lunar details as completely and systematically as his leisure and his instrumental means may permit.

[1] *Fraser's Magazine* for January, 1870.

CHAPTER V.

LUNAR CELESTIAL PHENOMENA.

IN discussing the nature of the celestial phenomena presented to lunarians, if such there be, we have considerations of two classes to deal with.   In the first place, there are demonstrable facts respecting the apparent motions of the sun, earth, stars, and planets, the progress of the lunar seasons, year, and so on ; in the second, we have other points to consider respecting which we can only form opinions more or less probable, —as the possible existence of a lunar atmosphere of small extent, the nature and effects of such an atmosphere, the question whether life—animal or vegetable —exists on the moon, with other matters of a similar nature.

But the only point of a doubtful nature respecting which I propose to speak at any length in this chapter, is the possible existence of a lunar atmosphere.   All celestial phenomena must be so importantly affected by the presence or absence of an atmosphere that it is desirable to inquire carefully into the evidence bearing on the subject.

Remembering that our air is a mixture of oxygen

and nitrogen (in the main), not a chemical compound of these gases, we see that there is no absolute necessity for the proportion in which these gases appear in our atmosphere. In the atmosphere of another body they might be differently proportioned. Moreover, carbonic acid gas, which forms a comparatively small part of the terrestrial atmosphere, might form a much larger proportion of the atmosphere of another planet. It is also conceivable that other and denser gases might be present in other atmospheres.

But even when all such considerations as these have been taken into account, it remains certain that unless we assume the existence on the moon of gases unknown on earth, a lunar atmosphere would have a specific gravity, under like conditions of pressure, differing in no marked degree from that of our earth's atmosphere. It would be a somewhat bold assumption to take for the average specific gravity of the lunar atmosphere that of carbonic acid gas, which, as we know, is almost exactly half as great again as that of air. But even if we supposed the lunar atmosphere composed of a gas as heavy as chlorine (which has a specific gravity nearly $2\frac{1}{2}$ times as great as that of air), or to be like phosgene gas, which is nearly $3\frac{3}{4}$ times as heavy as air, the argument which follows would not be seriously affected.

Our air is sufficient in quantity to form a layer about $5\frac{1}{2}$ miles in depth over the whole surface of the earth, and as dense throughout as air at the sea-level. This air, according to the laws of gaseous pressure,

P

adjusts itself so that at any given height the density corresponds to the quantity of air above that height. The air above any height acts, in fact, as a weight pressing upon the air at that height, and compressing its elastic substance until it has a density proportional to the pressure so produced. Obviously, therefore, the density of the air at any given level depends on the amount of the earth's attraction. For every weight on the earth would be doubled if the earth's attraction were doubled, and halved if the earth's attraction were halved, and so on ; and this applies as fully to the air as to any other matter having weight. Accordingly, if the earth's gravity were reduced to the value of gravity at the moon's surface ($0·16$ where the earth's gravity is represented by unity), the pressure of the air at the sea-level, and consequently the density of the air there, would be reduced to less than one-sixth of its present value. Of course, a given quantity of air at the sea-level would then occupy more space ; and the whole atmosphere would expand correspondingly. Instead of having to attain a height of about $3\frac{1}{2}$ miles, as at present, before the pressure would be reduced to one-half that at the sea-level (or to $\frac{1}{12}$ that at present existing at the sea-level), it would be necessary to attain a height more than six times as great, or nearly 22 miles. In other words, instead of one half of the whole atmosphere lying as at present below the height of $3\frac{1}{2}$ miles, the lower half of the atmosphere would then extend to a height of nearly 22 miles.

Accordingly, if on the moon there were an atmo-

sphere constituted like ours, and sufficient in quantity
to cover the moon's surface to a depth of about 5½
miles of uniform specific gravity equal to that of our
air at the sea-level, then such an atmosphere under
the moon's smaller attracting power would expand so
greatly that the half nearest the moon would extend
to a height of about 22 miles.[1]   At the mean level of
the moon's surface,—that is, a level corresponding
pretty nearly to our sea-level, so as to be as much
above the greatest lunar depressions as below the
greatest lunar heights,—the pressure would be about
one-sixth that at our sea-level.   Thus it is seen that
even though the lunarians had as much air per mile
of surface as we have on the earth, they would have a
much rarer atmosphere.   At a height of seven miles
from the earth, a greater height than has ever yet
been attained, or than could be attained by man,[2] the

---

[1] Here I take no account of the reduction of the moon's attracting power at this height from the surface.   The consideration of
such reduction would be important, however, in estimating the
height to which the rarer strata would extend.

[2] 'In the celebrated ascent by Messrs. Glaisher and Coxwell, in
which the greatest height yet reached by man was attained, Mr.
Glaisher became insensible before the balloon had attained a height
of six miles.   Mr. Coxwell, after endeavouring to rouse Mr. Glaisher,
found that he was himself losing his strength.   Indeed, he was
unable to use his hands, and had he not succeeded in pulling the
valve-string with his teeth, he and his companion must inevitably
have perished.   The height attained before the string was pulled
would seem, from an observation made by Mr. Coxwell, to have
been about 6½ miles.   At this time the temperature was 12° below
zero, and the neck of the balloon was covered with hoar frost.'—
(From my article on the balloon in Rodwell's *Science Dictionary*.)
'It is worth noticing, however,' I proceed, ' that although it would
seem from this experience that no man accustomed to breathe the

air is still one-fourth as dense as at the sea level. So
that, even though the lunarians had so large a quantity
of air as I have supposed, they must still be constituted
very differently from men, since men would perish at
once if placed in an atmosphere so attenuated.

But there is a more important point to be considered.
We see that an atmosphere of a given quantity per
square mile of lunar surface would reach much higher
than a similar atmosphere on the earth.   One half of it
would lie above a height of 22 miles—that is, enormously
above the summits of the highest lunar mountains. Far
the greater portion of the atmosphere would lie above
the lunar high lands.   Supposing the atmosphere differently constituted, and of specific gravity six times
as great as our air's under the same circumstances of
pressure, yet even then we should have only the same
density at the moon's level as at the earth's.   That
density could only be due to the pressure of the super-
incumbent parts of the atmosphere.   Diminishing with
height above the moon's mean surface, according to the

air at ordinary levels can hope to attain a greater height than
6½ miles, it is not impossible that those who pass their lives at a
great height, as the inhabitants of Potosi, Bogota, and Quito, might
safely ascend to a far greater height.   We know that De Saussure
was unable to consult his instruments when he was at no higher
level than these towns, and that even his guides fainted in trying
to dig a small hole in the snow; whereas the inhabitants of the
towns thus exceptionally placed are able to undergo violent exercise.   We may assume, therefore, that their powers are exceptionally
suited to such voyages as those in which Glaisher and Coxwell so
nearly lost their lives.'   Nevertheless it may be regarded as certain
that no race of men could exist even for a few minutes in an
atmosphere having a specific gravity less than one-sixth that of our
own air.

laws of gaseous pressure, it would extend as high above
the moon's surface as our air above the earth's, even on
the supposition of its having so remarkable a specific
gravity compared with that of common air.

We see, then, that if we were to suppose the atmospheric pressure at the moon's surface equal to that at
the earth's, we should have to suppose either that this
atmosphere is composed of gases of very great specific
gravity, or else that it extends to a much greater
height than our own atmosphere. In either case, it is
obvious that we should expect to find very marked
effects produced by such an atmosphere.

In the first place, when the moon was carried by
her motion over a star, the place of the star would be
affected by refraction, not only when the moon's edge
was very close to the star, but for some considerable
time before. If the lunar atmosphere were actually
as dense near the moon's mean surface as our air is at
the sea-level, then a star would not be occulted at all,
even though the moon passed so directly over the star's
true place on the heavens that the geometrical line
joining the star and the observer's eye passed through
the moon's centre. This is easily seen. For the moon's
semidiameter subtends an angle of less than 16'.
Now the sun appears wholly in view when in reality
he is below the level of the horizon, our atmosphere
having sufficient refractive power to raise the sun's
image by about 34' (his diameter is about 31'). And
this action is produced on rays which have only passed
through the atmosphere to reach the earth tangen-

tially. In passing out again, such rays would be deflected through 34′ more, or in all by about 68′· Accordingly, since 16′ is less than a quarter of 68′, if the moon's atmosphere possessed only a fourth part of the refractive power of our own atmosphere, a star in reality behind the centre of the moon's disc would appear as a ring of light. Nor would this ring be very faint. The light of the star would not be diluted or spread over the ring, and therefore reduced in corresponding degree : on the contrary, the moon's atmosphere would act the part of an enormous lens, increasing the total quantity of light received from the star, in the same way that the lens of a telescope's object-glass increases the quantity of light received from any celestial object.[1]

In the case supposed, as the moon really passed over a star we should see the star gradually approaching the edge of the moon (and perhaps slightly changing in tint), until at length, when the star was centrally behind the moon, it would appear as a ring around her disc.

The actual circumstances of an occultation of a star by the moon are very markedly contrasted with those here mentioned. In nearly all cases a star disappears

[1] An effect, indeed, somewhat similar to that here considered, may be produced by covering all but the outer ring of an object-glass with a black disc, and removing the eye-piece; if then the telescope be directed nearly towards a bright star, and shifted from that position until exactly directed on the star, the light from the star will be presented in the form of an arc, gradually ex-tending farther and farther round until it forms a complete circular ring.

instantly, when the moon's edge reaches the star's
place. There is no perceptible displacement of the
star, no change of colour, no effect whatever such as a
refractive atmosphere would produce. In certain instances, the brightness of a star has been observed to
diminish just before disappearance ; but we cannot be
sure that, where this has happened, the star may not
be really multiple, or perhaps nebulous. In the case
of the star κ Cancri, according to some observers, the
star has seemed suddenly reduced by about one half of
its light, and almost instantly after to vanish; but
these phenomena, only noticed in the case of this star,
may be fairly explained by supposing the star to be a
close binary. Again, there have been instances where
a star has seemed to advance for some distance upon
the moon's disc before vanishing; but it is by no means
unlikely that the star has in such a case chanced to cross
the moon's limb where a valley or ravine has caused a
notch or depression which is too small to be indicated
by any ordinary method of observation.[1] There is

[1] It is to be remembered that such disappearances as these
always take place opposite the bright limb of the moon, for the
dark limb, even when the moon is nearly new, cannot be properly
seen. Accordingly irradiation comes into play, as well, of course,
as the ordinary optical diffraction of the images of points forming
the lunar limb, both these causes tending to remove all trace of
minute notches really existing on the limb. But when a star is
occulted at such a notch, it of course remains visible, despite the
irradiation of the moon's limb ; so that it seems to be shining *through*
the moon's substance. That this explanation is sound, seems to be
confirmed by the circumstance that observers at stations not very
far apart recognise different appearances. Take, for instance, the
following passage from Smyth's *Celestial Cycle* :—' One of the
most remarkable projections of a star on the moon's disc which

every reason to believe that when a single star is occulted opposite a smooth part of the moon's limb,
the disappearance of this star is absolutely instan-
taneous.

Moreover, the evidence thus obtained has been
strengthened by spectroscopic evidence. Mr. Huggins
has watched the occultation of the spectrum of a
star,—that is to say, he has watched the spectrum of a
star until the moment when the star itself has been
occulted. He has found that the spectrum disappears
as instantaneously as the star itself. Now this is well
worth noticing; for it might be supposed that any
atmosphere existing round the moon would affect the
red rays more than the other; as our atmosphere, for
example, refracts the red light of the sun more fully
than the rest. Hence it might be expected that
the blue end of the spectrum would disappear a

I ever observed, was that recorded in the fifth volume of the
Astronomical Society's Memoirs, p. 363, of 119 Tauri, on December 18,
1831. On that occasion the night was beautiful, the moon nearly
full, and the telescope adjusted to the star which passed over
the lunar disc, and did not disappear till it arrived between two
protuberances on the moon's bright edge. This was also noted by
Mr. Snow, p. 373 of the same volume; but Sir James South saw
nothing remarkable, although in a few minutes afterwards he
observed the star 120 Tauri perform a similar feat.' 'Such
anomalies,' adds Smyth, 'are truly singular.' I cannot but think,
however, that they are to be expected as a natural consequence of
the unevennesses which certainly characterise certain parts of the
lunar limb. Such unevennesses on the limb must be minute to
escape detection, through the effects of irradiation; and accordingly
a very slight difference in the position of two observers would
suffice to render the observed phenomena at their two stations
altogether different.'

moment or two before the red end. But this did not happen.

The spectroscope has also afforded direct evidence of the non-existence of a lunar atmosphere of any considerable extent. For when the spectrum of the lunar light has been observed (by Mr. Huggins first, and later by others), it has been found to be absolutely similar to the solar spectrum,—that is, there is no trace whatever of absorptive action exerted by a lunar atmosphere upon the solar rays which are reflected by her to the earth. This evidence is, of course, not demonstrative of the absolute want of air of any sort on the moon, because a very rare and shallow atmosphere would produce no appreciable absorptive effect; but it confirms the other evidence showing that any lunar atmosphere must not only be extremely shallow but extremely rare. That is, there is not, as had been suggested by a well-known physicist, a dense atmosphere so shallow as not to rise above the summit of the lunar mountains. It is difficult, indeed, to conceive how such an atmosphere could be supposed to exist, since, as we have seen above, a gas six times as dense (under the same conditions) as our air, would on the moon only be as dense as our air, if so great in quantity as to reach as high as our air. An atmosphere sufficient in quantity to give traces of its presence in lunar shallows, but not extending higher than the summits of the lunar mountains, must be of a specific gravity so greatly exceeding (under the same conditions) that of common air, or indeed of any gas known to us on earth, that we are justified in regarding the theory of its existence as altogether unsupported by evidence.

But perhaps the strongest evidence we have to show that the moon has either no atmosphere or so little that she may be regarded as practically airless, is to be found in the phenomena of solar eclipses. It is certain, in the first place, that if the moon had an atmosphere resembling the earth's, the sun would not disappear at all, even at the moment of central eclipse, and when the sun was at his smallest and the moon at her largest. The moon's atmosphere would act as a lens (or as part of a lens) and reveal the sun to our view as a ring of blazing lustre—as really sunlight as the light of our setting sun. If the moon's atmosphere were at her mean surface but about one-fourth as dense as ours at the sea-level, the central part even of the sun's disc would be transmuted into a ring of light close to the moon's edge, while the parts nearer the sun's edge would form outer and brighter parts of the ring of glory round the moon. A very shallow lunar atmosphere indeed would suffice to bring the parts close to the edge of the sun's disc into view. It was, indeed, once supposed that the sierra of red light seen round the moon's disc during total eclipse was produced by the refraction of the sun's light by the moon.[1] We now know that no part of the

---

[1] Thus Admiral Smyth wrote in 1844:—'The red flames or protuberances of light, observed during total eclipses, and so correctly noted by the Astronomer Royal and Mr. Baily during that of July, 1842, seemed to be attributable to an atmospheric effect, albeit

light outside of the moon during totality is sunlight
refracted by the moon, simply because the part where

there may be no distinguishable atmosphere. So long ago as 1706,
Captain Stannyan, at Berne, observed of the sun, "that his getting
out of the eclipse was preceded by blood-red streaks of light from
the left limb, which continued not longer than six or seven seconds
of time." On this Flamsteed remarks in a letter to the Royal
Society :—" The Captain is the first man I ever heard of that took
notice of a red streak of light preceding the emersion of the sun's
body from a total eclipse ; and I take notice of it to you, because it
infers *that the moon has an atmosphere* ; and its short continuation of only six or seven seconds of time tells us that its height
is not more than the five- or six-hundredth part of her diameter."
This phenomenon was again noted during the total eclipse of the
sun in April, 1715, by Charles Hayes, the author of *A Treatise
on Fluxions*, who states in his philosophical dialogue *Of the
Moon* that there was a streak of "dusky but strong red light" preceding the sun's reappearance. There is much uncertainty, however, in all these observations, from their being liable to so many
conditions of place, weather, instrument, and wind.' I quote the
remainder of Admiral Smyth's remarks as bearing importantly on our
subject :—' From more than one observation, I had worked myself
up to a belief that the globes of Saturn and Jupiter were more
affected under occultation than could be assigned to the inflection
of their light in passing by the lunar surface ; and I also thought
that I had seen the satellites of Jupiter change their figure at the
instant of immersion. Thus prejudiced, so to say, I prepared to
establish the point by the occultation of the 1st of June, 1831, and
certainly observed it under a train of favouring circumstances ; but
my result, as stated in the second volume of the *Astronomical
Society's Memoirs*, p. 37, is this : Although the emersions of the
satellites were perfectly distinct, they were certainly not so instan-
taneous as those of the small stars, which I think was owing more
to light than disc. Jupiter entered into contact rather sluggishly ;
but though the lunar limb was tremulous from haze, there was not
the slightest loss of light. Faint scintillating rays preceded the
emersion, which was so gradual, that, as the planet reappeared, the
edge of the moon covered it with a perfectly *even* and black seg-
ment, which cut the belts distinctly, and formed clear sharp cusps
slowly altering until the whole body was clear. There was no
appearance of raggedness from lunar mountains, and Jupiter's belts

such refracted light would be strongest gives its own
proper spectrum quite distinct from the spectrum of
sunlight. But strong as this evidence is, there is yet
stronger evidence. It has been discovered by Prof.
Young that the sun has a relatively shallow atmosphere (say from two hundred to five hundred miles
in height), whose existence is only rendered discernible by spectroscopic analysis, *aided by the moon.*
As the moon passes over the face of the sun, the
visible sickle of the sun's disc grows narrower and
narrower, until at last it vanishes; at that moment
the shallow solar atmosphere is not yet covered, but
is just about to be covered. For a moment or two
the spectroscope gives the spectrum of this atmosphere, and this spectrum is found to consist of
myriads of bright lines,—the reversed Fraunhofer lines
in fact. These are visible only for a second or two,
and in the ordinary condition of the shallow atmosphere they vanish so suddenly that their disappear-

were superbly plain while emerging; but there was not the slightest
distortion of figure, diminution of light or change of colour. . . .
Schröter concluded that there existed a lunar atmosphere, but he
estimated it to be only 5,742 feet high; and Laplace considered it
as being more attenuated than what is termed the vacuum in an
air-pump. The slowness of the moon's motion on its axis may
account for such result.' (There is, however, no basis for this supposition.) . . . 'MM. Mädler and Beer, whose selenographical
researches have been carried to an unprecedented extent, arrive at
the conclusion that the moon is not without an atmosphere, but
that the smallness of her mass incapacitates her from holding an
extensive covering of gas, and they add, " it is possible that this
weak envelope may sometimes, through local causes, in some
measure dim or condense itself," the which would explain some of
the conflicting details of occultation phenomena.'

ance has been compared to the vanishing of rocket stars.[1]

Now if the moon had an atmosphere comparable even with what is called the vacuum of an air-pump, the recognition of the delicate phenomena attesting the existence of the shallow solar atmosphere would be wholly impossible. The slightest residue of sunlight brought into action by the refractive power of such an atmosphere would suffice to obliterate the beautiful but delicate spectrum of the complex solar atmospheric envelope.

The evidence derived from the non-existence of any twilight circle on the moon, or the extreme narrowness of any such zone which may exist, need not here be closely considered. The only observations yet made which appear to indicate the existence of lunar twilight, seem explicable as due to the fact that the sun is not a point of light illuminating the moon's surface, but presents, as seen from the moon, a disc

---

[1] During the annular eclipse of June, 1872, the lines were seen by Mr. Pogson, Government Astronomer at Madras, for about 2 or 3 seconds when the annulus was completed, and for about 6 or 7 seconds when the annulus broke, showing a variable condition of the solar atmosphere. Moreover, the lines did not vanish suddenly in the latter case, as when the phenomenon was observed by Young in December, 1870, and by Tennant, Maclear, and others, in December, 1871. These peculiarities have no bearing on the question of the moon's atmosphere, but I thought it desirable to mention them, lest the reader should derive erroneous impressions from the account given above. The general subject of the sun's complex shallow atmosphere is fully discussed in my treatise on *The Sun*, in the first edition of which I adopted the theory that such an atmosphere must exist, while as yet the decisive observations remained to be effected.

as large as she shows to us.   Thus there would be in
the case of a smooth moon, a penumbral fringe border-
ing the illuminated hemisphere, and about 32′ of the
arc of a lunar great circle in width.   This would
correspond to a breadth of nearly ten miles, and would
be readily discernible from the earth.   In the case of
a rough body like the moon, there would be no regular
penumbral fringe, but along some parts of the border-
line between light and darkness the effect would be
reduced, while along other parts it would be exaggerated.   On the whole, there would result appearances closely resembling those due to a twilight circle
of small extent; and we can reasonably ascribe the
supposed twilight effects hitherto recognised to this
cause,—that is, to the fact that the sun, as seen from
the moon, is not a point of light but a disc.

The conclusion to which we seem forced by all the
evidence obtainable, is that either the moon has no
atmosphere at all (which scarcely seems possible), or
that her atmosphere is of such extreme tenuity as not
to be perceptible by any means of observation we can
apply.   I must, however, make some remarks here on
a theory which has been advocated by astronomers
of repute, and even discussed by Sir John Herschel
as not wholly incredible,—the theory, namely, that a
lunar atmosphere (and lunar oceans) may possibly exist
on the hemisphere of the moon which is turned directly
away from the earth.

This theory is based on another,—the theory, namely,
that the moon's centre of gravity is nearer to us than
farther

her centre of figure. Thus Professor Hansen considers that an observed discrepancy between the actual lunar motions and the results of the theoretical examination of the moon's inequalities, is removed if the centre of gravity of the moon is assumed to be $33\frac{1}{2}$ miles farther from the earth than her centre of figure. This result —which, however, Professor Newcomb questions— appears to have been confirmed by the comparison of photographic pictures of the moon, taken at the times of her extreme eastern and western librations. In the year 1862, M. Gussew, Director of the Imperial Observatory at Wilna, carefully examined two such pictures taken by Dr. De la Rue. The result of the examination may be thus stated :—The outer parts of the visible lunar disc belong to a sphere having a radius of 1,082 miles, the central parts to a sphere having a radius of 1,063 miles; the centre of the smaller sphere is about 79 miles nearer to us than the centre of the larger; the line joining the centres is inclined at an angle of about 5° to the line from the earth at the epoch of mean libration : thus the central part of the moon's disc is about 60 miles nearer to us than it would be. if the moon were a sphere of the dimensions indicated by the disc's outline. If we suppose the invisible part of the moon's surface to belong to the larger sphere, and the density of the moon's substance uniform, it would follow from this conformation that the centre of gravity of the moon is about 30 miles farther from the earth than is the middle point of the lunar diameter directed

towards the earth, that is, than is the centre of the
moon's apparent figure.   This result accords sufficiently
well with Hansen's theoretical conclusion.

On this Sir John Herschel remarks :—' Let us now
consider what may be expected to be the distribution
of air, water, or other fluid on the surface of such a
globe, supposing its quantity not sufficient to cover
and drown the whole mass.   It will run towards the
lowest place, that is to say, not the nearest to the
centre of figure, or to the central point of the mere
space occupied by the moon, but to the centre of the
mass, or the centre of gravity.   There will be formed
there an ocean of more or less extent, according to
the quantity of fluid directly over the heavier nucleus,
while the lighter portion of the solid material will
stand out as a continent on the opposite side. . . .
In what regards its assumption of a definite level, air
obeys precisely the same hydrostatical laws as water.
The lunar atmosphere would rest upon the lunar
ocean, and form in its basin a *lake of air*, whose upper
portions, at an altitude such as we are now contem-
plating, would be of excessive tenuity, especially
should the lunar provision of air be less abundant in
proportion than our own.   It by no means follows,
then, from the absence of visible indications of water
or air on this side of the moon, that the other is
equally destitute of them, and equally unfitted for
maintaining animal or vegetable life.   Some slight
approach to such a state of things actually obtains on
the earth itself.   Nearly all the land is collected in one

of its hemispheres, and much the larger portion of the sea in the opposite. There is evidently an excess of heavy material vertically beneath the middle of the Pacific; while, not very remote from the point of the globe diametrically opposite, rises the great table-land of India and the Himalaya chain, on the summits of which the air has not more than a third of the density it has on the sea-level, and from which animated existence is for ever excluded.'

But pleasing though the idea' may be that on the farther hemisphere of the moon there may be oceans and an atmosphere, it is impossible to accept this theory. In the first place, it has not been demonstrated, and is in fact not in accordance with theoretical considerations, that the moon is egg-shaped, or bi-spherical, according to Gussew's view. The farther part may also project as the nearer part does (supposing Gussew's measurements and inferences to be trustworthy). But even if we assume the moon to have the figure assigned to it by Gussew, the invisible part is not that towards which the atmosphere would tend. The part of the surface opposite the centre of the visible disc is in fact not nearest to the centre of gravity, but (assuming the unseen part spherical, and of the radius indicated by the visible disc) is 30 miles farther from the centre of gravity than are points on the edge of the visible disc. The band or zone of the moon's surface lying on this edge is the region where oceans and an atmosphere should be collected [1] (if

[1] The argument is presented in another form in a paper con-

water and air existed in appreciable quantity) on the
moon's surface.

tributed by me to the *Monthly Notices of the Astronomical Society*,
as follows :—Let us assume, with Hansen, that the moon's surface
is formed of two spherical surfaces, the part nearest to us having
the least radius, so that in fact the moon is shaped like a sphere to
which a meniscus is added, said meniscus lying on the visible hemisphere. If we imagine the meniscus removed, the lunar atmosphere
would dispose itself symmetrically round the moon's spherical surface. Now, suppose that while this state of things exists, the lunar
air within the region now occupied by the meniscus of solid matter
is suddenly changed to matter of the moon's mean density, what
could be the effect of this change, by which new matter would be
added on the side of the moon towards the earth ? Surely not that
the remaining atmosphere would tend to the farther side of the
moon, but, on the contrary, that it would be attracted towards the
nearer side by the new matter there added.   The lunar air would
be shallower on this nearer side, no doubt, because the air thus
drawn to it would not make up for the air supposed to be changed
into the solid form ; but at the parts which form the edge of the
disc there would be an access of air, without this diminishing cause,
and the air would therefore be denser there than elsewhere.   But
in this final state of things there would be equilibrium ; we learn
then what are the conditions of equilibrium for a lunar atmosphere,
assuming the moon's globe to have the figure supposed by Hansen.
There would be a shallow region in the middle of the visible disc,
and a region slightly shallow directly opposite, while the mid-zone
would have the deepest atmosphere.   But it is around this zone
precisely that no signs of a lunar atmosphere have as yet been
recognised.   I may remark that this reasoning may be extended
to the earth.   Assuming the waters of the earth drawn towards
the South Pole because of a displacement in the earth's centre of
gravity, we may regard the surface of the sea in the southern
hemisphere as standing above the mean surface of the globe, and
a part of the southern seas as therefore constituting a meniscus
like that conceived by Hansen to exist in the case of the moon.
It would follow, then, if my reasoning is correct, that we should
have the atmosphere shallowest in high southern latitudes—shallow,
but only slightly so, in high northern latitudes, and densest between
the tropics.   This, as is well known, is precisely the observed
arrangement.

We seem justified in considering the phenomena presented to an observer supposed to be stationed on the moon, as practically those which would be seen if the moon had no atmosphere at all.

These phenomena may be divided into celestial and lunarian.

Of lunarian phenomena,—that is, of the appearance presented by lunar landscapes,—I shall say little ; because, in point of fact, we know far too little respecting the real details of lunar scenery to form any satisfactory opinion on the subject. If a landscape-painter were invited to draw a picture presenting his conceptions of the scenery of a region which he had only viewed from a distance of a hundred miles, he would be under no greater difficulties than the astronomer who undertakes to draw a lunar landscape, as it would actually appear to anyone placed on the surface of the moon. We know certain facts,—we know that there are striking forms of irregularity, that the shadows must be much darker as well during the lunar day as during an earth-lit lunar night, than on our own earth in sunlight or moonlight, and we know that whatever features of our own landscapes are certainly due to the action of water in river, rain, or flood, to the action of wind and weather, or to the growth of forms of vegetation with which we are familiar, ought assuredly not to be shown in any lunar landscape. But a multitude of details absolutely necessary for the due presentation of lunar scenery are absolutely unknown to us. Nor is it so easy as many imagine to draw a landscape which shall be correct even as respects the circumstances known to us. For instance, though I have seen many pictures called lunar landscapes, I have never seen one in which there have not been features manifestly due to weathering and to the action of running water. The shadows again are never shown as they would be actually seen if regions of the indicated configuration were illuminated by sun-light but not by sky-light. Again, aërial perspective is never totally abandoned, as it ought to be in any delineation of lunar scenery.

I do not profess to have done better, myself, in the so-called lunar landscapes (Plates IV. and V.) which illustrate this chapter. I have, in fact, cared rather to indicate the celestial than the lunarian features shown in these drawings. Still, I have selected a class of lunar objects which may be regarded as on the whole more characteristic than the mountain scenery usually exhibited. And by picturing the greater part of the landscape as at a considerable distance, I have been freer to reproduce what the telescope actually reveals. In looking at one of these views, the observer must suppose himself stationed at the summit of some very lofty peak, and that the view shows only a very small portion of what would really be seen under such circumstances in any particular direction. The portion of the sky shown in either picture extends only a few degrees from the horizon, as is manifest from the dimensions of the earth's disc; and thus it is shown

PLATE IV.

that only a few degrees of the horizon are included in the landscape.

Next let us consider the celestial phenomena visible from the moon's surface.

The stars must be visible day and night, since the lunar sky in the daytime must be perfectly black, except where the sun's corona and the zodiacal light spread a faint light over it ; and even where there is this light, the stars must be quite clearly visible. Secondly, many orders of stars below the faintest discernible by our vision must be visible in the lunar heaven to eyesight such as ours, by day as well as by night. The Milky Way, in particular, must present a magnificent spectacle.[1]

The apparent motions of the stars correspond to the moon's rotation. Since she turns on her axis once in 27·322 of our days, and in the same direction that our earth turns, it follows that the star-sphere turns round from east to west as with us, but at a rate more than twenty-seven times slower. The pole of the lunar heavens lies close to the pole of the ecliptic, since the inclination of the moon's axis is only 1½ degree. But the pole shifts more quickly than the pole of our heavens, completing its circuit around the pole of the ecliptic, in a circle 3 degrees in diameter, in 18·6 years. Thus in the course of a lunar day the pole of the heavens shifts appreciably in position, and there-

[1] I have not ventured to include any part of the Milky Way in the pictures illustrating this chapter,—for this reason simply, that no ordinary engraving could give the slightest idea of the splendour of the galaxy as seen from an airless planet.

fore the stars do not travel in true circles, nor remain
at a constant distance from the pole of the heavens
(as our stars appreciably do). This noticed, the
motion of the star-sphere, except as to rate, corresponds latitude for latitude with that of our star-sphere.
The northern and southern poles of the heavens
are overhead to observers placed respectively at the
northern and southern poles of the moon ; and as the
lunarian travels towards the equator from a northern
or southern station, the pole descends along a northerly
or southerly meridian respectively until at the lunar
equator the two poles are both on the horizon. The
equator of the lunar star-sphere lies always close to
the ecliptic, the points corresponding to those parts
of our celestial equator which lie farthest from the
ecliptic being only $1\frac{1}{2}$ degree instead of about $53\frac{1}{2}$
degrees, as with us, from the ecliptic. These points
and the nodes of the equator shift round so as to perform a complete circuit of the ecliptic in 18·6 years.

The motions of the sun bear the same relation to
the star-motions as in the case of our own celestial
phenomena. As our solar day exceeds the sidereal day
on account of the sun's advance on the ecliptic, so the
solar day on the moon exceeds the sidereal lunar day,
—amounting to 29·531 of our terrestrial days, instead
of 27·322 days.

But while the lunar day is much longer than ours,
the lunar year is considerably shorter. For the precession of the nodes is, as we have seen, much more rapid
in the moon's case than in the earth's ; and the lunar

tropical year, which is of course the year of seasons, is
correspondingly shortened by the rapid motion of the
vernal and autumnal equinox-points to meet the sun as
he advances along the ecliptic. We know precisely what
the lunar tropical year is, from the result stated at
p. 112. It lasts 346·607 of our days, or 11·737 lunar
days. Thus on the average each lunar season—spring,
summer, autumn, or winter—lasts 2·934 lunar days, or
nearly three days. But the seasons are not very marked,
since the sun's range is only from $1\frac{1}{2}°$ north to $1\frac{1}{2}°$ south
of the ecliptic, which is rather less than the range of
our sun during four days before and after either equinox,
vernal or autumnal. It appears to me that this state
of things scarcely warrants Sir W. Herschel's statement that 'the moon's situation with respect to the
sun is much like that of the earth, and by a rotation on
its axis it enjoys an agreeable variety of seasons and of
day and night.'

Differences of climate exist, however, on the moon;
and the circumstance is one to be carefully borne in
mind in discussing the physical condition of our satellite. Day and night are nearly equal everywhere on the
moon's surface, and during all the year of twelve long
days. Moreover, the sun everywhere and at all times
rises nearly due east and sets nearly due west. But his
meridian altitude varies with latitude precisely as the
meridian altitude of our spring or autumn sun varies
with latitude. Along the lunar equator he rises to the
point overhead, or very near to it, at mid-day; and the
same may be said of all places within the lunar tropical

zone (three degrees only in width). Near the lunar
poles, on the contrary, the mid-day sun is close to the
horizon. And in mid latitudes the mid-day sun has an
intermediate altitude, which is greater or less according
as the place is nearer or farther from the equator.

The motions of the planets as seen from the moon
need not be fully discussed. It may be noted that all
the motions of advance and retrogression observed from
the earth can be seen from the moon also. The principal differences in the view of the planets obtained
from the lunar station consists first in the visibility of
Venus and Mercury when close to the sun, so that the
varying illumination of these planets can be traced
during their complete circuit around the sun, and
secondly, in the visibility not only of Uranus, Neptune,
and whatever other planets may travel beyond Neptune,
but of many hundreds, and perhaps thousands, of the
asteroids. If any planet or planets travel within the
orbit of Mercury, lunarian astronomers, if such there be,
must be well aware of the fact, supposing their powers
of vision equal to ours.

The solar surroundings, as the prominences, corona,
zodiacal, meteor systems, comet-families, and so on,
must be perfectly visible from the moon ; and in particular, before sunrise and after sunset these objects
must form a very striking feature of the lunar
heavens. I shall presently give a brief ideal sketch of
some of the more remarkable circumstances of the
scene presented to a supposed lunar observer, as these
and other phenomena pass in review before him. The

reader will find in this sketch a description of the probable appearances presented during an eclipse of the sun by the earth.

But it is in the phenomena presented by our earth herself that our imagined lunarians must find their most interesting and difficult subject of study. On her they have an object of contemplation utterly unlike any known to our astronomers.

Of course on the farther side of the moon, at least on those parts which are never brought into view by libration, the lunarians never see the earth at all. On the hither side she is at all times visible, though under very varying conditions of illumination. On the zone including places on the moon which alternately pass into view and out of view, she is alternately seen and concealed, but to varying degrees.

Thus let us begin with the 'parallactic fringe' $pmem'p'$, next to the illuminated region, shown in fig. 33. The inner edge of this fringe (the left-hand edge in the figure) indicates a line on the moon where the earth's centre in extreme librations just descends to the horizon, but never below the horizon. The outer edge marks a line where the earth's whole disc just disappears in extreme librations. Thus on places within this fringe-region the earth sometimes descends so low as to show less than half her disc above the horizon. If a fringe equally wide were drawn just within the inner edge of this fringe, it would include all places where the earth in extreme librations descends so low that some part of her disc (less than half) is concealed below the horizon.

The space marked as the 'Region carried out of view by libration' is the lunar zone where the earth passes out of view, in extreme librations, but is for the greater part of the time in view, wholly or partially. The space marked as the 'Region brought into view by libration' is the lunar zone where the earth passes into view in extreme librations, but is for the greater part of the time wholly or partially concealed.

Lastly, let us take the parallactic fringe p m e m' p'. Here the edge next to the unseen region indicates a line on the moon where, in extreme librations, the earth's edge just touches the horizon, no part of the earth becoming visible. The other edge indicates a line on the moon where, in extreme librations, the earth's centre just reaches the horizon. On any place, therefore, within the fringe, a part of the earth's disc, but always less than a half, becomes visible in extreme librations. A fringe as wide on the other side of the line p m e m' p', includes places on the moon where, in extreme librations, more than the half of the earth's disc becomes visible, but not the whole disc; and its right-hand edge is a line on the moon where, in extreme librations, the whole disc of the earth *just* becomes visible, touching the horizon at its lower edge.

It would be idle, however, to enter into further details on these points, simply because the result would have no value. It is indeed instructive to consider the general features of the heavens as seen from any celestial body, and the general fact that the earth, as seen from each lunar station on the visible hemisphere, has

such and such a mean position, and sways libratingly
around or across that position, is sufficiently interesting.
But the special circumstances of these librations have no
interest, because in no sense affecting the physical habi-
tudes of the different lunar regions. Moreover, a volume
much larger than the present would be required for
their adequate discussion.

It is manifest that at each lunar station the earth
changes in phase precisely as the moon changes with us.
When we see the moon full, the lunarians have the
earth ' new,' that is, wholly dark; when we see the
moon at her third quarter, the earth, as seen from the
moon, is at her first quarter; when the moon is new,
the earth is ' full; ' and lastly, when the moon is at her
first quarter, the earth is at her third quarter. But in
the case of the earth seen from the moon, the changes
are all gone through while she is in one and the same
part of the heavens; and though they necessarily depend
on the sun's distance from the earth, this distance changes
by the sun's apparent motion around the lunar heavens,
and not, as in the case of the moon, by the motions
chiefly of the lesser luminary. Moreover, it is manifest
that the earth's phases occur at different hours of the
lunar day at different stations. When the earth is
seen on the meridian, ' new earth ' necessarily occurs at
noon-day, ' first quarter ' at sunset, ' full earth ' at midnight, and ' third quarter ' at sunrise. Where the earth
is seen on the east of the meridian, ' new earth ' occurs
in the forenoon, ' first quarter ' in the afternoon, ' full
earth ' between sunset and midnight, and ' third quarter '

between midnight and sunrise.   Where the earth is seen on the west of the meridian, ' new earth ' occurs in the afternoon, ' first quarter ' between sunset and midnight, ' full earth ' between midnight and sunrise, and third quarter in the forenoon.

Again the earth changes in aspect to the lunarians on account of the inclination of her axis.   When the moon is north of the equator, the lunarians see the north polar regions, or have a view of the earth resembling a summer sun-view of the earth; when the moon is south of the equator, the lunarians see the south polar regions, or a view resembling a winter sun-view of the earth.   These changes correspond exactly, in sequence, with the varying sun-views of the earth during a year, since the moon, like the sun, passes alternately north and south of the equator as she travels towards the east on the heavens.   But the period of these changes, in the case of the moon, is of course the period occupied by the moon in passing from the equator to her greatest northerly declination, thence to the equator, again to her greatest southerly declination, and finally to the equator once more, and this period has a mean value equal to a nodical month.   It will be manifest from fig. 28, p. 119, and the explanation, that the range of the earth's apparent sway, by which her north and south poles are brought alternately into view, varies from 18° 18′ to 28° 35′ on either side of the mean position (when both poles are on the edge of her visible disc).   The period in which these changes are completed is of course that of the revolution of the moon's nodes, or 18·6 years.

In the considerations here dealt with, the student who has sufficient leisure will find the necessary materials for the complete discussion of the varying aspect and position of the earth as supposed to be seen from any lunar station.

Before drawing this chapter to a conclusion, however, I shall venture to attempt the description of some of the chief events of a lunar month, as they might be supposed actually to present themselves if an inhabitant of earth could visit the moon and observe them for himself. I select time and place so as to include in the description the phenomena of an eclipse of the sun by the earth. The reader will perceive that neither of the views illustrating this chapter corresponds with the relations considered in the following paragraphs,—in fact, it was absolutely necessary to select for pictorial illustration a lunar station where the earth would be low down, whereas for descriptive illustration it was manifestly better to take a station having the earth high above the lunar horizon.

To an observer stationed upon a summit of the lunar Apennines on the evening of November 1, 1872, a scene was presented unlike any known to the inhabitants of earth. It was near the middle of the long lunar night. On a sky of inky blackness stars innumerable were spread, amongst which the orbs forming our constellations could be recognised by their superior lustre, but yet were almost lost amidst myriads of stars unseen by the inhabitants of earth. Nearly overhead shone the Pleiadse, closely girt round by hundreds of

lesser lights.　From them towards Aldebaran and the
clustering Hyads, and onwards to the belted Orion,
streams and convolutions of stars, interwoven in fan-
tastic garlands, marked the presence of that mysterious
branchlike extension of the Milky Way which the observer on earth can with unaided vision trace no farther
than the winged foot of Perseus.　High overhead, and
towards the north, the Milky Way shone resplendent,
like a vast inclined arch, full ' thick inlaid with patines
of bright gold.'　Instead of that faint cloud-like zone
known to terrestrial astronomers, the galaxy presented
itself as an infinitely complicated star region,

> ' With isles of light and silvery streams,
> And gloomy griefs of mystic shade.'

On all sides, this mighty star-belt spread its out-
lying bands of stars, far away on the one hand towards
Lyra and Bootes, where on earth we see no traces of
milky lustre, and on the other towards the Twins and
the clustering glories of Cancer,—' the dark constellation ' of the ancients, but full of telescopic splendours.
Most marvellous too appeared the great dark gap
which lies between the Milky Way and Taurus; here,
in the very heart of the richest region of the heavens,
—with Orion and the Hyades and Pleiades blazing
on one side, and on the other the splendid stream
laving the feet of the Twins,—there lay a deep black
gulf which seemed like an opening through our star
system into starless depths beyond.

Yet, though the sky was thus aglow with star-light,

though stars far fainter than the least we see on the clearest and darkest night were shining in countless myriads, an orb was above the horizon whose light would pale the lustre of our brightest stars. This orb occupied a space on the heavens more than twelve times larger than is occupied by the full moon as we see her. Its light, unlike the moon's, was tinted with beautiful and well-marked colours. At the border, the light of this globe was white, while somewhat to the left of the uppermost point, and as much to the right of the lowest, a white light of peculiar purity and brilliancy extended for some distance upon the disc. But whereas the upper passed farthest round the disc's edge, and seemed on the whole to be the most extensive, the lower spread farther in upon the disc, and appeared rounded into an oval shape. Corresponding to this peculiarity was the circumstance that the greater part of the disc's upper half was occupied by a misty and generally whitish light, amidst which spots of blue could be seen on the right and left, and brownish and yellowish streaks near the middle ; while, on the contrary, the lower half of the disc was nearly free from misty light, and occupied on the sides by widely-extended blue regions, and in the middle by green tracts on a somewhat yellowish background. To an inhabitant of earth it would not have been difficult to recognise in this last-named region the continent of South America bathed in the full light of a southern summer sun.

The globe which thus adorned the lunar sky and illuminated the lunar lands with a light far exceeding

that of the full moon was our earth.   The scene was
not unlike that shown to Satan when Uriel,

> ' one of the seven
> Who in God's presence, nearest to the throne,
> Stand ready at command,'—

pointing earthwards from his station amid the splendour
of the sun, said to the archfiend,—

> ' Look downward on that globe whose hither side
> With light from hence, though but reflected, shines :
> That place is earth, the seat of man ; that light
> His day, which else, as th' other hemisphere,
> Night would invade.'

In all other respects the scene presented to the
spectator on the moon was similar ; but as seen from the
lunar Apennines the glorious orb of earth shone high
in the heavens ; and the sun, source of the light then
bathing her oceans and continents, lay far down below
the level of the lunar horizon.

And now, as hour passed after hour, a series of
changes took place in the scene, which were unlike any
that are known to our astronomers on earth.   The stars
passed, indeed, athwart the heavens on a course not
differing from that followed by the stars which illumine
our skies, but so slowly that in an hour of lunar time
they shifted no more than our stars do in about two
minutes.   And, marvellous to see, the great orb of earth
did not partake in this motion.   Hour by hour passed
away, the stars slowly moved on their course westwards,
but they left the earth still suspended as a vast orb of
light high above the southern horizon.   She changed,

indeed, in aspect. The two Americas passed away towards the right, and the broad Pacific was presented to view. Then Asia and Australia appeared on the left, and as they passed onwards the East Indies came centrally upon the disc. Then the whole breadth of Asia could be recognised, but partly lost in the misty light of the northern half, while the blue of the Indian Ocean was conspicuous in the south. And as the hours passed on, Europe and Africa came into view, and our own England, foreshortened and barely visible, near the snow-covered northern region of the disc.

But although such changes as these took place in the aspect of the earth, her globe remained almost unchanged in position. It was indeed traversing the ecliptical zone, along which the sun and moon and planets pursue their course; and this star-zone was itself being carried slowly round the lunar sky: but these motions were so adjusted that the earth herself appeared at rest. The zone of the ecliptic was carried round from east to west behind the almost unmoving globe of the earth. When South America was in view, she had been close to the eastern border of Aries; and now Aries had passed away westwards, and Taurus was behind the earth. And yet it could not be said that the earth by advancing along the ecliptic was hiding the stars of the zodiacal constellations; rather it appeared as though these stars were hiding themselves in turn behind the earth.

But the stars are not hidden as they are when the moon passes over them. The terrestrial astronomer in

R

such a case observes that a star vanishes instantly, and
reappears with equal suddenness when the due time
has arrived.   But the passage of the multitudinous stars
of the lunar sky behind the earth was accomplished in
a different manner.   The border of the earth's disc was
seen to be full of a light far more resplendent than that
of the disc itself.   As the stars on their passage to the
region behind the earth approached this border, their
light was seen to be merged in the ring of splendour.
This ring was, in fact, produced by the mingled lustre
of all the stars which were behind the earth's disc ; and,
speaking correctly, these stars did not vanish at all.   The
earth's atmosphere, like a gigantic lens, brought them
all into view, and became filled with their diffused
light, just as the object-glass of a telescope is seen to
be filled with a star's light when we remove the eye-
glass.

Here then was another feature in which the earth,
seen as a celestial body from the moon, differed wholly
from any celestial orb visible to terrestrial astronomers.
Her orb, beautiful from its size and splendour, beautiful
also in its variegated colours, was girt around with a
ring of star-light, a ring infinitely fine as seen from the
moon by vision such as ours, yet conspicuous because of
the quality of the light which produced it.

It may seem surprising that, though the orb of earth
was shining so splendidly above the lunar horizon, stars
could be seen which the far fainter lustre of the full
moon obliterates from our skies ; and not these alone,
but countless thousands of other stars, which only the

telescopist can see from a terrestrial station. But the observer on the moon has no sky, properly so called. Above and around him is the vault of heaven, while the atmosphere which forms our sky, not only in the splendour of day, but in the darkest night, when the stars seem to shine as on a background of intense blackness, is wanting on the moon. The blackness of our darkest skies is as the light of day by comparison with the darkness of space on which the stars of the lunar heavens are seen projected. The glorious orb of the earth was there at the time we speak of, and her light would have lit up an atmosphere like our own, so that the whole sky would have been aglow; but on the moon there was no atmosphere to illuminate, so that above and around the observer there was no sky.

Yet the lunar lands were lit up with the splendour of earth-light. The mountainous region around shone far more brightly than a similar terrestrial scene under the full moon, and the glory of the earth-lit portions were rendered so much the more remarkable by the amazing blackness of the parts which were in shadow. But the lustre of the stars was not dimmed. There was no veil of light to hide the stars, as when the full moon pours her rays upon the terrestrial air. Homer's famous description of a moonlit night corresponds far better with the lunar scene than with night on the earth. For whereas on earth the glory of the moon hides the heaven of stars from our view, on the moon, in the far greater splendour of the full earth,—

'the stars about the *Earth*
Look beautiful. . . . .
And every height comes out, and jutting peak
And valley, and the immeasurable heavens
Break open to their highest, and all the stars
Shine.

The long hours passed, measured by the stately
motion of the stars behind the scarce-moving earth, and
by the changing aspect of her globe, as continents and
oceans were carried from left to right across her face by
her rotation. And gradually her orb lost its roundness.
The ring of brilliant star-light which encircled her disc
remained perfectly round indeed, but within this ring
on the right a dark sickle began to be seen, and, slowly
spreading, invaded the disc on that side. The earth
was no longer full, but had assumed a gibbous phase,
like the moon a day or two after full. Yet her aspect
was wholly unlike that of the gibbous moon. The ring
of light surrounding her true orb would of itself have
made her appear unlike the moon ; but besides this
peculiarity, there was a marked contrast in the appearance of the darkened portion. Instead of that sharply-
defined edge presented by the gibbous moon, there was
in the case of the earth a softening off of the light by
gradations so gentle that no eye could perceive where
the enlightened hemisphere terminated and the dark
hemisphere began. As night on our earth comes on
with stealthy pace, the shades of evening closing in so
gradually that we can hardly say when day ends and
night begins, so from the station of the lunar observer
the shading on the earth's darkened side which showed

where night was coming on, presented no recognisable outlines. One familiar with the earth and with the ways of her inhabitants could not but picture to himself how, as country after country was carried by the earth's rotation into that darkened region, the labours of men were being drawn towards a close for the day.

When about a week had passed, the earth had become a half-earth. The shape of the darkened half of the disc could still be recognised by the ring of star-light, which always surrounds her as she is seen from the moon, and remains nearly always bright and conspicuous, though sometimes, when many and bright stars are behind the earth, the ring is brighter than at others. This, in fact, had been the case when the Milky Way, where it crosses Gemini, had been carried behind the earth, which now, however, had passed beyond that region, and was entering the constellation of the Lion.

The aspect of the earth had in the meanwhile altered in another respect. The southern polar regions had been turned more fully than before towards the moon,—more fully than towards the sun.

We may pass, however, from the further consideration of changes in the earth's aspect, to describe a far more interesting series of phenomena which had already commenced to be discernible in the eastern part of the heavens.

At all times the zodiacal light is visible in the lunar heavens, forming a zone completely round the zodiac, and perfectly distinct in appearance from the Milky

Way. It is far more brilliant, even when faintest, than the zodiacal light we recognise through our air, at once dense enough to conceal, and sufficiently illuminated, whether by twilight, moonlight, or starlight, to spread a veil over the delicate light of the zodiacal. But near the sun's place the zodiacal has an aspect utterly unlike that of even the brightest portions seen by us. Its complicated structure becomes discernible, and its colour indicates its community of nature with the outer parts of the solar corona. At the epoch we are considering, the corona itself was rising in the east, and its outer streamers could be seen extending along the ecliptical zone far into the bright core of the zodiacal.

. Infinitely more wonderful, however, and transcending in sublimity all that the heavens display to the contemplation of the inhabitants of the earth was the scene presented when the sun himself had risen. I shall venture here to borrow some passages from an essay entitled 'A Voyage to the Sun,' in which I have described the aspect of the sun as seen from a station outside that atmosphere of ours which veils the chief glories of the luminary of day. 'The sun's orb was more brilliantly white than when seen through the air, but close scrutiny revealed a diminution of brilliancy towards the edge of the disc, which, when fully recognised, presented him at once as the globe he really is. On this globe could be distinguished the spots and the bright streaks called faculæ. This globe was surrounded with the most amazingly complex halo of glory. Close around the bright whiteness of the disc, and shining far more beautiful by contrast with that whiteness than as seen against the black disc of the moon in total eclipses—stood the coloured region called the chromatosphere, not *red*, as it appears during eclipses, but gleaming with a mixed lustre of pink and green, through which, from time to time, passed the most startlingly brilliant coruscations of orange and golden yellow light. Above this delicate circle of colour towered tall prominences and multitudes of smaller ones. These, like the chromatosphere, were not red, but beautifully variegated. In parts of the prominences colours appeared which were not seen in the chromatosphere,—and in particular, certain blue and purple points of light which were charmingly contrasted with the orange and yellow flashes continually passing along the whole length of even the loftiest of these amazing objects. The prominences round different parts of the sun's orb presented very different appearances; for those near the sun's equatorial zone and opposite his polar regions differed very little in their colour and degree of light from the chromatosphere. They also presented shapes resembling rather those of clouds moving in a perturbed atmosphere, than those which would result from the tremendous processes of disturbance which astronomers have lately shown to be in progress in the sun. But opposite the spot-zones the prominences presented a totally different appearance. They resembled jets of molten matter intensely bright, and seemingly moving with immense velocity. They formed and vanished with amazing rapidity, as when in terrestrial conflagrations a flame leaps suddenly to a great height and presently disappears.' . . . 'Around the sun a brightly luminous envelope extended to about twice the height of the loftiest prominences, while above even the faintest signs of an atmosphere, as well as through and amidst both the inner bright envelope and the fainter light surrounding it, there were the most complex sprays and streams and filaments of whitish light, here appearing as streamers, elsewhere as a network of bright streaks, and yet elsewhere clustered into aggregations which can be compared to nothing so fitly, though the comparison may seem commonplace, as to hanks of glittering thread. All these streaks and sprays of light appeared perfectly white, and only differed among themselves in that whereas some appeared like fine streaks of a uniform silvery lustre, others seemed to shine with a curdled light. The faint light outside the glowing atmosphere surrounding the prominences was also whitish ; but the glowing atmosphere itself shone with a light resembling that of the chromatosphere, only not so brilliant. The pink and green lustre,—continually shifting, so that a region which appeared pink at one time would shine a short time after with a greenish light,—might aptly be compared in appearance to mother-of-pearl. The real extension of the white streaks and streamers was not distinguishable, for they became less and less distinct at a greater and greater distance from the sun, and finally became imperceptible.'

Much more might be said on this inviting subject,

only that the requirements of space forbid, obliging me to remember that the moon, and not the sun, is the subject of this treatise. The reader, therefore, must picture to himself the advance of the sun with his splendid and complicated surroundings towards the earth, suspended almost unchangingly in the heavens, but changing gradually into crescent form as the sun drew slowly near. He must imagine also, how, in the meantime, the star-sphere was slowly moving westwards, the constellations of the ecliptic in orderly succession passing behind the earth at a rate slightly exceeding that of the sun's approach, so that he, like the earth, only more slowly, was moving eastwards so far as the star-sphere was concerned, even while the moon's slow diurnal rotation was carrying him westwards towards the earth.

At the station we are considering, the lunar eclipse which took place on November 15, 1872, was only partial. Here, therefore, though the sun actually passed in part behind the earth, a portion of his orb remained unconcealed. But owing to the refractive power of the earth's atmosphere the rest of his disc was also brought into view, amazingly distorted, and forming a widely-extended crescent of red light—true sun-light—around a large arc of the earth's edge, the visible portion of the solar disc being at the middle of this crescent.

To an observer near the north pole of the moon, the eclipse was total, at least in our terrestrial mode of considering lunar eclipses : the true shadow of the earth fell on that portion of the moon. From a station so placed then, no part of the sun's disc could be seen, by the Lunarian ; nevertheless a crescent of sun-light was visible in this case also, the crescent extending farther round the earth's disc than in the former case, and in fact round considerably more than a semicircle, the brightest part of the crescent being opposite the part of the earth's disc behind which the sun's disc was in reality placed.

I must, however, leave the reader to conceive the slow processes of change by which, as the sun advanced to the position here indicated, his disc became gradually modified into this crescent of true sun-light, this distorted image of the *whole* sun, thus seen through the spherical shell of the earth's atmosphere, and how passing onwards towards the west, he gradually reappeared. Space will not permit me to dwell as I should wish on the multitude of interesting relations presented as the solar surroundings passed in their turn behind the earth, either before the sun as he approached the earth, or after the sun as he moved on westwards. Enough has been said to indicate to the thoughtful reader the general nature of the phenomena presented during the whole course of the sun's passage from the eastern to the western horizon, as well as those which followed after he had set, until the lunar month was complete, and the earth again seen, on November 30, 1872, with fully illuminated orb upon the lunar sky.

CHAPTER VI.

CONDITION OF THE MOON'S SURFACE.

IF the study of our earth's crust—or the science of geology—is capable of throwing some degree of light on the past condition of other members of the solar system, the study of those other orbs seems capable of at least suggesting useful ideas concerning the past condition of our earth. There are members of the solar system respecting which it may reasonably be inferred that they are in an earlier stage of their exist- ence than the earth. Jupiter and Saturn, for instance, would seem—so far as observation has extended—to be still in a condition of intense heat, and still the seat of forces such as were once probably at work within our earth. We see these planets enwrapped, to all appear- ance, within a double or triple coating of clouds, and we are compelled to infer, from the behaviour of these clouds, that they are due to the action of forces belong- ing to the orb which they envelope; we have, also, every reason which the nature of the case can afford to suppose that our own earth was once similarly cloud- enveloped. We can scarcely imagine that in the long- past ages, when the igneous rocks were in the primary stages of their existence, the air was not loaded heavily with clouds. We may, then, regard Jupiter and Saturn as to some degree indicating the state of our own earth at a long-past epoch of her existence. On the other hand, it has been held, and not without some degree of evidence in favour of the theory, that in our moon we have a picture of our earth as she will be at some far-distant future date, when her period of rotation has been forced into accordance with the period of the moon's revolution round the earth, when the internal heat of the earth's globe has been radiated almost wholly away into space, and when her oceans and atmosphere have disappeared through the action of the same circumstances (whatever they may be) which have caused the moon to be air-less and ocean-less. But whether we take this view of our earth's future, or whether we consider that her state has been from the beginning very different from that of the moon, it nevertheless remains probable that we see in our moon a globe which has passed through a much greater proportion of its history (so to speak) than our earth ; and accordingly the study of the moon's condition seems capable of giving some degree of information as to the future (possibly also as to the past) of our earth.

I wish here to consider the moon's condition from a somewhat different point of view than has commonly been adopted. It appears to me that the study of the moon's surface with the telescope, and the consideration of the various phenomena which give evidence on the question whether air or water exist anywhere upon or within her, have not as yet led to any satisfactory inferences as to her past history. We see the traces of tremendous sublunarian disturbances (using the word ' sublunarian,' here and elsewhere, to correspond to the word ' subterranean ' used with reference to the earth), and we find some features of resemblance between the effects of such disturbances and those produced by the subterranean forces of our earth ; but we find also as marked signs of difference between the features of the lunar and terrestrial crusts. Again, comparing the evidences of a lunar atmosphere with those which we should expect if an atmosphere like our own surrounded the moon, we are able to decide, with some degree of confidence, that the moon has either no atmosphere or one of very limited extent. But there our knowledge comes to an end ; nor does it seem likely that, by any contrivances man can devise, the further questions which suggest themselves respecting the moon's condition can be answered by means of observation.

Yet there are certain considerations respecting the moon's past history which seem to me likely, if duly weighed, to throw some light on the difficult problems presented by her for our study.

In the first place, it is to be noted that the peculiar relation between the moon's rotation and revolution possesses a meaning which has not hitherto, so far as I know, been considered. We know that *now* there is an absolutely perfect agreement between the moon's rotation and revolution,—in this respect, that her mean period of rotation on her axis is exactly equal to her

mean period of revolution.   (Here either sidereal rotation and revolution or synodical rotation and revolution
may be understood, so long as both revolution and rotation are understood to be of the same kind.)   I say
' mean period of rotation,' for although as a matter of
fact it is only the revolution which is subject to any
considerable variation, the rotation is also not perfectly
uniform.   We know, furthermore, that if there had
been, long ago, a *near* agreement between the mean
rotation and revolution, the present exact agreement
would have resulted, through the effects of the mutual
attractions of the earth and moon.   But, so far as I
know, astronomers have not yet carefully considered the
question whether that close agreement existed from
the beginning, or was the result of other forms of
action than are at present at work.   If it existed from
the beginning,—that is, from the moon's first existence
as a body independent of the earth,—it is a matter
requiring to be explained, as it implies a peculiar relation between the moon and earth before the present
state of things existed.   If, on the contrary, it has been
brought about by the amount of action which is now
gradually reducing the earth's rotation-period, we have
first of all to consider that an enormous period of time
has been required to bring the moon to her present
condition in this respect, and secondly, that either an
ocean existed on her surface or that her crust was once
in so plastic a condition as to be traversed by a tidal
wave resembling, in some respects, the tidal wave in
our own ocean.   This, at any rate, is what we must

believe if we suppose, first, that the main cause of the lengthening of the terrestrial day is the action of the tidal wave as a sort of brake on the earth's rotating globe, and secondly, that a similar cause produced the lengthening of the moon's day to its present enormous duration. It may be, as we shall presently see, that other causes have to be taken into account in the moon's case.

Now we are thus, either way, brought to a consideration of that distant epoch when—according to the nebular theory, or any admissible modification of it— the moon was as yet non-existent as an orb distinct from the earth. We must suppose, on one theory, that the moon was at that time enveloped in the nebulous rotating spheroid out of which the earth was to be formed, she herself (the moon) being a nebulous sub-spheroid within the other, and so far coerced by the motion of the other that her longer axis partook in its motion of rotation. Unquestionably in that case, as the terrestrial spheroid contracted and left the other as a separate body, this other, the lunar spheroid, would exhibit the kind of rotation which the moon actually possesses. On the other theory, we should be led to suppose that primarily the lunar spheroid rotated independently of its revolution; but that the earth's attraction acting on the outer shells, after they had become first fluid and then (probably) viscous, produced waves travelling in the same direction as the rotation, but with a continual brake-action, tending slowly to reduce the rotation until it had its present value, when dynamical equilibrium would be secured.

But, as I have said, in either case we must trace back the moon's history to an epoch when she was in a state of intense heat. And it seems to me that we are thus led to notice that the development of the present state of things in the moon must have taken place during an era in the history of the solar system differing essentially from that which prevailed during the later and better-known geological eras of our own earth. Our moon was *shaped*, so to speak, when the solar system itself was young, when the sun may have given out a much greater degree of heat than at present, when Saturn and Jupiter were brilliant suns, when even our earth and her fellow minor planets within the zone of asteroids were probably in a sunlike condition. Putting aside all hypothesis, it remains clear that, to understand the moon's present condition, we must form some estimate of the probable condition of the solar system in distant eras of its existence ; for it was in such eras, and not in an era like the present, that she was modelled to her present figure.

It appears to me that we are thus, to some extent, freed from a consideration which has proved a difficulty to many who have theorised respecting the moon. It has been said that the evidence of volcanic action implies the existence, at least when that action was in progress, of an atmosphere capable of supporting combustion,— in other words, an atmosphere containing oxygen, for other forms of combustion than those in which oxygen plays a part may here be dismissed from consideration.

But the fiery heat of the moon's substance may have been maintained (in the distant eras to which we are now referring the formation of her crust) without combustion. Taking the nebular hypothesis as it is commonly presented, the moon's globe may have remained amid the intensely hot nebulous spheroid (which was one day to contract, and so form the globe of the earth) until the nebula left it to cool thenceforth rapidly to its present state. Whatever objections suggest themselves to such a view are precisely the objections which oppose themselves to the simple nebular hypothesis, and may be disposed of by those who accept that hypothesis.

But better, to my view, it may be reasoned, that the processes of contraction and of the gathering in of matter from without, which maintained the heat of the nebulous masses, operated to produce all the processes of disturbance which brought the moon to her present condition, and that thus there was not necessarily any combustion whatever. Indeed, in any case, combustion can only have commenced when the heat had been so far reduced that any oxygen existing in the lunar spheroid would enter into chemical combination with various components of the moon's glowing substance. If there were no oxygen (an unlikely supposition, however), the moon's heat would nevertheless have been maintained so long as the contraction of the moon's substance on the nucleus continued to supply the requisite mechanical sources of heat-generation. In this case there would not necessarily have been any gaseous or vaporous matter, other than the matter retained in the gaseous

S

condition by intensity of heat, and becoming first liquid and afterwards solid so soon as the heat was sufficiently reduced.

Nothing hitherto advanced has explained at all satisfactorily the structure of the great crateriform mountain-ranges on the moon. The theory that there were once great lakes seems open to difficulties at least as grave as the one I have just considered, and to this further objection, that it affords no explanation of the circular shape of these lunar regions. On the other hand, Sir John Herschel's account of the appearance of these craters is not supported by any reasoning based on our knowledge of the actual circumstances under which volcanic action proceeds in the case of our own earth. 'The generality of the lunar mountains,' he says, 'present a striking uniformity and singularity of aspect. They are wonderfully numerous, occupying by far the larger portion of the surface, and almost universally of an exact circular or cup-shaped form, foreshortened, however, into ellipses towards the limb; but the larger have for the most part flat bottoms within, from which rises centrally a small, steep, conical hill. They offer, in short, in its highest perfection, the true volcanic character, as it may be seen in the crater of Vesuvius; and in some of the principal ones, decisive marks of volcanic stratification, arising from successive deposits of ejected matter, may be clearly traced with powerful telescopes. What is, moreover, extremely singular in the geology of the moon is, that although nothing having the character of seas can be traced (for the dusty spots which are commonly called seas, when closely examined, present appearances incompatible with the supposition of deep water), yet there are large regions perfectly level, and apparently of a decided alluvial character.'

It is obvious that in this description we have, besides those features of volcanic action which might, perhaps, be expected on the moon, a reference to features essentially terrestrial. Alluvial deposits can have no existence, for example, save where there are rivers and seas, as well as an atmosphere within which clouds may form, whence rain may be poured upon the surface of wide land regions. It is not going too far to say that we have the clearest evidence to show that in the moon none of these conditions are at present fulfilled. But it is probable that in former ages lunar oceans and seas and a lunar atmosphere may have existed ; though it is certain that most of the evidence we have is negative, save only those extremely doubtful signs of glacier action recognised by Professor Frankland. I venture to quote from Guillemin's 'Heavens' a statement of Frankland's views, in order that the reader may see on how slender a foundation hypotheses far more startling than the theory I have suggested have been based by a careful reasoner and able physicist. 'Professor Frankland believes,' says the account— 'and his belief rests on a special study of the lunar surface—that our satellite has, like its primary, also passed through a glacial epoch, and that several, at least, of the *valleys, rills,* and *streaks* of the lunar surface are not improbably due to former glacial action. Notwithstanding the excellent definition of modern telescopes, it could not be expected that other than the most gigantic of the characteristic details of an ancient glacier-bed would be rendered visible. What, then, may we expect to see ? Under favourable circumstances, the terminal moraine of a glacier attains enormous dimensions ; and consequently of all the marks of a glacier valley, this would be the one most likely to be first perceived. Two such terminal moraines, one of them a double one, have appeared to observers to be traceable upon the moon's surface. The first is situated near the termination of the remarkable streak which commences near the base of Tycho, and passing under the south-eastern wall of Bullialdus, into the ring of which it appears to cut, is gradually lost after passing Lubiniezky. Exactly opposite this last and extending nearly across the streak in question, are two ridges forming the arcs of circles whose centres are not coincident, and whose external curvature is towards the north. Beyond the second ridge a talus slopes gradually down northwards to the general level of the lunar surface, the whole presenting an appearance reminding the observer of the concentric moraines of the Rhône glacier. These ridges are visible for the whole period during which that portion of the moon's surface is illuminated ; but it is only about the third day after the first quarter, and at the corresponding phase of the waning moon, when the sun's rays, falling nearly horizontally, throw the details of this part of the surface into strong relief, and these appearances suggest this explanation of them. The other ridge answering to a terminal moraine, occurs at the northern extremity of that magnificent valley which runs past the eastern edge of Rheita.'

Here are two lunar features of extreme delicacy, and certainly not incapable of being otherwise explained, referred by Frankland to glacier action. It need hardly be said that glacial action implies the existence of water and an atmosphere on the moon; and not only so, but there must have been extensive oceans, and an atmosphere nearly equal in density to that of our own earth, if the appearances commented upon by Frankland were due to glacial action. It is admitted by Frankland, of course, that there is now no evidence whatever of the presence of water, ' but, on the contrary, all selenographical observations tend to prove its absence. Nevertheless,' proceeds the account from which I have already quoted, ' the idea of former aqueous agency in the moon *has received almost universal acceptation*' (the italics are mine). 'It was entertained by Gruithuisen and others. But, if water at one time existed on the surface of the moon, whither has it disappeared? If we assume, in accordance with the nebular hypothesis, that the portions of matter composing respectively the earth and the moon once possessed an equally elevated temperature, it almost necessarily follows that the moon, owing to the comparative smallness of her mass, would cool more rapidly than the earth; for whilst the volume of the moon is only about 1-49th (and its mass, it might be added, only about 1-81st part), its surface is nearly 1-13th that of the earth. This cooling of the mass of the moon must, in accordance with all analogy, have been attended with contraction, which can scarcely be conceived as occurring without the development of a cavernous structure in the interior. Much of this cavernous structure would doubtless communicate, by means of fissures, with the surface, and thus there would be provided an internal receptacle for the ocean, from the depths of which even the burning sun of the long lunar day would be totally unable to dislodge more than traces of its vapour. Assuming the solid mass of the moon to contract on cooling at the same rate as granite, its refrigeration, though only 180° F., would create cellular space equal to nearly fourteen and a half millions of cubic miles, which would be more than sufficient to engulf the whole of the lunar oceans, supposing them to bear the same proportion to the mass of the moon as our own oceans bear to that of the earth.'

A similar theory was earlier propounded by Seeman in Germany and by Sterry Hunt in America, while more recently the theory has been advanced (independently, no doubt) by Stanislas Meunier in France. It should be noted that actual cavities cannot be supposed to form in the interior of a cooling globe like the moon, or anywhere except near the surface—that is, within a distance not exceeding, perhaps, some twenty or thirty miles. For the pressure existing at greater depths would render the hardest solids plastic, so that, though their molecular condition would still be that of solid bodies, they would behave (under that pressure) as fluids. Cavities could no more form in cooling solid matter under such pressure than they could form in cooling fluids. The only kind of spaces which could form for the reception of the lunar waters would be capillary spaces like those in certain porous solid bodies.

The great objection to this view of the moon's past history consists in the difficulty of accounting for the lunar atmosphere. It must be remembered that, owing to the smallness of the moon's mass, an atmosphere composed in the same way as ours would have a much greater depth compared with its density at the mean level of the moon's surface than our atmosphere possesses compared with its pressure at the sea-level. If there were exactly the same quantity of air above each square mile of the moon's surface as there is above each square mile of the earth's surface, the lunar air would not only extend to a much greater height than ours, but would be much less dense at the moon's surface. The atmospheric pressure would in that case be about 1-6th that at our sea-level, and instead of the lower half of such an atmosphere (that is, the lower half in actual quantity of air) lying within a distance of about $3\frac{1}{2}$ miles from the mean surface, as in the case of our earth, it would extend to a distance of about 22 miles from the surface. Now this reasoning applies with increased force to the case of an atmosphere contained within the cavernous interior of the moon, for there the pressure due to the attraction of the moon's mass would be reduced. It is very difficult to conceive that under such circumstances room would not only exist for lunar oceans, but for a lunar atmosphere occupying, one must suppose, a far greater amount of space even before its withdrawal into these lunar caverns, and partially freed from pressure so soon as such withdrawal had taken place. That the atmosphere should be withdrawn so completely that no trace of its existence could be recognised, does certainly appear very difficult to believe, to say the least.

Nevertheless, it is not to be forgotten that, so far as terrestrial experience is concerned, water is absolutely essential to the occurrence of volcanic action. If we are to extend terrestrial analogies to the case of our moon, notwithstanding the signs that the conditions prevailing in her case have been very different from those existing in the case of our earth, we are bound to recognise at least the possibility that water once existed on the moon. Moreover, it must be admitted that the theory seems to accord far better with lunar facts than any of the others which have been advanced to account for the disappearance of all traces of water or air. The theory that oceans and an atmosphere have been drawn to the farther side of the moon cannot be entertained when due account is taken of the range of the lunar librations. Sir John Herschel, indeed, once gave countenance to that somewhat fanciful theory; but he admitted, in a letter addressed to myself, that the objection I had based on the circumstances of libration was sufficient to dispose of the theory. The hypothesis that a comet had whisked away the lunar oceans and atmosphere does not need serious refutation ; and it is difficult to see how the theory that lunar seas and lunar air have been solidified by intense cold can be maintained in presence of the fact that experiments made with the Rosse 3-feet mirror indicate great intensity of heat in the substance of those parts of the moon which have been exposed to the full heat of the sun during the long lunar day.

If there ever existed a lunar atmosphere and lunar seas, then Seeman's theory seems the only available means of accounting for their disappearance. Accordingly we must recognise the extreme interest and importance of telescopic researches directed to the inquiry whether any features of the moon's surface indicate the action of processes of *weathering,* whether the beds of lunar rivers can anywhere be traced, whether the shores of lunar seas can be recognised by any of those features which exist round the coast-lines of our own shores.

One circumstance may be remarked in passing. If the multitudinous lunar craters were formed before the withdrawal of lunar water and air into the moon's interior, it is somewhat remarkable that the only terrestrial features which can be in any way compared with them should be found in regions of the earth which geologists regard as among those which certainly have not been exposed to denudation by the action of the sea. Thus Sir John Herschel, speaking of the extinct volcanoes of

the Puy de Dôme, remarks that here the observer sees
' a magnificent series of volcanic cones, fields of ashes,
streams of lava, and basaltic terraces or platforms,
proving the volcanic action to have been continued for
countless ages before the present surface of the earth
was formed ; here can be seen a configuration of surface
quite resembling what telescopes show in the most volcanic districts of the moon ; for half the moon's face is
covered with unmistakable craters of extinct volcanoes.'
But Lyell, speaking of the same volcanic chains, describes them as regions ' where the eruption of volcanic
matter has taken place in the open air, and where the
surface has never since been subjected to great aqueous
denudation.' If all the craters on the moon belonged
to one epoch, or even to one era, we might regard them
as produced during the withdrawal of the lunar oceans
within the still heated substance of our satellite. But
it is manifest that the processes which brought the
moon's surface to its present condition must have occupied many ages, during which the craters formed earliest
would be exposed to the effects of denudation, and to
other processes of which no traces can be recognised.

It is not likely, however, that the withdrawal of the
lunar oceans into the moon's cavernous interior can
have taken place suddenly. Up to a certain epoch the
entry of the waters within the moon's mass would be
impossible, owing to the intense heat, which, by maintaining the plasticity of the moon's substance, would
prevent the formation of cavities and fissures, while any
water brought into contact with the heated interior

would at once be vaporised and driven away. But when once a condition was attained which rendered the formation of cavities possible, the contraction of the moon's substance would lead to the gradual increase of such cavities, and so, as time proceeded, room would be formed for all the lunar oceans.

We are next led to the inquiry whether the contraction of the moon's substance may not have played the most important part of all in producing those phenomena of disturbance which are presented by the moon's surface. Quite recently the eminent seismologist Mallet has propounded a theory of terrestrial volcanic energy, which not only appears to account—far more satisfactorily than any hitherto adopted—for the phenomena presented by the earth's crust, but suggests considerations which may be applied to the case of the moon, and in fact are so applied by Mallet himself. It behoves us to inquire very carefully into the bearing of this theory upon the subject of lunar seismology, and therefore to consider attentively the points in which the theory differs from those hitherto adopted.

Mallet dismisses first the chemical theory of volcanic energy, because all known facts tend to show that the chemical energies of the materials of our globe were almost wholly exhausted prior to the consolidation of its surface. This may be regarded as equally applicable to the case of the moon. It is difficult to see how the surface of the moon can have become consolidated while any considerable portion of the chemical activity of her materials remained unexhausted.

' The mechanical theory,' proceeds Mallet, ' which finds in a nucleus still in a state of liquid fusion a store of heat and of lava, &c., is only tenable on the admission of a very thin solid crust ; and even through a crust but 30 miles thick, it is difficult to see how surface-water is to gain access to the fused nucleus ; *yet without water there can be no volcano.* More recent investigation on the part of mathematicians has been supposed to prove that the earth's crust is not thin.' He proceeds to show that, without attaching any great weight to these mathematical calculations, there are other grounds for believing that the solid crust of the earth is of great thickness, and that ' although there is evidence of a nucleus much hotter than the crust, there is no certainty that any part of it remains liquid ; but if so, it is in any case too deep to render it conceivable that surface-water should make its way down to it. The results of geological speculation and of physico-mathematical reasoning thus oppose each other ; so that some source of volcanic heat closer to the surface remains to be sought. The hypothesis to supply this, proposed by Hopkins and adopted by some, viz. of isolated subterranean lakes of liquid matter, in fusion at no great depth from the surface, remaining fused for ages, surrounded by colder and solid rock, and with (by hypothesis) access of surface-water, seems feeble and unsustainable.'

Now in some respects this reasoning is not applicable to the moon, at least so far as real evidence is concerned ; though it is to be noticed that, if a case is made out for any cause of volcanic action on the earth, we are led by analogy to extend the reasoning (or at least its results) to the case of the moon.   But it may be remarked that the solidification of the moon's crust must have proceeded at a more rapid rate than that of the earth's, while the proportion of its thickness to the volume of the fused nucleus would necessarily be greater for the same thickness of the crust.   The question of the access of water brings us to the difficulty already considered, —the inquiry, namely, whether oceans originally existed on the moon.   For the moment, however, I forbear from considering whether Mallet's reasoning must necessarily be regarded as inapplicable to the moon if it should be asserted that there never were any lunar oceans.

We come now to Mallet's solution of the problem of terrestrial volcanic energy.

We have been so long in the habit of regarding volcanoes and earthquakes as evidences of the earth's subterranean forces,—as due, in fact (to use Humboldt's expression), to the reaction of the earth's interior upon its crust,—that the idea presents itself at first sight as somewhat startling, that all volcanic and seismic phenomena, as well as the formation of mountain-ranges, have been due to a set of cosmical forces called into play by the *contraction* of our globe.   According to the new theory, it is not the pressure of matter under the crust outwards, but the pressure of the earth's crust inwards, which produces volcanic energy.   Nor is this merely substituting an action for reaction, or *vice versâ*.

According to former views, it was the inability of the
crust to resist pressure from within which led to volcanic explosions, or which produced earthquake-throes
where the safety-valve provided by volcanoes was not
supplied.   The new theory teaches, in fact, that it is a
deficiency of internal resistance, and not an excess,
which causes these disturbances of the crust.   'The
contraction of our globe,' says Mallet,[1] 'has been met,
from the period of its fluidity to its present state,—
first, by deformation of the spheroid, forming generally
the ocean-basins and the land; afterwards by the foldings over and elevations of the thickened crust into
mountain-ranges, &c.; and, lastly, by the mechanism
which gives rise to volcanic actions.   The theory of
mountain-elevation proposed by C. Prévost was the only
true one—that which ascribes this to tangential pressures propagated through a solid crust of sufficient
thickness to transmit them, these pressures being produced by the relative rate of contraction of the nucleus
and of the crust; the former being at a higher temperature, and having a higher coefficient of contraction
for equal loss of heat, tends to shrink away from beneath
the crust, leaving the latter partially unsupported.
This, which during a much more rapid rate of cooling
from higher temperature of the whole globe, and from
a thinner crust, gave rise in former epochs to mountain-

---

[1] I quote throughout from an abstract of Mallet's paper in the
Philosophical Magazine for December, 1872. The words are probably, for the most part, Mallet's own; but I have not the original
paper by me for reference. I believe, however, that the abstract is
from his own pen.

elevation, in the present state of things gives rise to volcanic heat.'   By the application of a theorem of Lagrange, Mr. Mallet proves that the earth's solid crust, however great may be its thickness, 'and even if of materials far more cohesive and rigid than those of which we must suppose it to consist, must, if even to a very small extent left unsupported by the shrinking away of the nucleus, crush up in places by its own gravity, and by the attraction of the nucleus.   This is actually going on; and in this partial crushing,' at places or depths dependent on the material and on conditions which Mr. Mallet points out, he discerns 'the true cause of volcanic heat.[1]   As the solid crust sinks

[1] 'In order to test the validity of his theory by contact with known facts' (says the *Philosophical Magazine*), 'Mr. Mallet gives in detail two important series of experiments completed by him;— the one on the actual amount of heat capable of being developed by the crushing of sixteen different species of rocks, chosen so as to be representative of the whole series of known rock-formations, from oolites down to the hardest crystalline rocks; the other on the coefficients of total contraction between fusion and solidification, at existing mean temperature of the atmosphere, of basic and acid slags analogous to melted rocks. The latter experiments were conducted on a very large scale; and the author points out the great errors of preceding experimenters, Bischoff and others, as to these coefficients. By the aid of these experimental data, he is enabled to test the theory produced when compared with such facts as we possess as to the rate of present cooling of our globe, and the total annual amount of volcanic action taking place upon its surface and within its crust. He shows, by estimates which allow an ample margin to the best data we possess as to the total annual vulcanicity, of all sorts, of our globe at present, that less than one-fourth of the total heat at present annually lost by our globe is upon his theory sufficient to account for it; so that the secular cooling, small as it is, now going on, is a sufficient *primum mobile,* leaving the greater portion still to be dissipated by radiation. The author then brings his views into contact with known facts of

together to follow down after the shrinking nucleus, the *work* expended in mutual crushing and dislocation of its parts is *transformed into heat,* by which, at the places where the crushing sufficiently takes place, the material of the rock so crushed and of that adjacent to it are heated even to fusion. The access of water to such points determines volcanic eruption. Volcanic heat, therefore, is one result of the secular cooling of a terraqueous globe subject to gravitation, and needs no strange or gratuitous hypothesis as to its origin.'

It is readily seen how important a bearing these conclusions have upon the question of the moon's condition. So far, at any rate, as the processes of contraction and the consequent crushing and dislocation of the crust are concerned, we see at once that in the case of the moon these processes would take place far more actively than in the earth's case. For the cooling of the moon must have taken place far more rapidly and the excess of the contraction of the nucleus over that of the crust must have been considerably greater. Moreover, although the force of gravity is much less on the moon than on our earth, and therefore the heat developed by any process of contraction correspondingly reduced, yet, on the one hand, this would probably be

vulcanology and seismology, showing their accordance. He also shows that to the heat developed by partial tangential thrusts within the solid crust are due those perturbations of hypogeal increment of temperature which Hopkins has shown cannot be referred to a cooling nucleus and to differences of conductivity alone.'

more than compensated by the greater activity of the lunar contraction (*i.e.* by the more rapid reduction of the moon's heat), while, on the other, the resistance to be encountered in the formation of elevations by this process would be reduced precisely in the same proportion that gravity is less at the moon's surface.   It is important to notice that, as Mr. Mallet himself points out, his view of the origin of volcanic heat ' is independent of any particular thickness being assigned to the earth's solid crust, or to whether there is at present a liquid fused nucleus,—all that is necessary being a *hotter* nucleus than crust, so that the rate of contraction is greater for the former than for the latter.'   Moreover, ' as the play of tangential pressures has elevated the mountain-chains in past epochs, the nature of the forces employed sets a limit ' to the possible height of mountains on our globe.   This brings Mr. Mallet's views into connection with ' vulcanicity produced in like manner in other planets, or in our own satellite, and supplies an adequate solution of the singular, and so far unexplained fact, that the elevations upon our moon's .surface and the evidences of former volcanic activity are upon a scale so vast when compared with those upon our globe.'

All that seems wanted to make the explanation of the general condition of the moon's surface complete, according to this theory, is the presence of water in former ages, over a large extent of the moon's surface, —*unless* we combine with the theory of contraction the further supposition that the downfall of large

T .

masses on the moon produced that local fusion which is
necessary to account for the crateriform surface-contour.
It is impossible to contemplate the great mountain-
ranges of the moon (as, for instance, the Apennines
under favourable circumstances of illumination) without seeing that Mallet's theory accords perfectly with
their peculiar corrugated aspect (the same aspect,
doubtless, which terrestrial mountain-ranges would
exhibit if they could be viewed as a whole from any
suitable station). Again, the aspect of the regions
surrounding the great lunar craters—and especially the
well-studied crater Copernicus—accords closely, when
sufficient telescopic power is employed, with the theory
that there has been a general contraction of the outer
crust of the moon, resulting in foldings and cross-fold-
ings, wrinkles, corrugations, and nodules. But the
multiplicity of smaller craters does not seem to be explained at all satisfactorily ; while the present absence
of water, as well as the want of any positive or direct
evidence that water ever existed upon the moon, com-
pels us to regard even the general condition of the
moon's surface as a problem which has still to be explained. If, however, it be admitted that the processes
of contraction proceeded with sufficient activity to produce fusion in the central part of a great region of con-
tracting crust, and that the heat under the crust
sufficed for the vaporisation of a considerable portion
of the underlying parts of the moon's substance, we
might find an explanation of the great craters like
Copernicus, as caused by true volcanic action. The

masses of vapour, however, which, according to that view, sought an outlet at craters like Copernicus must have been enormous. Almost immediately after their escape they would be liquefied, and flow down outside the raised mouth of the crater. According to this view we should see, in the floor of the crater, the surface of what had formerly been the glowing nucleus of the moon : the masses near the centre of the floor (in so many cases) might be regarded as, in some instances, the *débris* left after the great outburst, and in others as the signs of a fresh outburst proceeding from a yet lower level; while the glistening matter which lies all round many of the monster craters would be regarded as the matter which had been poured out during the outburst.

We need not discuss in this connection the minor phenomena of the moon's surface. It seems evident that the *rilles*, and all forms of *faults* observable on the moon's surface, might be expected to result from such processes of contraction as Mallet's theory deals with.

It is, in fact, the striking features of the moon's disc—those which are seen when she is examined with comparatively low telescopic powers—which seem to tax most severely every theory which has yet been advanced. The clustering craters, which were compared by Galileo to ' eyes upon the peacock's tail,' remain unaccounted for hitherto ; and so do the great dark regions called seas. Mallet's theory explains, perhaps, the varieties of level observed in the moon's surface-contour, but the varieties of tint and colour remain seemingly inexplicable.

There is one feature of the lunar globe which presents itself to us under a wholly changed aspect if we adopt Mallet's theory. I refer to the radiations described at pp. 177–182. According to any theory which accounted for these features as due to internal forces acting outwards, it was exceedingly difficult to interpret the fact that along the whole length of these rays there can be observed a peculiar difference of brightness under direct illumination, while, nevertheless, such features of the surface as craters, mountain-ranges, plains, and so on, extend unbroken over the rays. I do not know that the theory of contraction serves to meet the difficulty completely ; in fact, the difference of tint in the rays, and the circumstance that the rays can only be well seen under full illumination, appear to me to be among the most perplexing of the many perplexing phenomena presented by the moon's surface. But so far as the mere formation of radiations of enormous length is concerned, it seems to me that we have a far more promising interpretation in the theory of contraction than in any theory depending on the action of sublunarian forces. For whenever an outer crust is forced to contract upon an enclosed nucleus a tendency can be recognised to the formation of radially-arranged corrugations. Nevertheless, it may be questioned whether—when this tendency is most clearly recognised —there is not always present some centre of resistance round which the radiations are formed ; and it is not difficult to see how such centres of resistance would exist in the case of the lunar crust. We certainly cannot very naturally entertain the notion that matter arriving from without has produced these sublunarian *knots*, if one may so speak, whose presence is not directly discernible, but is nevertheless strikingly indicated at the centres of some of these series of radiating streaks.

The circumstance already referred to, that these rays can only be well seen when the moon is full, has long and justly been regarded as among the most mysterious facts known respecting the moon. It is difficult to understand how the peculiarity can be explained as due merely to a difference of surface-contour in the streaks ; for it is as perplexing to understand how the neighbouring regions could darken from this cause just before full moon, and remain relatively dark during two or three days, as to explain the peculiarity by supposing that the rays themselves grow relatively bright. It is true that there are certain surfaces which appear less bright under a full than under an oblique illumination, —using the words 'full' and 'oblique' with reference to the general level of the surface. But the radiations occupy arcs of such enormous length upon the moon's surface, that the actual illumination of different parts of the radiations varies greatly, and of course there is a like variation in the illumination of different parts of the regions adjacent.

Before leaving the consideration of the evidence afforded by the moon's disc respecting her past history, I deem it desirable to indicate the bearing of certain recent inquiries, and especially of certain geological discoveries, upon this interesting subject.[1]

In two directions results have been obtained which enable us to examine with advantage the perplexing problems presented by the surface of the moon. On the one hand, astronomical observations on bodies of a very different class—the stars—have corrected the old idea that the various orbs peopling space are probably formed of very different materials. Dr. Whewell was perhaps the last to maintain this doctrine (in his ' Plurality of Worlds '), though we still occasionally hear a form of the doctrine advanced in the utterly

[1] There are few points in modern scientific inquiry more important or more interesting than the application of each newly recognised truth to all the varied matters on which it bears. The most striking example of this process may be found in the application of spectroscopic analysis to the heavenly bodies ; only in this case it chanced that though spectroscopic analysis is in reality an optical method of pursuing chemical inquiries, it was originally (counting from the detection of the dark lines in the spectrum) suggested by astronomical research. Men inquired into the meaning of the dark lines in the solar spectrum long before they had any idea that in the spectral analysis of light they had a most effective method of chemical research. It seemed natural enough, then, in that case, to apply the principles discovered in the laboratory to the work of the astronomer in the observatory. But with many discoveries made in special lines of research this has not been the case. The workers in one field have been too busily employed to note either on the one hand the value of their results for other fields than their own, or on the other, the advantage they might obtain from employing in their own field other workers' results. Hence the necessity, which Spencer and others have pointed out, for scientific overseers, who, not working especially in any field, but having a general knowledge of what is going on in all, may note what the workers themselves would be apt to overlook,—the general rather than the special significance of the results obtained in the various fields of scientific labour.

untenable theory that in the solar system the outer planets are formed of the lighter elements, the inner planets of the heavier,—a theory inconsistent with physical and dynamical possibilities. We now see that in all probability all the orbs in space are aggregations of matter in which the various elements, though not present in precisely the same proportions, are yet not 'very diversely represented. This doctrine applied to the moon at once defines the general nature of the problems we have to deal with, and suggests the line on which their interpretation must be sought. On the other hand, geologists have recognised the fallacies underlying their old ideas respecting the formation of the various features of the earth's surface-contour.

They no longer regard mountain ranges as portions of matter thrust upwards by the earth's interior forces, or these interior forces as products of the interior fires of the earth. On the contrary, they regard the great mountains of the earth as among the latest products of the exterior forces, the action of sea, rain, wind, snow, and so forth—as resulting from processes of deposition in long trough-like hollows, the deposited masses being eventually raised by side pressures. Again, they no longer regard mountain ranges as the oldest but rather as among the very youngest features of the earth's crust, the loftier mountains being younger generally than those of less elevation, while some of the smaller hills in certain regions are actually the wrecks of forms of elevation of which (at any rate on their old scale) no examples now remain upon the earth. Here, again,

are changes of view which alter entirely the character
of the problems presented by the moon's peculiarities
of surface-contour, and may also serve to direct us to
the proper lines of thought for their solution, as well
as to new methods of observation for obtaining fresh
evidence in regard to our companion planet.

That the moon is, or rather has been, a planet there
can be very little doubt, though whether she was ever
a planet like our earth may be reasonably questioned.
She is now so utterly unlike the earth that it becomes
rather difficult to imagine that there was ever even
such general resemblance as is implied in the remark
that she was once a planet. She is not only arid and
airless, but even were she clothed with sea and air she
would yet be utterly unlike the earth because of her
long day of more than four weeks. We know, however,
that that is a result of terrestrial influence,—and that
in the fulness of time our earth must undergo a similar
change. Indeed this peculiarity, telling us as it does
of the immense age of the moon, enables us more
readily to understand her death-like surface. It shows
us that the moon has existed long enough as a planet
to have aged and died, even as we see she has.

There is no difficulty, now, in understanding that
even if formed as long ago, or later, the moon would
have been much older than the earth. With 81 times
as much mass and only $13\frac{1}{2}$ times as large a surface, our
earth would have cooled through the various stages of
her life much more slowly,—in fact each stage would
have lasted just as much longer as 81 exceeds $13\frac{1}{2}$, or

be six times as long. Suppose the earth and moon both white-hot 60 millions of years ago, then the moon would have reached the earth's present stage 50 millions of years ago, corresponding to 300 millions of years of earth-life,—so that the moon would tell us of the earth's condition 300,000,000 years hence. And though this result is based on assumptions, it yet presents truly the general inference we may safely form that the earth will not be in the same stage of planetary life as the moon for many millions of years. (If each stage of the earth's life is six times as long as the corresponding stage of the moon's, then—on any assumption whatever—the earth will only reach the moon's condition after a period five times as long as the interval which has elapsed since they were both simultaneously in the same stage, or running neck and neck in the race of planetary life.)

But even with this knowledge it remains difficult to understand why the moon should be so unlike the earth. The waters of the earth may soak their way beneath the crust (as our underground caves, and even our hot· wells and volcanic outbursts, show they are doing) till they all disappear. Our air can hardly, however, become thinned to the condition of the lunar air. And even if it did, and every trace of water had vanished, the earth would not be as the moon is. There are no great craters on the earth as on the. moon, there are scarcely any great mountain ranges on the moon as on the earth. In these chiefly, but in other important respects also, the moon and the earth are so unlike that the uniformitarian theory seems to fail.

But so soon as we apply to the moon the two lines of reasoning which were touched on above, we at once find reason for expecting just such differences as actually exist. Made of the same materials, proportioned probably in much the same way, the moon and the earth would have very different histories. To begin with, as we have just seen, the stages of the moon's life would be very much shorter than those of the lifetime of our earth, and therefore, even under the same conditions, the power of producing great changes of contour would be far less in the moon's case. But the conditions would not be the same. With 81 times as much matter, and presumably about 81 times as much water—spread over a surface only $13\frac{1}{2}$ times as large—the earth would have had six times as much water per square mile as the moon: this would have made a great difference in the efficiency of all those forms of denuding action (and they are altogether the most important) which depend on the action of water in its various forms: it would also have greatly increased the duration of the action of these forces upon the earth, as compared with that of the action of the similar but much feebler forces on the moon. But an even more remarkable difference appears in regard to the probable density of the lunar air when she was passing through that stage of her life which corresponded with the present state of our earth's life. For, while precisely the same reasoning would apply to the air, so that the quantity over each square mile of the moon would probably have been but one-sixth of the quantity over each square mile of the earth, that

smaller quantity would have been compressed only by
the small force of lunar gravity, about one-sixth of terrestrial gravity. Thus the density of the lunar air would
have been but one-thirty-sixth of the density of the air
we breathe.   Air so tenuous as this would not only be
unfit to support life, it would have very small efficiency
as a denuding agent, whether we consider its direct
action, or its power in conjunction with water.

On the whole, subaërial denudation on the moon
must in all probability have been so exceedingly slow in
its action, and the time during which it acted so exceedingly short, that the wonder is how any denudation at all can have taken place on the moon's surface.
We may probably ascribe such denudation as is indicated
by the condition of the crater-covered regions, and by
the aspect of the mountain ranges—indeed by the very
existence of any mountain ranges at all—to the time
when the lunar atmosphere, like the earth's air in past
ages, was laden with carbonic acid (carbon dioxide),
sulphurous acid, sulphuretted hydrogen, boracic acid,
and so forth.   The earth's air when so constituted was
immensely more dense than it is at present, and all the
processes of denudation went on far more rapidly than
they have done since.   The lunar atmosphere at that
stage of the moon's history was probably about as
dense as our own atmosphere is now ; but even if less
dense, its constitution and its high temperature in connection with the high temperature of the crust would
lead to changes at least as rapid and effective (while
they lasted) as those which have taken place on the

earth since the earliest ages of which geological records
remain.

Thus, while we would not expect to find the great
craters belonging to the early stages of the moon's
vulcanian history converted into such wrecks as alone
attest on this earth the former existence of similar
terrestrial crater-mountains, we may yet fairly look for
evidence of considerable denudation during the time,
short-lasting though it may have been, when the moon's
atmosphere and oceans were capable of doing effective
denuding work.   Accordingly we find that, while the
immense craters remain still the most striking features
of the moon's surface, they attest the action of subaërial
denudation during a period which, though it may have
been short compared with the corresponding period of
our earth's history, must still be measured by hundreds
of thousands of years.

And while the great craters, grand though their
remains are compared with the mere wrecks which (as
in Mull and Skye) remain to show on our earth how
large terrestrial craters once were, show yet signs of
denudation, we see also in lunar mountain ranges the
products of such denuding work.   The great range
called the Lunar Apennines attests, for example, on
the moon the long-continued action of denuding forces
by which the whole tract now occupied by the Sea of
Serenity and the Sea of Showers was covered with
matter worn by the action of sea and storm, river, rain,
snow, and wind, from the surface of the lunar continents
around.   In a vast trough-like depression running

athwart what was once the floor of an immense sea, covering both the great regions just named, the products of denudation were deposited in greater quantity than on either side. Then as the region thus heavily laden with deposited matter sank more and more deeply, the matter was collected, to the depth of many miles, out of which the future mountain range was to be formed. When at length this process ceased, and the shrinking of the moon's crust compelled this seam of sedimentary deposit to rise, forced upwards by side pressure, the range of mountains rose, rounded and dome-shaped then, but presently to become into the precipitous pinnacled forms now recognised in the Lunar Apennines. The side pressures no doubt generated enormous heat, converting the sedimentary strata into various kinds of crystalline rock, the harder materials resisting best the still active denuding forces of the lunar atmosphere, and forming the higher peaks of the range as we know it now.

But we see in the evidence of such denuding action the last important traces of subaërial denudation in the moon. Not there, as on this earth, have lands and seas interchanged after the manner described by Tennyson when he says—

> There rolls the deep where grew the tree :
>   Oh earth, what changes hast thou seen !
>   There, where the loud street roars, hath been
> The stillness of the central sea.

> The hills are shadows, and they flow
>   From form to form, and nothing stands ;
>   Like mists they melt, the solid lands,
> Like clouds they shape themselves and go.

One interchange of land and water, and one only, can be recognised on the moon. The floors of the great seas tell of buried continents. The very shapes of sand-covered craters, as large as any now remaining uncovered, can be recognised—shadowy and ghost-like, but still clearly recognisable—in the broad dark tracks called seas, which doubtless are the floors of what were once great lunar seas.

Thus do the most characteristic features of the moon's surface (except the immense ray systems which belong to an earlier stage yet) find satisfactory interpretation in the comparative shortness of the stages of the moon's vulcanian history. There are many great craters, because there was not time or power to wear them down. There are few great mountain ranges, because there was not time or power to fashion many. But some work was done in this way, and the broad, dark sea-floors attest the energy with which for awhile such work was done; while the ghosts of craters buried beneath the sands of those lunar seas show that once, if no more, sea replaced land even in the moon.

It may be well, in considering these more delicate markings, to inquire how far it is probable (1) that real processes of change take place on the moon's surface, and (2) that it is to these processes that we owe the greater or lesser distinctness with which certain features present themselves.

We have seen that Mr. De la Rue was led, by his photographic researches into the moon's condition (for we may fairly thus describe his experience in lunar photography), to the conclusion that processes resembling vegetation take place on the moon, the period during which the vegetation passes through its series of changes being a lunar month, and that the moon may have an atmosphere of great density, but of small extent.

It is important to notice that photography shows the light near the terminator to be less bright than it appears to the eye. It may be, of course, that the distinction resides mainly or entirely between the photographic power and the luminosity of these portions; there may, for example, be an excess of yellow light and a deficiency of green, while the greater photographic power of the parts under full solar illumination may indicate an increase of green light due to some process of vegetation. It is, however, important to inquire whether the greater part of the difference may not be due to a physiological cause; whether, in fact, the neighbourhood of the dark portion of the disc may not cause the illuminated parts near the terminator to appear, through contrast, brighter than they really are.

On the answer which may be given to this question depends, in a great degree (as it seems to me), the opinion we are to form of those recent researches which have appeared to indicate that the floor of Plato grows darker as the sun rises higher above it. Taking these researches in their general aspect, it cannot but be recognised that it is a matter of the utmost importance to determine whether they indicate a real change or one which is only apparent. If it is really the case that Plato grows darker under a rising sun, we should have to infer that in the case of Plato certainly, and probably in the case of other regions similarly placed, processes of change take place in each lunation which correspond (fairly) with what might be expected if these regions became covered with some sort of vegetation as the lunar month (or, which is the same thing, the lunar day) proceeds. Other explanations—meteorological, chemical, or mechanical—might indeed be available, yet in any case conclusions of the utmost interest would present themselves for consideration.

It must be remembered, however, that thus far these observations have been based on eye-estimations. Nothing has yet been done to apply any photometric test to the matter; nor has the floor of Plato been brought alone under observation, but other light, of varying degrees of intensity, has always been in the field of view. Plato is seen bright when near the 'terminator,' and growing gradually darker as the sun rises higher and higher above the level of the floor of the crater. The point to be decided is, how far the brightness of Plato near the terminator is an effect of contrast. Photographic observations go far to prove (they at least strongly suggest) that contrast has much to do with the matter. They show that, photographically, the parts near the terminator are not so bright as they look. May it not be that they look brighter than they are in reality? We have only to suppose that the photographic results represent pretty accurately the true relative luminosity of different parts of the moon to answer this question at once in the affirmative.

It seems to accord with this view, that the greater darkness of the floor of Plato agrees with the time when the sun attains his greatest elevation above the level of the floor.   For if the action of the sun were the cause of the darkening, we should expect the greatest effect to appear some considerable time after the sun had culminated (as supposed to be seen from the floor of Plato). We know that on our own earth all diurnal solar effects, except those which may be described as optical, attain their maximum after the sun has reached his highest point on the heavens, while all annual solar effects attain their maximum after midsummer.   If an observer on Venus could watch the forests of our north temperate zones as they became clothed with vegetation, and were afterwards disrobed of their leafy garment during the progress of the year, it would not be on the 21st of June that he would recognise the most abundant signs of vegetation.   In July and August vegetation most richly clothes the northern lands of our earth.   It is then also that the heat is greatest ; *that* is the time of true midsummer as distinguished from astronomical midsummer.   And in like manner the true heat-noon is at about two o'clock in the afternoon, not at the epoch when the sun is highest, or at astronomical noon. The difference in either case amounts to about one-twelfth part of the complete period in question : in one case we find the maximum of heat a month or twelfth part of the year after the time of the sun's greatest

U

northerly declination ; in the other we find the time of
greatest heat two hours, or one-twelfth part of a day,
after the time of the sun's greatest elevation.   If we
take a corresponding portion of the lunar month, we
find that the greatest effect of any solar action on the
floor of Plato might be expected to take place about
two and a half days after the sun had attained his
greatest elevation.   This appears to show that either
the effect is physiological, or that it is purely an optical
peculiarity—that is, due to the manner in which the
light falls on a surface of peculiar configuration.

It does not appear to me, I may remark further, that
the occurrence of real variations in the condition of the
spots upon the floor of Plato has been demonstrated.
It has been ascertained that some of these are at times
relatively darker or brighter than at others, and that
this is not a mere physiological effect is proved by the
fact that the result has been obtained by comparing
the spots *inter se.*   Nevertheless it must not be forgotten how largely the presentation of the floor of Plato
towards the terrestrial observer is affected by libration,
now tilting the floor more fully towards the observer
and presently tilting it away from him ; at one time
tilting the floor eastwards, at another westwards, and
at intermediate periods giving every intermediate
variety of tilt ; these changes, moreover, having their
maximum in turn at all epochs of the lunation.   Com-
bining this consideration with the circumstance that
very slight variations in the presentation of a flattish
surface will cause certain portions to appear relatively

dark or relatively light, it appears to me that a case has not yet been made out for real selenographical changes as the interpretation of these phenomena. Let us consider this point more closely. In all terrestrial comparisons to determine processes of change, the observer or experimenter is careful always to keep the circumstances unchanged under which the object of research is examined. If he desired to ascertain whether some distant and (let us say) inaccessible surface underwent changes, he would, to speak plainly, be careful to look at that surface in the same way throughout his experiments, and also to select occasions when the atmosphere was in some given condition.

Now, first, the conditions under which any lunar object is observed necessarily change with the progress of the lunar day. As the sun gradually rises higher and higher above the horizon of any lunar place, the shadows not only decrease in length, but shift in direction ; and as the sun passes down again towards the horizon, the shadows, though they increase again in length, are yet thrown in quite a different direction from that in which they fell in the earlier part of the day. The effect of such changes will depend partly on the nature of the surface ; but all parts of the moon's surface where one would look for changes due to volcanic action, or to the effects of expansion and contraction, would be certainly very much affected by changes of illumination. Thus it is found that the whole aspect of a lunar region at morning time differs from its noon aspect, and its noon aspect again from the aspect it presents when its evening is in progress. We can take the diurnal changes into account in successive lunations, because (weather permitting) we can observe any given lunar region repeatedly at about the same hour of the lunar day. But we cannot do this with perfect exactness ; for the lunar day—that is, the lunation—is not commensurable with our day. Since one lunation in fact contains approximately 29·53 of our mean days, we see that if any lunar feature is observed in a given part of our sky, at a given lunar hour in one lunation, then, in the next lunation, that part of the lunar day will correspond to a time when the moon is nearly 12 hours of diurnal rotation from that part of the sky. For instance, if true full moon occurs at midnight in one lunation, so that a place on the moon's central meridian is observed at its noon and at our midnight, then, in the next lunation, the noon of that place will occur nearly at our mid-day, and the moon was on the meridian about half a day of our time before, or will be on the meridian about half a day of our time after, the time of true noon for places on the central meridian of the moon ; in half a day of our time a place on the moon undergoes a considerable change of illumination. Since two lunations amount to 59·06 days,—that is, to 59 days and nearly an hour and a half,—we see that, in the next lunation but one, there will be a much smaller difference of illumination if any lunar region is observed at almost the same hour of terrestrial time ; for an hour and a half of our time corresponds to only about three minutes of lunar time,[1] and, as we know, the sun's position does not change much in three minutes. But then a great change will have taken place in the moon's diurnal course, simply because the moon's position with respect to the equator, at any given phase, varies as the sun's does (sometimes more, sometimes less, according to the position of the nodes of the moon's orbit, but always to a considerable degree), since the inclination of the moon's orbit to the equator is never less than 18°; accordingly a long time elapses before there is a close approach to identity in the lunar and terrestrial conditions under which a lunar region is observed.

And it is to be noted that when, so far as the moon's motion in her orbit is concerned, there would otherwise be a close approach to identity in the conditions, the continual change in the inclination of the orbit causes a marked difference in the elevation at which the moon is seen above the horizon.

If we add to these considerations the fact that the moon has seasons, though they are not very marked, and that the sun's elevation at lunar noon thus varies through an arc of about 3°, we see that a very long interval must elapse before there is any very near approach

---

[1] Since the lunar day contains 29·53 of our days, it follows that the lunar hour, or the 24th part of the day, corresponds to 1·23 terrestrial day, or 29·53 terrestrial hours. Again, one terrestrial day corresponds to 1÷29·53 of a lunar day, or to rather less than 48m. 46s. of lunar time supposed to be divided as ours (that is, the day into 24 equal parts, to be called lunar hours, the hour into 60 minutes, and the minute into 60 seconds). These two relations are sufficient for the ready conversion of terrestrial into lunar time and *vice versâ*.

to the conditions, lunar as well as terrestrial, under which any lunar region is observed.

As yet we have taken no account whatever of the lunar librations. These occasion a distinct class of differences. The varying solar elevation affects the actual aspect of any lunar region as it would be seen from one and the same standpoint; and varying lunar elevations, by causing the moon to be observed under different conditions of terrestrial atmosphere, must manifestly produce varying effects. But the lunar librations correspond to an actual change of place on the observer's part.

Let it be noticed, that the point which is at the centre of the moon's disc when there is no libration is carried by the librations so as to occupy in turn every part of a lunar area appreciably rectangular, some $15\frac{1}{2}°$ wide in lunar longitude and some $13\frac{1}{2}°$ wide in lunar latitude—the space A G A G′ of fig. 28, p. 118. Thus the lunar region occupied by this point is viewed in every direction corresponding to these limits. We see it squarely when it is in its mean position, we see it tilted $7\frac{3}{4}°$ on either side of its mean position in longitude, and $6\frac{3}{4}°$ on either side of this position in latitude, and in every possible mean position as well as with every possible combination of tilt in longitude and latitude. In fine, if O (fig. 28) be its mean and central position, then this point occupies in turn (and in the course of time) every part of the area A G G′ A′.

Now this has only been stated to show the actual librational sway of the moon, not to indicate the im-

portance of the effects due to such libration.   For it is
manifest that the region about O cannot be very much
affected in appearance by being shifted even to the
point A, or to G, or to G', or to A'—that is, to its maximum amount.   If we were looking at the summit and
slopes of any hills or craters, when the central region
was at O, we should also be looking at those summits
and slopes when the region was at A, G, G', or A',—
unless, indeed, the slopes were exceedingly steep.

Of course the two opposite slopes of a ridge (sup-

Fig. 34.

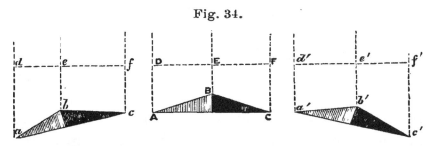

pose) would be seen in different proportion at A, G, G',
and A', and if they were differently tinted, a different
effect would be produced, whether we could see such
slopes separately or not.

Thus if such a ridge as A B C (fig. 34) were looked
at directly when at O, we should see the slopes A B,
B C, of apparently equal width, as shown by the equality
of D E and E F drawn square across the parallels from
A, B, and C towards the eye ; whereas, if the base A C
were inclined to the position a c or a' c', we should in
one case see b c the wider, and in the other see a' b' the
wider, as shown by the inequality of the lines d e, e f,
and d' e', e' f'.   Such changes would necessarily produce

some effect; and the effect might be deceptive, and indicate change where there had been no change, if a surface were covered with ridges such as A B C, too minute to be individually discernible, and having the side towards C darker or lighter than the side towards A. The same would hold also if the slopes A B and B C were not, as in the imagined case, inclined equally to the base A C.

But it will be manifest that these effects, though they might be appreciable, would be insignificant com-

Fig. 35.

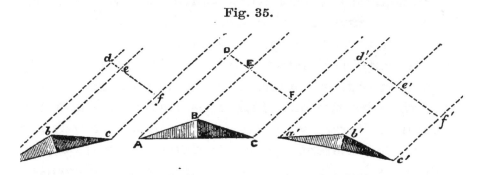

pared with those which libration might produce, in certain circumstances, on points at a considerable distance from the centre of the disc. Thus, take such a case as is illustrated in fig. 35, where a ridge, A B C, instead of being looked at squarely, is viewed at an angle of 40°, corresponding to a position removed 50° from O in fig. 28. Then lines being drawn from A B C, and, at an angle of 40°, to A C, and parallel lines from the corresponding points of the same ridge tilted on either side of its mean position as before, we see that the inequality between D E and E F is much less than that between d e and e f, and much greater than that between d' e' and e' f'. The effects of libration may thus be very considerable indeed on places considerably removed from O (fig. 28). It is indeed clear that places which, when the moon is in mean libration, are near the lunar limb, but not near enough to be carried actually out of view, must be very importantly affected, since d e (fig. 35) would vanish altogether with a slight reduction of the angle at which the parallels of the figure are inclined to A C.

Remembering that every point of the visible lunar hemisphere undergoes libration, and that in every lunar month there is a complete oscillation of the point O over a certain libration-ellipse, which is continually varying in different months as well in position and size as in the direction in which it is traversed, while the maximum libratory effects (always considerable) are attained at different epochs in different lunations, we see that we have here a very important cause of changes of appearance. It is utterly impossible that any surface like the moon's could, as a whole, undergo such remarkable librations without some noteworthy changes of appearance being produced, even without those changes of illumination which have been referred to above. Further evidence on this point will presently be cited.

Now the cycle of libratory changes for the moon, regarded without reference to her phases, is a long one. It amounts, on the average, to almost exactly six years; and we may say that the same libratory condition is not restored until this period has elapsed. There are

momentary coincidences of position, but these positions
are arrived at, and passed away from, in different ways,
until at the end of the long cycle the same series of
changes is recommenced.   But this is not all.   We
must consider *phase* in this inquiry ; indeed, it is the
most important consideration of all.   Now, the six-yearly
period brings back the same libratory condition, but
not the same phase when given libration effects are
produced.   This is manifest if we consider that the
node regredes only 19° 21' per annum, and therefore in
six years regredes little more than 116°, having, therefore, a totally different position with respect to ecliptical longitude.   In two six-yearly periods it regredes
rather more than 233°, or has still a totally different
position.   In three six-yearly periods it regredes 348°
23' 24", or is now 11° 36' 36" from its first position.
This is the nearest approach.   The fourth, fifth, and
sixth six-yearly periods bring the node to 23° 13' 12"
from its first position.   We may call this a second
eighteen-yearly period.   Ten such eighteen-yearly
periods bring the node 116° 6' from its first position,
and one other six-yearly period then brings it into all
but perfect coincidence with its first position.   But 186
years have then elapsed, and though the conditions are
nearly reproduced so far as libration is concerned, the
astronomer who made a first series of observations at
the beginning of this period is not alive to repeat them
under like conditions, even if like conditions existed.
Even this, however, is not the case absolutely, since
the lunation would be in another part of its progress at

any given season of the year, at the end of the long period named.

Of course I would not have it understood that there is not, within much shorter periods, an approach to the restoration of given relations.   Two or three times, perhaps, in ten years, any given feature in the moon may be seen under conditions so nearly alike as to produce a great similarity of aspect; and if the weather is favourable on such occasions, a legitimate comparison may be instituted for the purpose of ascertaining if any change has taken place.   But it may safely be asserted that the opportunities presented during the life of any single astronomer for a trustworthy investigation of any portion of the moon's surface, under like conditions, are few and far between, and the whole time so employed must be brief, even though the astronomer devote many more years than usual to observational research.

Nevertheless it cannot be insisted on too strongly that it is from the detailed examination of the moon's surface that we can now alone hope for exact information as to its present condition and past history.   I would even urge, indeed, that the detailed examination at present being carried out is not sufficiently exact in method.   I should be glad to hear of such processes of examination as were applied by Mr. Dawes to the solar spots.   In particular it seems to me most important that the physiological effects which render ordinary telescopic observation and ordinary eye-estimates of size, brightness, and colour, deceptive, should be as far as possible eliminated.   This might be done by so arranging the observations that the conditions under which each part of the moon should be studied might be as far as possible equalised during the whole progress of the lunation. Thus, returning to the case of the floor of Plato ; this region should not be examined, whether when Plato is near the terminator or at the time of full moon, with the rest of the moon's disc or large portions of it in the field of view ; the eye of the observer should be protected from all light save that which comes from the floor itself ; and moreover, the artificial darkness produced for this purpose should be so obtained that the general light of the full moonlight should be excluded as well as the direct light from the disc. Then differences of tint should be carefully estimated either by means of graduated darkening-glasses, or by the introduction of artificially illuminated surfaces into the field of view for direct comparison with the lunar region whose brightness is to be determined.

When observations thus carefully conducted are made, and when the effects of libration, as well as of the sun's altitude above the lunar regions studied, are carefully taken into account, we should be better able than we are at present to determine whether the moon's surface is still undergoing changes of configuration. I cannot but think that such an inquiry would be made under more promising circumstances than those imagine who consider that the moon's surface has reached its ultimate condition, and that therefore the search for signs of change is a hopeless one. So far am I from considering it unlikely that the moon's surface is still undergoing change, that, on the contrary, it appears to me certain that the face of the moon must be undergoing changes of a somewhat remarkable nature, though not producing any results which are readily discerned with our imperfect telescopic means.

It is not difficult to show reasons for believing that the face of the moon must be changing more rapidly than that of our earth. On the earth, indeed, we have active subterranean forces which may, perhaps, be wanting on the moon. On the earth, again, we have a sea acting constantly upon the shore,—here removing great masses, there using the *débris* to beat down other parts of the coast, and by the mere effect of accumulated land-spoils acquiring power for fresh inroads. We have, moreover, wind and rain, river action and glacier action, and lastly, the work of living creatures by land and by sea, while most of these causes of change may be regarded as probably, and some as certainly, wanting in the case of our satellite. Nevertheless, there are processes at work out yonder which must be as active as any of those which affect our earth. In each lunation, the moon's surface undergoes changes of temperature which should suffice to disintegrate large portions of her surface, and, with time, to crumble her loftiest mountains into shapeless heaps. In the long lunar night of fourteen days, a cold far exceeding the intensest ever produced in terrestrial experiments must exist over the whole of the unilluminated hemisphere ; and under the influence of this cold all the substances composing the moon's crust must shrink to their least dimensions—not all equally (in this we find a circumstance increasing the energy of the disintegrating forces), but each according to the quality which our physicists denominate the co-efficient of expansion.   Then comes on the long lunar day, at first dissipating the intense cold, then gradually raising the substance of the lunar crust to a higher and higher degree of heat, until (if the inferences of our most skilful physicists, and the evidence obtained from our most powerful means of experiment can be trusted) the surface of the moon burns (one may almost say) with a heat of some 300° F.   Under this tremendous heat all the substances which had shrunk to their least dimensions must expand according to their various degrees ; not greatly, indeed, so far as any small quantity of matter is concerned, but to an important amount when large areas of the moon's surface are considered.

Remembering the effects which take place on our earth, in the mere change from the frost of winter to the moderate warmth of early spring, it is diffi-cult to conceive that such remarkable contraction and expansion can take place in a surface presumably less coherent than the relatively moist and plastic sub-stances comprising the terrestrial crust, without gra-dually effecting the demolition of the steeper lunar elevations.   When we consider, further, that these pro-cesses are repeated not year by year, but month by month, and that all the circumstances attending them are calculated to render them most effective because so slow, steadfast, and uniform in their progression, it certainly does not seem wonderful that our telescopists should from time to time recognise signs of change in the moon's face. So far from rejecting these as incredible, we should consider the wonder rather to be that they are not more commonly seen, and more striking in their nature. Assuredly there is nothing which should lead our telescopists to turn from the study of the moon as though it were hopeless to seek for signs of change on a surface so desolate. Rather they should increase the care with which they pursue their observations, holding confidently the assurance that there are signs of change to be detected, and that in all probability the recognition of such change may throw an instructive light on the moon's present condition, past history, and probable future.

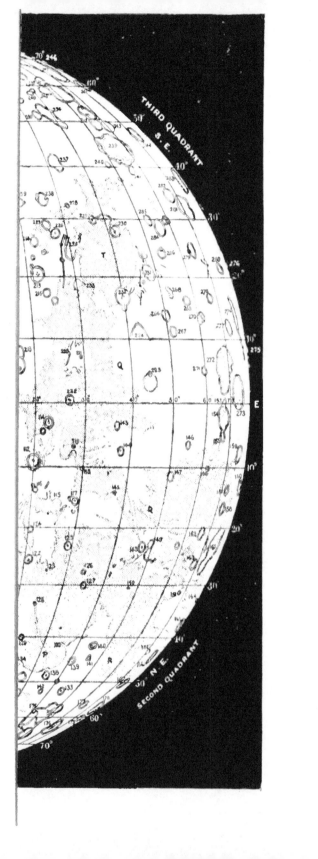

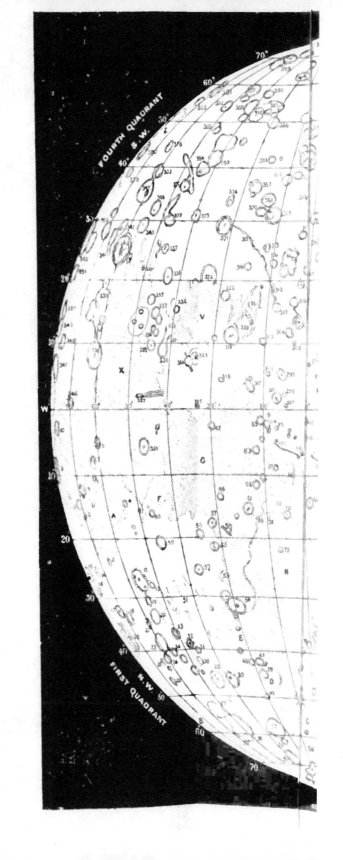

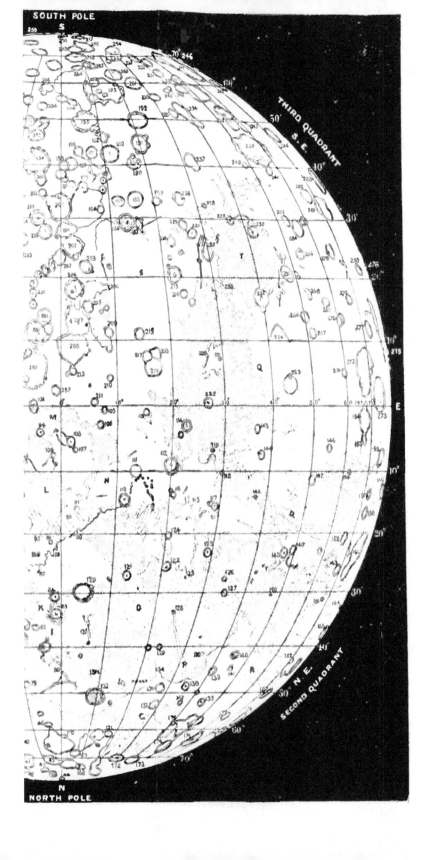

INDEX TO THE MAP OF THE MOON.

TABLE I.

GREY PLAINS, USUALLY CALLED SEAS.

A. Mare Crisium
B. —— Humboldti-anum
C. —— Frigoris
D. Lacus Mortis
E. —— Somniorum
F. Palus Somnii
G. Mare Tranquilli-tatis

H. Mare Serenitatis
I. Palus Nebula-rum
K. —— Putredins
L. Mare Vaporum
M. Sinus Medii
N. —— Æstuum
O. Mare Imbrium
P. Sinus Iridum

Q. Oceanus Pro-larum
R. Sinus Roris
S. Mare Nubiur
T. —— Humor
V. —— Nectari
X. —— Fœcunc tatis
Z. —— Austral

TABLE II.

CRATERS, MOUNTAINS, AND OTHER OBJECTS.

Numbered as in the Map.

1. Promontorium Agarum
2. Alhazen
3. Eimmart
4. Picard
5. Condorcet
6. Azout
7. Firmicus

8. Apollonius
9. Neper
10. Schubert
11. Hansen
12. Cleomedes
13. Tralles
14. Oriani
15. Plutarchus

16. Seneca
17. Hahn
18. Berosus
19. Burckhardt
20. Geminus
21. Bernouilli
22. Gauss
23. Messala

390. Nearchus
391. Hagecius
392. Biela
393. Nicolai

394. Lilius
395. Jacobi
396. Zach
397. Schomberger

398. Boguslawsky
399. Boussingault
400. Mutus

TABLE III.

Alphabetical Table of Lunar Nomenclature.

Abenezra, 310
Abulfeda, 305
Agatharchides, 223
Agrippa, 102
Airy, 291
Albategnius, 289
Alfraganus, 300
Alhazen, 2
Aliacensis, 296
Almanon, 306
Alpetragius, 205
Alphonsus, 207
Alps, 80
Altai Mts., 315
Anaxagoras, 168
Anaximander, 174
Anaximenes, 173
Ansgarius, 349
Apennines, 85
Apianus, 294
Apollonius, 8
Arago, 63
Aratus, 86
Archimedes, 120
Archytas, 46
[Argæus, Mt.] 58
Ariadæus, 100
Aristarchus, 148
Aristillus, 83

Aristoteles, 78
Arnold, 39
Arzachel, 204
Atlas, 28
Autolycus, 84
Azophi, 309
Azout, 6

Bacon, 360
Bailly, 245
Baily, 49
Barocius, 359
Barrow, 45
Bayer, 235
Beaumont, 322
Behaim, 350
Bernouilli, 21
Berosus, 18
Berzelius, 33
Bessarion, 145
Bessel, 73
Bettinus, 251
Bianchini, 138
Biela, 392
Billy, 266
Biot, 329
Blancanus, 260
Bode, 107
Boguslawsky, 398

Bohnenberger, 332
Bonpland, 218
Borda, 337
Boscovich, 98
Bouguer, 142
Boussingault, 399
Bouvard, 283
Bradley, Mt., 89
Briggs, 163
Buch, 361
Bullialdus, 213
Burckhardt, 19
Burg, 50
Büsching, 362
Byrgius, 279

Cabeus, 257
Calippus, 76
Campanus, 226
Capella, 324
Capuanus, 238
Cardanus, 157
Carlini, 128
Carpathus, Mt., 115
Casatus, 254
Cassini, 81
Catharina, 321
Caucasus, Mt., 75
Cavalerius, 155

TABLE IV.

ELEMENTS OF THE MOON.   EPOCH, JANUARY 1, 1801.

(Earth's equatorial diameter is taken as 7925·8 miles.)

Mean longitude of moon at epoch . . .	118° 17′ 8″·3
Ditto node	13° 53′ 17″·7
Ditto perigee	266° 10′ 7″·5
Mean distance from the earth (earth's radius 1) .	60·2634
Same in miles	238,818
Maximum distance in miles (maximum eccentricity)	252,948
Minimum do. do. do. do. .	221,593
Mean eccentricity of orbit	0·05490807
Maximum do.	0·066
Minimum do.	0·044
Mean equatorial horizontal lunar parallax . .	57′ 2″·7
Maximum do. do.	1° 1′ 28″·8
Minimum do. do. . . .	53′ 51″·5
Moon's mean apparent diameter	31′ 5″·1
Moon's maximum do. . , . . .	33′ 30″·1
Moon's minimum do.	29′ 20″·9
Moon's diameter in miles	2159·6
Moon's surface in square miles	14,600,000
Moon's diameter (earth's equatorial diameter as 1)	0·2725
Earth's equatorial diameter (moon's as 1) . .	3·670
Moon's surface (earth's as 1)	0·0742
Earth's surface (moon's as 1)	13·471
Moon's volume (earth's as 1)	0·0202
Earth's volume (moon's as 1)	49·441
Moon's mass (earth's as 1)	0·01228
Earth's mass (moon's as 1)	81·40
Density (earth's as 1)	0·60736
Density (water's as 1, and earth's assumed = 5·7) .	3·46
Gravity, or weight of one terrestrial pound . .	0·16547
Bodies fall in one second in feet	2·65
Mean inclination of orbit	5° 8′
Maximum do. do.	5° 13′
Minimum do. do.	5° 3′
Inclination of axis	1° 30′ 11″·3

Y

Synodical revolution in days . . . . . 29·53059
Sidereal   do.   do.   . . . . . 27·32166
Tropical   do.   do. . . . . . 27·32156
Anomalistic do.   do. . . . . . 27·55460
Nodical   do.   do. . . . . . . 27·21222
Maximum evection . . . . 1° 20′ 29″·9
Maximum variation . . . . 35′ 42″·0
Maximum annual equation . . . . . 11′ 12″·0
Maximum libration in latitude . . . . . 6° 44′
Ditto   do.   in longitude . . . . 7° 45′
Maximum total·libration (from earth's centre) . . 10° 16′
Maximum diurnal libration . . . . . 1° 1′ 28″·8
Surface of moon never seen (whole as 10,000, and
    diurnal libration neglected) 4198
Surface seen at one time or other   do.   do.   . 5802
Ditto.   do.   never seen if diurnal libra-
    tion be taken into account 4111
Ditto   do.   seen at one time or other do. 5889
Mean revolution of nodes (retrograde) in days . . 6793·391
Ditto   do.   do.   in years . 18·5997
Mean regression of nodes per annum . . . 19° 21′ 18″·3
Mean regression of node between successive con-
    junctions of sun and rising node . . . 18° 22′ 3″·2
Mean interval between such conjunctions in days . 346·607
Mean revolution of perigee (advancing) in days . . 3232·575
Ditto   do.   in years . . . 8·8505
Mean advance of perigee per annum . . . 40° 40′ 31″·1
Ditto   do.   between successive con-
    junctions of sun and perigee . . . . 45° 51′ 23″·7
Mean interval between such conjunctions in days . 411·767

PRINTED BY
SPOTTISWOODE AND CO., NEW-STREET SQUARE
LONDON.

WORKS BY R. A. PROCTOR.

The SUN ; Ruler, Light, Fire, and Life of the Planetary System. By R. A. PROCTOR, B.A. With Plates and Woodcuts. Crown 8vo. 14s.

The ORBS AROUND US ; a Series of Essays on the Moon and Planets, Meteors and Comets, the Sun and Coloured Pairs of Suns. With Chart and Diagrams. Crown 8vo. 5s.

OTHER WORLDS than OURS ; the Plurality of Worlds Studied under the Light of Recent Scientific Researches. With 14 Illustrations. Crown 8vo. 5s.

The MOON : her Motions, Aspects, Scenery, and Physical Condition. With Plates, Charts, Woodcuts, and Lunar Photographs. Crown 8vo. 10s. 6d..

UNIVERSE of STARS ; presenting Researches into and New Views respecting the Constitution of the Heavens. With 22 Charts and 22 Diagrams. 8vo. 10s. 6d.

LIGHT SCIENCE for LEISURE HOURS ; Familiar Essays on Scientific Subjects, Natural Phenomena, &c. 3 vols. Crown 8vo. 5s. each.

LARGER STAR ATLAS for the Library, in Twelve Circular Maps, with Introduction and 2 Index Plates. Folio, 15s. or Maps only, 12s. 6d.

NEW STAR ATLAS for the Library, the School, and the Observatory, in 12 Circular Maps (with 2 Index Plates). Crown 8vo. 5s.

TRANSITS of VENUS ; a Popular Account of Past and Coming Transits, from the First Observed by Horrocks in 1639 to the Transit of 2012. With 20 Lithographic Plates (12 Coloured) and 38 Illustrations engraved on Wood. 8vo. 8s. 6d.

STUDIES of VENUS-TRANSITS ; an Investigation of the Circumstances of the Transits of Venus in 1874 and 1882. With 7 Diagrams and 10 Plates. 8vo. 5s.

PLEASANT WAYS in SCIENCE. Crown 8vo. 6s.

MYTHS and MARVELS of ASTRONOMY. Cr. 8vo. 6s.

ELEMENTARY PHYSICAL GEOGRAPHY. With 33 Maps, Woodcuts, and Diagrams. Fcp. 8vo. 1s. 6d.

LESSONS in ELEMENTARY ASTRONOMY ; with an Appendix containing Hints for Young Telescopists. With 47 Woodcuts. Fcp. 8vo. 1s. 6d.

London : LONGMANS, GREEN, & CO.

ImTheStory.com

Personalized Classic Books in many genre's

Unique gift for kids, partners, friends, colleagues

Customize:

- Character Names
- Upload your own front/back cover images (optional)
- Inscribe a personal message/dedication on the
  inside page (optional)

Customize many titles Including
- Alice in Wonderland
- Romeo and Juliet
- The Wizard of Oz
- A Christmas Carol
- Dracula
- Dr. Jekyll & Mr. Hyde
- And more...